AT HOME AT LOS ISLOTES

Finding Our Way On This Veraguas Coast

Kathleen Peddicord

Published by Lahardan Books

Published by Lahardan Books

Copyright © Kathleen Peddicord, 2023
All rights reserved

ISBN 978-1-958583-02-9

Book and Cover Design by Cristian Landero

No part of this publication may be reproduced, stored in, or introduced into a retrieval system, or transmitted, in any form, or by any means (electronic, mechanical, photocopying, recording, or otherwise), without the prior written permission of both the copyright owner and the publisher of this book.

The scanning, uploading, and distribution of this book via the Internet or via any other means without the permission of the publisher is illegal and punishable by law. Please purchase only authorized electronic editions, and do not participate in or encourage electronic piracy of copyrighted materials. Your support of the author's rights is appreciated.

For Ariadne,
the real reason we found Los Islotes

Also By Kathleen Peddicord:

Your New Life Overseas: Portugal (The Algarve)

Your New Life Overseas: Belize

How To Retire Overseas: Everything You Need To Know To Live Well (For Less) Abroad

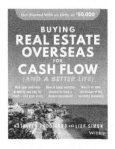

Buying Real Estate Overseas For Cash Flow (And A Better Life): Get Started With As Little As $50,000

"At Home" Series: At Home In Ireland

Acknowledgements

This book is part memoir, part invention. I've changed some names, created some characters, compressed some events, and reimagined some dialogue.

My aim is to showcase the hidden corner of Panama that my husband Lief Simon and I consider ourselves blessed to be able to call home. This tale is a thank-you to Veraguas, her unparalleled natural beauty, and her enigmatic people. Their bewitching reality should be known. Engaging with it has given me purpose I've long sought.

This book would not exist if not for my editor Rebecca Cole. Becky agreed to work with me on this project even though I know she knew I had no idea what story I wanted to tell. Then she helped me find the answer to that question.

Finally, I thank Dalys, my right hand at Los Islotes and our bridge to her world, for allowing me to share with you the confidences she has shared with me, and Lief, my partner in adventure on this coast, for finding Los Islotes in the first place. It took me too long to realize the gift in that discovery.

Contents

I	Machetes	15
II	Genesis	24
III	Other People's Money	37
IV	Beyond The Path Of Progress	54
V	Falling In Love With The New World	72
VI	False Starts	81
VII	Dalys	115
VIII	Ancestors	131
IX	Santiago	161
X	Martin	175
XI	Quebro Township	202
XII	Ariadne	214
XIII	Spirit Tree	223
XIV	Showdown	229
XV	La Bruja	244
XVI	Iya Janina	262
XVII	Old Ways	273
XVIII	New Ways	282
XIX	The Way Forward	286

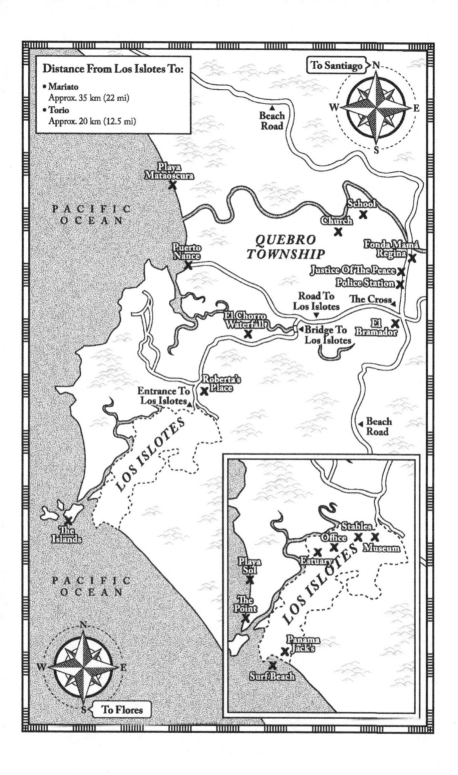

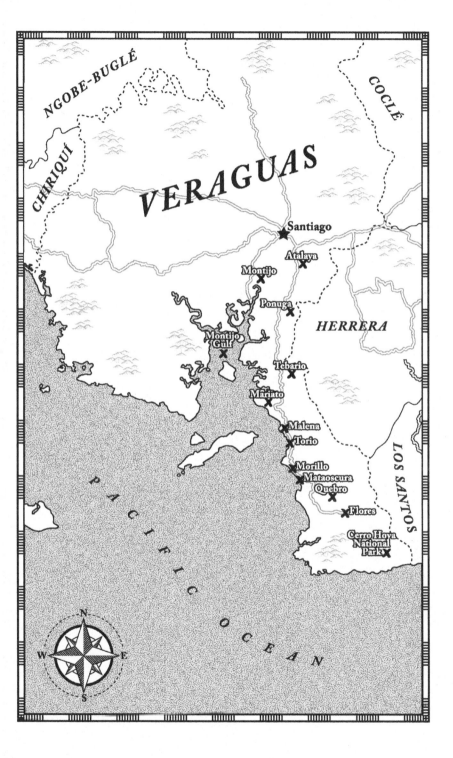

I

Machetes

LOS ISLOTES
2022

It was my third machete. My first was in Santiago where I watched a man use one to shave his chest. He sat in a wooden rocking chair on his front porch at about 10:00 o'clock in the morning, his red checkered shirt unbuttoned and open as he scraped the blade across his belly.

My second machete was at Panama Jack's, the tiki bar on our property at Los Islotes. My husband, Lief, used one to cut the head off a snake. It was late and most of the staff of our publishing business we'd invited to enjoy themselves at our beach were good and drunk. We were sunburned and tired and the evening was winding down when Valentine, our marketing director, pulled a cooler over to a table to sit on. Underneath was a long black snake coiled around itself. Exposed, it stretched out and darted across the floor. Everyone screamed. We were all in swimsuits and barefoot. We jumped up on chairs, onto the bar. Lief ran to the Prado

AT HOME AT LOS ISLOTES
Finding Our Way On This Veraguas Coast

and returned with the machete he keeps in the back. In a stroke, he decapitated the intruder. He picked up the severed head with his blade and flung it as far as he could into the darkness. He knew better than to leave it where it lay. Even separated from its body, the head can still bite.

Now our neighbor Roberta was swinging machete number three above her head while shouting in Spanish I couldn't follow. From the cab of our project manager Dalys' pick-up truck, Lief, Dalys, and I watched as five guys from our construction crew huddled together a meter away. They stood rigid and straight, whispering to each other but never taking their eyes off Roberta. Every one of them had a good three inches and fifty pounds on the woman losing her mind in the middle of our dirt road, but they were clearly afraid.

"What is she saying?" I asked Dalys. I've been spending time in Latin America for four decades and have lived in Panama for fifteen years. I should speak better Spanish than I do. Dalys is a local. I've let her become a crutch.

"She's yelling at them to get off her land, Señora Kathleen. She's saying that if they don't stop work on this fence, they will regret it." We've been feuding with Roberta over this fence for two years. We believe it's our right to build it on land we own. She disagrees. I knew the situation was coming to a head, but I never imagined it would escalate to physical violence. What could the woman be thinking?

MACHETES
Chapter I

Roberta moved toward our men, holding her machete straight out in front of her. Roberta is a small woman but strong. I've seen her carry stacks of concrete blocks and big tree trunks. Behind her was the two-room concrete structure that is both her house and her restaurant. A few yards behind it stood her wooden outhouse with its rusty tin roof. Roberta and her husband, Mateo, sleep in hammocks strung from trees in between.

The contrast between Roberta's homestead and our five-star community next door is jarring. Just outside our property line, chickens scratch in the dirt and feral dogs dart among piles of sand, broken car parts, and garbage. It doesn't say Welcome to Paradise. Passing by every day, I feel a twinge of shame although I shouldn't. The gap between the haves and the have-nots on display is undeniable. Roberta and Mateo resent us for being the big, bad, rich foreigners but we've tried every way we can think of to help them see that we respect them and their world and intend only good. Our project provides jobs and pumps money into the local economy. We hope they'll benefit along with everyone else.

Roberta stopped two inches from one of our guys, leaned back, looked up, and brought the tip of her blade within inches of his face. She stared at him a long second. Then she stepped to the next man. She assumed the same bent-backward posture with her arm straight out so her machete nearly touched the second man's cheek. She'd stopped shouting. All her energy was going into that stare. She moved to the third man in line and placed the tip of her

AT HOME AT LOS ISLOTES
Finding Our Way On This Veraguas Coast

blade a hair away from his throat.

"Lief, we need to do something. Someone's going to get hurt."

"We're building this fence," Lief said flatly. My husband is stubborn, and he can be contentious. But I'm too agreeable. I want everyone to be happy all the time and will twist myself into knots to try to make it so. Lief was right. Roberta had pushed us around long enough. Still, I didn't want bloodshed.

"I agree," I said, "but this is getting out of hand. I think we need to tell the men to come back inside the gate. Dalys can give them other work for today."

We'll come out the other side of this wiser and stronger, like we've done so many times before, I told myself, as I have about so many other things on so many sleepless nights since we embarked on this adventure fourteen years ago. But I'm finding it harder and harder to believe myself. We've tried diplomacy. We've enlisted help from the authorities. We've hired two sets of attorneys, one in Santiago and another in Panama City. Yet here we are. No one has been able to help. Our surveyor maps the area. Roberta's sons remove the boundary points. Our crew digs post holes. Roberta's sons fill them in overnight. Some of our men have quit rather than face Mateo's ceaseless taunts. Who needs the aggravation when you're breaking your back under the tropical sun for eight hours a day. I've never felt more frustrated or more vulnerable.

"If we back down again now, it'll only be harder to start up again later," Lief said. "I'm done backing down. I don't care what

MACHETES
Chapter I

Roberta wants. I want a fence." I glanced over at Dalys. She was sitting calmly, with her head lowered slightly, listening to our debate. Dalys recognizes the role she's grown into. She is often the voice of compromise between Lief's position and mine. I wanted to know what she was thinking.

"I understand, Señor Lief," Dalys said in answer to my unspoken question. "But this woman is crazy." *Thank you, Dalys.* She'd said what needed saying, and I knew it was better for Lief to hear it from her than from me. My contrarian husband can be counted on to take the opposing view to mine. I sometimes adopt positions I don't believe so he'll respond conversely. This situation was too serious for those games.

Roberta's machete was in the face of the final man in the huddle. Her screaming had resumed, now incoherent in any language. Then, suddenly, she stopped, dropped her machete to her side, and turned in our direction. She stood still and silent for a moment then raised her weapon again. She was pointing her machete at us. We'd turned off the engine in Dalys' truck when we'd parked. With no air conditioning, it was better than ninety degrees inside the cab, but as Roberta stared at the wall separating us from her, I shivered.

I thought back to how this had begun ten minutes earlier. Lief and I had just finished a conference call with the marketing team for our publishing business in Panama City when we heard Dalys call out, "Come quick, Señor Lief, Señora Kathleen!" I looked up

AT HOME AT LOS ISLOTES
Finding Our Way On This Veraguas Coast

to see her running down our front path. Dalys isn't easily ruffled. I'd never seen her run anywhere before. She stopped at the twisted tree in our front yard, the one we call the spirit tree, where she could see me looking out. "There's trouble at our gate. You need to come, please," she shouted so I could hear through the closed window. She cut through the garden where our allamandas are in full bloom. I don't have the heart to cut them, so they overgrow the path. Rising amidst the masses of yellow blossoms is the spirit tree. While the rest of the garden is thriving, the tree could be mistaken for dead. Its gnarled trunk is black with rot and every limb is leafless. Dalys had my attention, but I couldn't help searching the tree for proof of life as I do every time I look at it. I counted three small sprigs of green, same as yesterday. The tree will resurrect, I reassured myself. It always does.

Lief and I jumped up from our laptops to respond to Dalys' cry for help, but we weren't surprised by it. Nearly a decade-and-a-half into our adventures at Los Islotes, we take trouble for granted.

We've come to this Veraguas coast to create a resort. We've cut roads, dug wells, brought in electricity, and installed fiber-optic internet. Now we want to build a beautiful gate that announces our intentions and showcases the beauty of this place, welcoming people and inviting them to join our community. Our Los Islotes master plan calls for a grand arch with a bell tower and, between the arch and the gate, a wall and a fence. The problem is that Roberta insists that the land where we intend to build our entrance

MACHETES
Chapter I

is hers even though we have the title document to prove it's not. I've sometimes wondered whether, in the interest of keeping the peace, we could do without the fence in front of Roberta's house. Then I've reminded myself that this is our land. Why shouldn't we build a fence on it?

With Dalys as our emissary, we have been trying to reason with Roberta for months. Dalys has stopped by Roberta's house every day for two weeks to remind her of our plan. It's our land. We want to improve it with a fence. Roberta responds every time simply to say no. She will not allow a fence. She's been certain we wouldn't defy her. No one in these parts goes against Roberta. They call her *bruja*. We aren't from these parts, and where we come from people don't believe in witches.

I've encouraged Lief to give Roberta the benefit of the doubt. We're the invaders. We could have landed here from Mars. That's how much we have in common with the people of this Veraguas coast. They don't think they can trust us. They don't understand that we're well intentioned. They're afraid to let us in. All they know is that we're making big changes in a place that has remained largely unaffected by outsiders since the Spanish landed on these shores five centuries ago. We've assured Roberta that we want to be good neighbors. We've offered to send crew and equipment to create a new path to her place from the public road, but the more we've cajoled, the angrier Roberta has grown.

Finally, this morning, as Dalys had promised her they would,

AT HOME AT LOS ISLOTES
Finding Our Way On This Veraguas Coast

our guys appeared in the road in front of Roberta's place to dig more post holes. That's when the trouble began.

Dalys had driven us down the hill from our house in a hurry. Just before we reached the gate, I'd asked her to pull off to the side, behind our front wall. Lief and I wanted to take in the scene. I'd hoped Roberta wouldn't notice us. Now that we knew she knew we were watching, I felt cowardly. We needed to act.

Roberta turned again to face our men and raised her machete over her head as though to charge them. "Dalys is right, Lief," I said. "We've got to stop this. Dalys, let's have these guys join the crew working on the stables. Then would you please drive out to the justice of the peace's office to file a complaint against Roberta? While you're there, make another report with the police, too." The current situation was dramatic, but it was hardly the first time Roberta had interfered with our work. Dalys had met with local law enforcement many times. They just brush her off. Still, we wanted each incident on record.

"Sounds good," Dalys said as she opened her door. Wait. What? I nearly called out to object but stopped myself. I hadn't imagined Dalys would walk over to our men. I was thinking she'd drive us to them so we could manage their exodus from the safety of the truck. I was surprised but shouldn't have been. Dalys has lived her whole life in Quebro. She knows the Roberta stories. But, unlike our crew, she isn't afraid of the woman. I worried that maybe she should be as she walked calmly through our gate, past Roberta

MACHETES
Chapter I

and her machete, and over to our guys. I watched her give instructions to our men then help them collect their tools. All the while, Roberta kept her machete straight out in front of her, pointing it hard at Dalys and our crew as they walked away.

Every man, woman, and child up and down this coast would hear tell of this confrontation by lunchtime. Most of them don't have indoor plumbing, but they've all got WhatsApp on their cell phones. The twenty-first century's coconut telegraph. So be it, I thought. As Dalys turned the truck around, the doubts that'd become my constant companions bubbled to the surface. I could never keep them down for long. Maybe we don't belong here, and maybe our development plan is misguided. But we're too invested emotionally and financially to pull out now. And, if we did, it wouldn't be long before another developer took our place, and their agendas wouldn't be as well-meaning as ours, I'd guarantee it. The world is finding its way to Veraguas. As publisher of a magazine for Americans interested in living and investing overseas, I've watched what passes for progress along coasts and valleys across these Americas for decades. The after is rarely better than the before. I think our vision for how the inevitable modern-day invasion of Veraguas plays out is its best hope. If Roberta doesn't murder someone first.

II

Genesis

PARIS
2008

Los Islotes was Lief's idea. His thinking was straightforward. He wanted to make money. Lief's investment focus has always been real estate. Beachfront property is the most marketable, so he decided he'd find a piece of coastal land in a path of progress and subdivide it. It wasn't an unreasonable plan. We'd been watching other investors develop land for profit for decades.

Lief and I met in 1998 when I was a partner in a publishing company. Agora was based in Baltimore, where I'd grown up, but had offices across the globe and an appetite for expansion. Agora's owner, Bill Bonner, targeted Ireland as a next step in his global diversification program. I planned a tour of the country to scout options for where specifically to locate Agora's new EU presence and invited readers of the *International Living* magazine I published to come along. Lief, a longtime *IL* reader who was two months divorced and looking for a fresh start, signed up. Most on

GENESIS
Chapter II

the tour were shopping for a retirement home in the Auld Sod. Lief was looking for an investment opp. Our first morning in Dublin, I asked Lief for help downloading emails on my laptop. His response was so rude that, even though he did solve my Internet problems, I made a mental note after the exchange to avoid Lief Simon as much as possible. Then, over the two weeks to follow, the guy got under my skin. He was gruff and brusque but also sentimental and romantic. I happened upon him in an old barn in Sligo in cowboy boots and a Stetson leaning against a bale of hay and making notes in a journal. Lief spoke to me without looking up, engaging intimately, as though picking up a conversation with an old friend. I knew in that moment that this was the man I'd spend the rest of my life with.

We were engaged four months later and married the month after that. After a certain age, when you're sure, you're sure. Why waste time? Two weeks after our I-dos, Lief, my eight-year-old daughter, Kaitlin, and I moved to Waterford, where I'd decided to base Agora's Irish operations and where Lief had identified an investment play. Lief's real estate investment project fell through after a year of negotiations when the eccentric owner of the property he'd targeted changed his mind about selling. I persuaded my partners in Baltimore to let me hire Lief to help with the business I'd come to Ireland to start. I needed support and Lief needed something to do, but hiring my brand-new husband as my second was a predictably bad idea with life-altering consequences.

AT HOME AT LOS ISLOTES
Finding Our Way On This Veraguas Coast

Lief resented the job, the overlords at Agora, and eventually me. Lief and I fell in true love in a flash and are forever connected, but we struggled those early years more than most newly married couples to find balance. Fortunately, neither of us is a quitter. We stuck it out, made it work, and came out the other side of the battle like forged iron.

Seven years after moving to Waterford, we launched the second phase of our adventures abroad. Kaitlin wanted to study away in Paris. Why not go with her, I suggested to Lief. I'd dreamt of living in the City of Light since I was a young girl, and Agora was open to the prospect of a second EU office. By that time, our son Jackson was four years old. I'd been to Paris many times for business and pleasure but was jump-up-and-down-on-my-bed thrilled for the chance to rediscover my favorite city with my children. I appreciated Paris even more as a resident. The sights and sounds of the world's most beautiful city became my everyday reality and memories my children would carry with them all their lives. I wouldn't trade those years for anything.

But four years into our Paris move and after more than ten years reporting to his wife, Lief had had enough. He needed something of his own. Lief finally extricated himself from Agora but now what? He rambled around our apartment constantly grumpy and complaining about things that didn't matter. He told me years later that he was desperate in the months after he quit. He'd gone from working for his wife to being unemployed, in his

GENESIS
Chapter II

mind a kept man. The balance of power in our marriage was more out of whack than ever. Lief had to do something big to rescue his pride. He needed a high-profile project that would earn him more money than I made.

My husband is a man of few words, and I'm quiet, too. Every major development of our lives together from agreeing to marry after having known each other just a few months to moving to another country with no plan beyond showing up has come to pass without much discussion. We're both resourceful. We operate on the unspoken principle that together we can figure anything out on the fly. So I wasn't surprised when Lief mentioned unceremoniously one morning while we were dressing for the day that he was thinking of returning to the idea he'd had when we'd met. "I'm going to look for a piece of property to develop," he said simply as he followed me from the bedroom into the kitchen. "We'll sell lots and maybe build condos," he added as we sat down for breakfast with Kaitlin and Jackson. Finally, Lief had a plan that would make him master of his own destiny.

"Sounds great," I said and just like that our future was decided. It was another big life choice with unpredictable and potentially dramatic consequences, but I didn't blink. New is my favorite thing. My husband was suddenly animated, which isn't a word I'd ever associated with him before. This was far preferable to the old grouch I'd been living with. What would follow would follow.

"Hey, bud, hurry up," Lief said to Jackson across the table that fateful morning.. "It's nearly time to leave for school." Jackson's kindergarten was a fifteen-minute walk from our apartment. "Finish your cereal then go grab your backpack."

"I'll stop on the way back for supplies," Lief added, turning in my direction. "I'm going to set up an office in the spare room. I'll need a place to work." He was like a new man. That mattered more to me than the details of the undertaking, which I was a little afraid to ask about and didn't have time to focus on anyway.

Lief knew that France was no place for the kind of project he imagined. This was an idea best suited to a New World market. We'd both been spending time and doing business in Latin America for two decades, and we'd established small offices for *International Living* in a half-dozen countries across the region. We considered Nicaragua, Belize, Argentina, and Uruguay but landed on Panama. The country stacks up as an investment market better than any other either of us had known. The Canal makes this country the ultimate safe haven. The critical global trade route generates nearly US$4 billion a year. That's a lot of per-capita cashflow in a country of four million people. Panama's economy cycles up and down like any other, but its dips are less severe and shorter lived than most, certainly than any other country in the region. Plus the administration at the time was rolling out the welcome mat for foreign investors, big and small. It was the right choice for a legacy-level property play.

Launching a property development in Panama meant finding

GENESIS
Chapter II

property in Panama. Lief began a series of scouting trips that extended for more than two years. He was gone two weeks out of four. I didn't begrudge him the time away. He'd earned it after having supported my career for so long. But I got lonesome. I missed Lief when he was in Panama and couldn't let myself get used to him being home when he was because I knew he'd be leaving again in a matter of days.

About the time that Lief launched his Panama property search, Kaitlin departed for college in the States. That left Jackson and me alone in Paris for weeks at a time. My days as a single working mom relied on routine. I was up by 5:00 a.m. I'd dress myself then wake, dress, and feed Jackson, then we'd set off, hand-in-hand, for the walk to his school. I tried every morning to focus on the magic of the moment, leading my kindergardener along the Boulevard Saint-Germain as central Paris started her day. *These walks are a treasure*, I'd tell myself. *I'll miss them in years to come.* All the while, my mind was racing. Lief's new life plan had him hopping out of bed in the mornings. I was happy to see him so passionate but who knew how long until his project generated income. It'd require months or longer of investment before we could expect any return. My career had to stay on track. I needed to drop Jackson at École Chomel in time to dash around the corner to the Sèvres-Babylone Métro station so I could catch a train that'd deliver me two blocks from our office in Madeleine. My goal was to be at my desk before any staff arrived, but that almost

AT HOME AT LOS ISLOTES
Finding Our Way On This Veraguas Coast

never happened. I'd run back out the door of my office at 5:00 o'clock precisely so I could be back to Chomel before 6:00. That almost never happened either. The director and I got to know each other well. Every day I was late he'd be standing by the front door with my little guy. Jackson's hand in mine made up for the stress of leaving him waiting and I hoped mine in his had the same effect for him, but I was very aware that every other child's parent managed to get there on time. After dinner, it was homework, bath, then bed so we could get up before dawn to do it all over again the next day. I wanted Lief to have the satisfaction of building something for himself. I believed our marriage depended on me supporting his idea, but I wondered how long I could keep up the effort.

Lief's resentment for Agora had grown every year he'd worked there. By the time he left, he placed the blame for our struggles as a couple in Ireland squarely on the shoulders of everyone associated with the business that'd sent me there, and he was jealous of my continued attachment. I learned not to bring up work. The tension was always just beneath the surface, and any mention of anything to do with Agora sent Lief into a tailspin. We argued a lot. Six months after Lief embarked on his property development plan, Agora's CFO reneged on promises Bill had made during my contract renegotiation. I crashed. Taking care of young Jackson on my own and running a multi-million-dollar company with Lief gone half the time was too much. Bill told me I seemed tired

GENESIS
Chapter II

and stressed. He was worried about me. I was worried about me. I knew something had to give, but I couldn't imagine a life without Agora. It had been my universe since I'd graduated college, and Bill Bonner was like my second father. I knew it was time for me to move on, but I couldn't bring myself to admit it let alone to make a change.

One afternoon, after another Agora-related argument, without a word of warning, Lief picked up the phone. He called Agora's office in Baltimore, got Bill on the line, and told him that I quit. I was seated across the room. I couldn't hear Bill's side of the conversation, but he must have been pushing back. "It's time to let her go, Bill," I heard Lief insist. "Just let her go." I felt like I was having an out-of-body experience. I was in shock. I sleptwalked through the next few days, but I didn't call Bill back. I knew my husband had done the hard but necessary thing that I'd been incapable of doing for myself. Agora was my past. Lief and our family were my future.

Now, though, we were both without jobs as Lief was preparing to make a huge investment. Lief seemed certain, but I didn't know what to make of his plan. I could have given in to panic, but we had my partnership payout to keep us going, and I was tired. Plus, suddenly unemployed, I was free for the first time in my life to be a mother. Ambition had kept me from being a focused mom for Kaitlin when she was Jackson's age. That was the greatest regret of my life. I'd rationalized all along that we needed the money and

AT HOME AT LOS ISLOTES
Finding Our Way On This Veraguas Coast

we did, but that was a cover. The truth is I'm more driven by my appetite for advancement than budget concerns. I'd been making the same mistake with Jackson that I'd made with my daughter. Now I was the first mom in the queue to collect Jackson at the end of his day. The director greeted me with a smile each afternoon. And now we didn't have to rush home. We hung out in parks and whiled away hours in museums and bookstores. I hope the memories of these months are as sweet for Jackson as they are for me.

Lief's scouting trips continued. One November afternoon, Jackson and I returned to the apartment from our after-school walk to find him unpacking from his most recent expedition to Panama. He'd flown home a day early to surprise us. Jackson dropped his backpack on the living room floor and ran to his dad. "What did you bring me?" he asked his father. Lief pulled a tagua nut carved in the shape of a turtle from his pocket and handed it down to his son. Jackson hugged Lief around the legs then ran off to his room to find a place for his new treasure. His shelves were loaded with souvenirs from his dad's travels.

"How was the trip?" I asked as I collected Lief's dirty clothes from his open suitcase. *This is what it means to be a housewife*, I thought, *picking up after your husband each time he returns from another adventure.*

"I found it," Lief said, beaming. He stopped sorting his laundry and looked straight at me, which he almost never does. "It's every-

GENESIS
Chapter II

thing I've been hoping for. Mountainous so there are ocean views from nearly every spot on the entire property. Plus two beaches, one that stretches on for nine kilometers. The ocean there is strong, great for surfing. The other beach is smaller and protected, good for swimming. Between the two beaches is an elevated point of land with rocky cliffs all around. Very dramatic. Just offshore are three little islands. The ranch is named for them. 'Los Islotes.' You've got to see it to believe how beautiful it is. How perfect it is. On the plane ride back, I began planning my return trip. I need to walk the boundaries with a surveyor and then I'll meet with our attorney to confirm the details of an offer. I want you and Jackson to come with me. I want you to see this land before I go much further." I don't need an idea to be fully thought through to be on board. Lief's enthusiasm was contagious. Ready, fire, aim. I was in. If I had to choose one place to be indefinitely, it'd be Paris, but I thrive on discovery. I was ready for a change of scenery.

From the start, Lief had focused his search on the western side of Panama's Azuero Peninsula. Its Pacific coast is one of Panama's greatest assets. Everyone who can afford a house at the beach has one. Beachfront nearer to Panama City was already being aggressively developed by the time Lief set out scouting. The eastern coast of the Azuero Peninsula was in the crosshairs of international investment groups. The peninsula's western coast, in Panama's Veraguas Province, was a final frontier. Access was more difficult, but prices were one-third as much for land we found to

AT HOME AT LOS ISLOTES
Finding Our Way On This Veraguas Coast

be arrestingly more beautiful. Plus the sunsets along this coast are the best in the country.

After his first trip, word of the gringo shopping for land spread, and watermelon farmers and cattle ranchers sent messages to Lief's home base, a hotel in Santiago, to alert him that they had land to sell. Lief would drive down the coast then follow the local landowners on foot or horseback into the jungle to see what they had to offer. These were long, hot days that, much as I savor any chance to travel, I was happy to hear about rather than live through. I'd spent the previous two decades reconnoitering developing-world property markets as publisher of *International Living* magazine. If you've seen one parcel of unserviced jungle land at the end of a rutted dirt road, you can imagine them all. Now, though, it seemed Lief had identified something worth making a trip for.

"Wow, that's exciting," I said processing the implications. The large-scale investment Lief was suggesting would mean we'd need to live in Panama for at least a year. We knew Panama well. We had friends and investments in both Panama City and the interior. That's how Panamanians refer to anywhere in the country beyond the capital. Now we'd have the chance to become even more connected. I prize moving around, but I don't enjoy being a tourist. I want a reason to spend time in a place that allows me to get beneath the surface and connect with the local rhythms. I'm not good at playing. I like to work. After seven years in Ireland

GENESIS
Chapter II

and four in Paris, now I'd have a chance to try life in the New World and with a business agenda. These seem like big life changes, and they were, but I'd been reporting for Americans interested in spending time and money in other countries for two decades and Lief had been chasing a life beyond U.S. borders since grad school. We're built for big life changes. When too much time passes in between, we get bored.

"When are you thinking of going back?" I asked as I started a travel to-do list in my head. I'd need to get Jackson's summer clothes out of storage and make sure he had waterproof boots that fit.

"Jackson's Toussaint break starts in ten days," Lief said. "That's our window. I've checked dates with the investor I've been speaking with, and he's available. He can meet us in Panama City. I'll call the airline after I've unpacked to book tickets."

Hundreds of acres of raw land on one of the most remote coastlines in the world? I was sure Lief was right when he said it was beautiful. He'd seen beaches from Belize and Mexico to Thailand and Vietnam. If he said this was special, it was special. But what were we going to do with it? And how would we pay for it? My partnership payout would carry us for a long while, but eventually we'd need an income. Could a cattle farm on the Veraguas coast of Panama serve as the foundation of a business model to get the cash flowing again? I had doubts, but I wouldn't let myself throw water on his big idea.

"Great," I said. "I can't wait." And I left it at that. I didn't ask

AT HOME AT LOS ISLOTES
Finding Our Way On This Veraguas Coast

for particulars. If he told me the asking price for the land, I'd want to know how he planned to come up with the money. Lief would think I was doubting his ability to pull the deal together. I'd fail in my efforts to assure him that wasn't the case. We'd fight. There had been enough of that, and Jackson was just down the hall. I was choosing to trust my husband. I'm not a follower, but I was making a point of letting Lief take the lead. For too long I'd made the decisions about where we'd live and what we'd do with our money once we'd earned it. Some of my staff over the years, men who were older than I was, had referred to me as The Emasculator when they thought I couldn't hear and sometimes when I figured they hoped I could. I minded at first but came to wear the insult as a badge of honor. My husband was a strong man, but I can be stronger. Time for me to step to the side.

I loaded Lief's dirty clothes into the washing machine then put salmon on the stove and set the table. *We're buying a three-hundred-acre ranch in Panama*, I thought as I worked, turning the phrase over in my head. In fact, when I let it sink in in theory rather than in the context of our current circumstances, I loved the idea. I'm always up for doing the thing nobody else would think of. The financial implications were big, but I'm happy in ambiguity. My years with Lief in Ireland and Paris had only bolstered my natural receptiveness to taking chances. Every one had worked out so far. Making dinner for my family that night, I had no idea how severely my openness to the uncharted would be tested.

III

Other People's Money

LOS ISLOTES
2009

Once I was able to bring myself to ask how exactly the finances were going to work for this project, Lief told me that he intended to get rich using other people's money. My heart sank. It's a common investment strategy that has never made sense to me—neither the naked objective of getting rich nor the idea of leveraging third-party capital to do it. Taking money from someone, no matter the terms, means that person owns you. That may sound dramatic, but I've learned the hard way more than once that a partner can hijack control of an investment leaving you beholden to their agendas. When I married Lief, I accepted him as my partner in all things, including business. Otherwise, I've known since early in my career that I prefer to operate alone.

I've always wanted to be successful and can be too competitive for my own good. Competition is healthy and makes us stronger, but it can get in the way. My need to do more and better than

AT HOME AT LOS ISLOTES
Finding Our Way On This Veraguas Coast

everyone else and more and better than I did myself whenever I last did the thing I'm doing keeps me feeling like I'm constantly failing because of course I can't always do more and better though I expend a lot of time and energy trying. No matter how much I accomplish, it's never enough because I never let it be enough. A compulsion for growth and excellence drives me, and it's the rate of expansion not the money that matters as an ultimate objective. Cash in, cash out. I want to make it then spend it to build something and then make more to build more. That's how I grade my efforts. Profit-driven investors like my husband dismiss my perspective as naive. I say I'm seeing the bigger picture.

By November 2009, after twelve months of phone calls I'd found too embarrassing to listen to, Lief had connected with a potential investor. Dan was a money manager from Florida who seemed legitimately interested in the opportunity. He wanted to tour the property. Lief hadn't been begging in his calls with potential investors, but I saw it as a distinction without a difference. I don't like asking anyone, especially strangers, for anything, especially money, and I didn't fancy my husband putting his hand out either. These guys didn't care about Lief. Some of them demanded fees just to have a conversation. I hoped Dan would be the end of this phase of this project.

Dan wanted to diversify beyond U.S. markets and to have an adventure, not in that order of priority. During their final call before we were to meet Dan in Panama, Lief put him on speaker

Chapter III

phone so I could listen in the background. "I don't want to walk through life," Dan said. "I want to slide into it sideways holding a drink in one hand and screaming, 'Yahoo!'" *Lief could be right*, I thought. *This could be our guy.*

The first day of Jackson's fall break, Lief, Jackson, and I flew from Charles de Gaulle to Tocumen International, spent the night in Panama City, then picked Dan up from his hotel early the next morning for the three-hour drive to Santiago. I'd explored Panama coast to coast, islands to highlands, but I'd never been to Veraguas and hadn't met anyone who had. Even most Panamanians didn't know this part of the country, though this was changing. Santiago was attracting investor attention. The road from Santiago down the coast had just been paved for the first time, making travel to Azuero's western Veraguas coast easier than it'd ever been, and it wouldn't be long before forward thinkers seized the opportunity the improved access created. I was having trouble buying into Lief's investment strategy. What business did he and I have undertaking beachfront development on this scale? But the timing seemed good.

The trip from Panama City to the country's Pacific beaches is a straight shot. After you cross the Canal—on the original Bridge of the Americas or the newer Centennial Bridge, opened in 2004 to ease the traffic load—you follow the Pan-American Highway west. An hour later you're in Coronado, the oldest and most developed of Panama's City Beaches. These are the stretches of Pacific

AT HOME AT LOS ISLOTES
Finding Our Way On This Veraguas Coast

coast within weekend commuting distance of the capital. Both sides of the road here are crammed with shoulder-to-shoulder strip malls, fast-food franchises, and small, crappy houses. Weekends and holidays they're clogged with tourists. This is coastal development in the developing world at its worst and not a place Lief and I have ever been interested in spending time.

An hour beyond the City Beaches is Penonomé. The town is nondescript, but the land is fertile. Penonomé is home base to big farming operations. Passing through on the Pan-American Highway, the other thing you notice are the windmills. The rotating white giants stretch over tens of thousands of hectares. Next come thousands of hectares of sugarcane. Panama grows two-and-a-half-million tons of it a year, most destined to become the eighty-proof white liquor called seco. Panama makes rum, too. The local brand is Abuelo. Seco is more popular because it's cheaper and does the job quicker.

To reach the beach towns along the east coast of Panama's Azuero Peninsula, you turn south just beyond the cane fields, at Divisa. I knew that coast well. Its surf breaks and sportfishing had been attracting growing numbers of tourists for a decade, fueling development. The natural landscape was increasingly overshadowed by shopping centers and beach condos. I agreed with Lief that the opportunity was on the other side of this peninsula and was eager for a firsthand look.

We arrived in Santiago midday on Sunday, checked into

OTHER PEOPLE'S MONEY
Chapter III

our rooms at La Hacienda, regrouped over lunch, then toured Dan around the city. Long ignored, Santiago was now the fastest-growing town in Panama. The owner of La Hacienda, when we returned to his restaurant for dinner, told us that Mel Gibson had been a guest the week before. Like us, he was shopping for land. It seemed Lief wasn't the only one who recognized the potential of this terra incognita. I was encouraged but still skeptical. We didn't have Mel Gibson's resources. Much as I wanted to buy into Lief's idea, it was so grandiose. I was all in on the adventure, but as an income strategy the plan seemed detached from reality. I couldn't say that to Lief, so I chose to savor the experience. I was along for the ride, trying to keep an open mind, and hoping for the best.

When Lief, Jackson, Dan, and I climbed into our SUV Monday morning for the drive to Los Islotes, rain was falling so hard you couldn't see a foot ahead of where you stood. The rainy season in Panama begins in March with brief afternoon showers and builds steam month by month through November. We didn't realize until too late that we were touring our prospective investor at the worst possible time of year. The dramatic storm and the whole experience had Dan, who, he told us, had never been south of the Rio Grande before, hopped up on adrenaline. He jabbered nonstop. Lief didn't take his eyes off the road, which was barely visible. I was in the back with Jackson. I sat in silence, staring out at the weather. The heavy rain made it hard to see clearly,

AT HOME AT LOS ISLOTES
Finding Our Way On This Veraguas Coast

but I got the idea. This was nothing like this peninsula's eastern half. This coast was virgin. Here and there I could make out small homes. Otherwise, the just-paved two-lane road traversed dense, dark jungle.

As we continued through the storm, I grew worried about our Los Islotes road. Seeing our beach would be the main event of the day, but the road to it had been freshly cut, days before, on our dime, even though we still didn't actually own the land, in Dan's honor. The property was hilly, the new dirt road winding. In this rain, it'd be muddy and slick.

I should have been more concerned about the river just outside the Los Islotes gate. The hills around run with many, but Lief had mentioned one river in particular that we'd have to cross to reach the property. When we rounded the bend and the Quebrada El Salto came into view, I saw that it had broken its banks. "We'll build a bridge after the end of the rainy season," Lief offered for Dan's sake. "But right now the only way across this river is through it. Everybody ready?" he called out with what I recognized as overcompensating zeal. If it'd been just Lief, Jackson, and me, we would have turned around. Lief and I are cavalier travelers, but we're not fools. That raging river looked like it didn't want to be crossed. But Dan wouldn't be making a second visit. He'd tour Los Islotes today or he wouldn't tour it. I knew my husband. He'd share my concern over how fast the river was moving, but he'd push ahead anyway. Lief never doubts his ability to accomplish

Chapter III

a thing once he's set his mind to it. I find the trait both sexy and annoying. In that moment approaching the river with Dan, Lief's unflinching self-confidence seemed reckless. *No, Lief, I thought as he drove our Prado full speed into the water, I don't think we're going to make it across.* I looked over at Jackson who was looking out his window and smiling. Good. He wasn't scared. I'm not a nervous Nellie, but I realized I'd been holding my breath. I exhaled. *Lief is good in these kinds of situations,* I told myself. *If he believes we can get to the other side, maybe we can.* Just as I had that thought, the river slammed over the hood of the Prado, and the engine cut out. We were stalled mid-river with water flowing above the running boards and surging as high as the windshield. I'd been in hairy situations before scouting developing world property markets and had come through unscathed every time, but this felt more perilous. I reached for Jackson's hand. "Hey, bud, you okay?" I said as evenly as I could. He turned away from his window to look at me. His eyes were wide and bright, and he was grinning from ear to ear. Our intrepid explorer. Jackson took his first trans-Atlantic voyage when he was three weeks old, and he's been on the move ever since.

I relaxed. As long as Jackson was okay, so was I. When I was born, doctors diagnosed cataracts that couldn't be removed. I've never had vision in my right eye. I see the world in two dimensions. My brain and body have learned to adjust, but I know that

AT HOME AT LOS ISLOTES
Finding Our Way On This Veraguas Coast

things aren't always as I perceive them. I operate on half-blind faith and not only physically. If angels exist, one seems to watch over me. At times like this, I count on my unseen guardian.

I grabbed my backpack and took hold of Jackson's wrist. "Come on, bud, follow me," I said as I pushed the Prado door open. I jumped out of the car and into the river. Jackson was right behind me, climbing down as quickly as he could as water rushed inside. Still holding him by the wrist, I pushed the car door closed. "This way, bud," I said as I half-dragged, half-swam Jackson forward. The rain was blinding, the river muddy and dark. I thought about snakes. I'm terrified of them, and this storm would have them out in a frenzy. Fortunately, we didn't have far to go. We reached the bank in a couple of minutes. Pulling Jackson up onto it, I heard a great rattling and looked up to see a cattle rancher approaching fast from around the bend. I grabbed Jackson by the waist and pulled him aside as the truck sped past us. The cattle truck's tires were twice the size of ours. In a flash, it was through the river and out the other side. To my relief, rather than continuing on his way, the driver stopped and climbed down with a rope. He tied one end to the back of his vehicle then waded into the water. Our savior.

I took stock. Jackson had walked down to the river's edge to watch his father. He still seemed to be taking the day's excitement in stride. Dan, standing in the middle of the river with Lief, was laughing. He had come to Panama for a story he could tell his buddies back home, and he'd have one. The cattleman joined

OTHER PEOPLE'S MONEY
Chapter III

Lief and Dan in the water. The three men knelt together to tie the other end of the rancher's rope around the front hitch of our SUV. Then the farmer sloshed back through the river and climbed back up onshore. Inside his vehicle again, he punched the gas and pulled our car from the river, up the bank, and onto solid ground. Then he hopped out, untied the rope from our front bumper, and moments later was back in his truck. Our Good Samaritan must have been in a hurry. He was off without ever having spoken a word. He waved out his window as he pulled away. That's been my experience in places like this. In case of trouble on the frontier, you don't call 911 or AAA. There's no such thing. You wait for a neighbor. They'll stop to help if they can, and they won't expect anything in return. The four of us waved back to our friendly rancher, screaming *"Muchas gracias"* over and over hoping he could hear us above the rain and the rushing river.

 Lief and Dan pushed through the waist-high current to join Jackson and me onshore. The four of us were out of the river but still stranded. No way that car was starting. I figured we'd do what we've done under circumstances like these in the past. We'd start walking until we found someone who could tow the Prado to town. That'd mean writing off Dan's visit to the property, but I didn't see that we had any choice. My husband had a different perspective. He took me by the elbow and led me up the bank so Dan and Jackson couldn't hear the question I couldn't believe Lief had the nerve to ask.

"Could you take Jackson and lead Dan to the property while I go in search of help?" His tone was reluctant. It was a giant ask. First, in situations like this, splitting up is not a good idea. Second, Lief knew that I'd never been to the property before and he also knew that I can get lost in a big grocery store. What was he thinking? I knew what he was thinking. He was thinking that he needed Dan's investment and a little rain wasn't going to get in the way of it. He looked at me with his best pretty-please smile. *Seriously?* But what choice did I have?

"Yes, of course, no problem," I said as cheerfully as I could manage. What else was I going to say? I couldn't tell my husband no. He might never forgive me for letting him down in this hour of need. All I wanted was to get out of the rain. Instead, I found myself throwing my backpack over my shoulder and rallying my troops. "Dan, Jackson," I called out, "it looks like we three are on our own for a while. Bud, Dad is going to go find someone who can fix the car. You, Dan, and I will hike to the property. I'll need your help, okay?"

"Yes, sure, Mom," my little adventurer replied without hesitation.

"Dan, what do you think?" I asked. "We can go on ahead and Lief will catch up later after he's gotten someone to help him with the car." That was the theory anyway.

"Sounds good to me," Dan said. I couldn't imagine what he was thinking, and I didn't have time to care. This guy was a good sport. Most people would have called an audible long before now.

OTHER PEOPLE'S MONEY
Chapter III

"Take the first right then the first left and carry on straight until you reach the beach," Lief told me. "The first turn should be about five minutes down the road. Then look for a white house with excavation work nearby. The fork to the left is just past that point. That's the new road into the property. It continues all the way to the ocean." I tried to commit the directions to memory, suspecting that the trip wouldn't be as simple as Lief was making it out to be. This wasn't my first stranded-in-the-middle-of-nowhere experience. The way out is seldom easy.

Jackson, Dan, and I headed off into the deluge. Fifteen minutes later, we still hadn't reached a right turn. Maybe we were walking slower than normal because of the rain and the mud? Or maybe Lief had understated the distance so as not to scare me off the idea of heading up this expedition. We didn't reach the first road to the right for fifteen minutes more. At least we'd hit our first landmark. Forty-five minutes later, we came to a little white house at a fork. We went to the left.

At last, it stopped raining. We celebrated by taking a break. Dan leaned against a tree and Jackson knelt down to inspect a yellow butterfly resting on a red hibiscus flower. I looked up at the sunlight filtering through the trees. Birdsong came from every direction. Turning slowly in the middle of the lane, I smelled jasmine. A green iguana with a three-foot-long black-ringed tail darted across the road in front of us then disappeared into the jungle on the other side, which reminded me that snakes were

AT HOME AT LOS ISLOTES
Finding Our Way On This Veraguas Coast

probably hiding in the brush all around. I was glad for my leather boots. I'd been wearing them on jungle treks for years. I believed they'd protect against a snake's bite. Hopefully today wouldn't be the day that theory was put to the test. The sky cleared. Sunrays danced off the wet leaves of the trees and glistened on the white petals of the tiny flowers at our feet. I stopped turning. Motionless, with the sun on my face, I was at peace.

That isn't a sensation I know well. Since I was a young girl, an exhausting worry has followed me through my every day. No matter what I'm doing, I'm fighting back a sick feeling in my stomach caused by an acute awareness of all the things I'm not doing. Every night, I lay awake reviewing my mental scorecard. I count everyone I fear I've disappointed that day and everything I didn't check off my to-do lists, big and small, from scheduling Jackson's overdue dentist appointment to finishing copy for passing deadlines and coming up with new strategies for meeting business growth targets. I've heard people describe me as successful. I'd say I'm keeping failure just beyond the gate, never making enough progress in my efforts to achieve the objectives I've set for myself and very aware that every passing day is one less day I have to work with. It's nobody's fault but my own. My parents were supportive. They appreciated my accomplishments but didn't push unrealistically. I've always created the stress myself. It's how I'm wired. In elementary school, I'd panic before tests, worried I might get something less than an A. I almost never did, but

Chapter III

that didn't keep me from having to excuse myself from class on exam days to be sick in the girls' room. That wasn't fun. Neither is never getting a good night's sleep, which has been my reality as an adult. Still, I don't think I'd change my overly ambitious nature if I could. I like the results. Well, mostly. I hope my children have benefited from the lifestyle their Type A mother has created for them, but I know they've also paid a price. So have I. Carrying the constant dread that I'm running out of time is exhausting. That's why for that exhilarating moment, standing in that muddy lane with my head turned up to the sun, I was amazed to realize that I wasn't dissecting my current status or calculating my next move. I simply *was*. I wanted nothing more than to carry on being. I felt not myself. Bewitched.

"Mom, what are you doing?" Jackson asked, breaking my trance. "Hmmm? What, bud? I don't know. I mean... nothing. I'm not doing anything. Let's get going!" I said with forced conviction as I reached out for Jackson's hand.

We set off walking again. The puddles came to the tops of Jackson's red wellies, and the mud nearly sucked them from his feet. We slipped and stumbled. I gave up trying to keep Jackson upright and let him slide down the hills on his backside. Dan and I followed slowly behind, taking baby steps to keep from falling. At each summit, we'd look down to the next valley or around the next bend and ask each other again, "Should we continue?"

I had to give Dan credit. He didn't complain. "Onward" was his reply each time I checked in with him, though eventually it was more a question than a direction. Finally, we could see the frothy, pounding surf, the three little islands just offshore, and the long beach Lief had described. The views urged us on. We'd come this far. We couldn't retreat without putting our toes in the Pacific.

Nearly two-and-a-half hours after we'd left Lief at the river, we reached the end of the muddy road. And yet, still we weren't at the beach. That was ten meters away at the bottom of a cliff. We'd have to hack through the brush then shimmy down the rock face to get to the water's edge. "Can I take my boots off?" Jackson wanted to know. "They're giving me blisters." I worried about him cutting his feet on thorns and twigs but didn't argue. Whatever kept up his morale at this point was good with me. I picked up Jackson's wellies from where he'd dropped them then Dan and I followed him through the jungle and down the cliff. My arms were scratched and bleeding from pushing branches and brambles out of our way. Jackson's feet would be, too. Finally, we landed on the beach.

In that moment, all thoughts of Dan, our investment, and the deal vanished. The scene was spectacular. Lief hadn't oversold it. This was a hidden paradise. The jungle grew thick to a wide blue-pebble beach that extended into the distance. At the horizon, the land turned inward, creating a finger of rolling green hills against the soft blue sky. I felt like an explorer arriving on hitherto untrodden shores. The surf pounded. I ran to the ocean and waded

Chapter III

in, boots, clothes, and all. Dan and Jackson followed. I continued past them until I was in up to my waist with waves surging to my shoulders. The salt water rushed at me, washing away the mud and the sweat. A joyfulness came over me. I couldn't hold my position against the surging sea but didn't mind. I was underwater, upside-down, and laughing, coming up for air then succumbing again. What was going on? When we were kids, my sister would tease me because I wouldn't go into the ocean above my knees and would run inside if my face got wet. Here I was inviting the Pacific to have its way with me and thrilling in the release. My boots replanted on the sand of the ocean floor and my head back above water, I saw Jackson waving for me, again calling me out of my reverie. He and Dan had returned to shore. They were both wet from the waist down and grinning, enjoying the rush as much as I was. I started toward them.

"Come on, Mom," Jackson said when I was near enough to hear. "Let's go find Dad!"

We climbed back up the cliff then hiked back through the jungle until we reached the road we'd come in on. I stopped to catch my breath. To my right, through a screen of tall trees, was the second beach Lief had told me about. While the ocean we'd just come from was fierce and powerful, here in this sheltered cove it lapped gently against the dark sand. I turned to look behind me. There was the rocky point of land separating the two beaches that Lief remembered. As I watched, the clouds above separated and

AT HOME AT LOS ISLOTES
Finding Our Way On This Veraguas Coast

the sun reappeared. Lief had explained that the geology of this coast is unique. The rock formations are volcanic and millions of years old. This one was carpeted with emerald vegetation glimmering in the burst of light. The pinnacle called to me. I wanted to climb up and see the world from that perspective. No time for that today but maybe next time—if there were a next time.

I turned to check on Jackson. Still barefoot, he had sprinted ahead and had already reached the top of the second hill on the road back to civilization. As I started toward him, he stopped. "I see him," he shouted out with a big smile. "Daddy's back! He's in a truck!" Lief had found another rancher who'd towed our SUV to Mariato, a half-hour north. Then the rancher had offered to drive Lief back to pick us up.

A week later, after we'd returned to Paris, Lief told me that Dan passed on the investment opportunity. For a moment, I thought maybe that would be the end of Los Islotes. Basking in the sun in the jungle after the rain and again later in the throes of the surf I'd known a mixture of wild delight and total serenity like nothing I'd felt before. But, back to reality, the magic faded. Los Islotes was a paradise, no doubt, but we were just a couple of regular people with limited resources. This was too big a bite. I didn't admit it to Lief, but I was relieved when Dan opted out.

I felt a small surge of panic the next day, therefore, when Lief told me he'd decided that he would make his offer to the cattle ranchers who owned Los Islotes anyway. He said he had another

Chapter III

plan for how to raise the money. I feared I'd like Lief's new strategy for coming up with the capital to buy the finca he'd found at the edge of nowhere even less than his idea of taking angel money from Dan, and I was right.

IV

Beyond The Path Of Progress

PARIS
2009

After potential angel investor Dan took a pass, Lief pivoted. We'd known a developer in Nicaragua who had funded a land purchase by selling investor lot packages. Lief decided he'd do that, too. Three more months of phone calls later, he'd succeeded. Lief pre-sold enough lots to raise the necessary funds to close on the buy. Now rather than a single money guy, we had several. Lief was pumped. At last he had what he'd been wanting since the day I'd met him—a project all his own. Well, as long as you didn't count the half-dozen investors, but I seemed to be the only one concerned about them. More important to Lief was that I had nothing to do with the deal he'd put together.

Since our first months in Ireland, I'd been Lief's direct supervisor. He'd always had to run everything by me. I'd been in the direct-marketing publishing business for more than a dozen years by the time Lief arrived on the scene. My response to most of his

BEYOND THE PATH OF PROGRESS
Chapter IV

ideas was, "We've tried that already. It didn't work." I wasn't being controlling. I was doing my job, watching out for the business. But the dynamic was maddening for Lief. Los Islotes was his chance to set his own agendas and to make his own decisions. He'd go into the office he'd set up in our apartment in Paris each morning and close the door. I had no idea what happened after that and didn't ask. Lief told me what he wanted me to know over dinner. He wasn't keeping secrets. He was proving that he could make money on his own. He seemed to feel the need to demonstrate that both to me and to himself. I'd always been the primary breadwinner. Lief had come to think I didn't think he was capable, and to be honest, he wasn't completely off the mark. It wasn't that I didn't believe my husband could pull off any venture he set his mind to. I absolutely did. However, when considering any undertaking, I'm always of two minds. I believe blindly that things will work out while doubting everyone but myself. I take for granted that I can bob and weave to navigate any challenge, but I'm skeptical that anyone else can do the same. It's arrogant and obnoxious and one of the things I both value and want to fix about myself. For the sake of my marriage, I knew I needed to overcome my natural reluctance and learn to trust my husband the way I trust myself. This was my opportunity.

Six months into my departure from Agora, I'd improved my French with the help of an immersion language course, visited dozens of museums, and explored every corner of central Paris

AT HOME AT LOS ISLOTES
Finding Our Way On This Veraguas Coast

on foot. I was living a dream life with no responsibilities beyond Jackson. But I was restless. I've never been good at doing nothing, and since my accidental early retirement, that's what my days were filled with. One spring afternoon, after I'd whiled away another morning reading and watching the passersby in a café, I walked to the park across from Jackson's school and sat on a bench. I looked at my watch. Two p.m. Jackson wouldn't be out until 4:00 o'clock. Two more hours to kill. Never in my life had I had so much leisure time. It felt like the greatest imaginable waste. When I was in school, if I finished my homework early, I did extra credit. When I joined the workforce, I was the first one in the office each morning and the last one to leave at night. After my kids, I worked every evening after putting them to bed, including weekends. Now whole weeks were passing without measurable yield. I was beside myself, afraid I might start twitching. Enough. I'd taken the months since leaving Agora as they'd come but no more. I needed to be busy again. I wanted to race through every day without time to catch my breath and barely able to keep up with expectations, especially the ones I'd set myself. I was sorry for the implications for Jackson, but I required work. And, I realized as the thought formed, I didn't want another job. It was time to build something of my own. I'd parted ways with Agora to save my marriage. My departure had had nothing to do with the work. I loved the business model. It allowed me to create a scalable income as a writer. I'd do that again, this time for myself.

BEYOND THE PATH OF PROGRESS
Chapter IV

When Jackson and I returned home later that afternoon, I walked into Lief's office. He was hanging up from another conference call with his surveyors. "I'd like to start my own publishing business," I announced. "Online." Lief had known since the day I'd left Agora that I wouldn't be able to fritter away my life for long. "Okay," he said without looking up from the property map on his desk. "Panama will be a good place for that." Another major life decision made in the course of a two-minute conversation.

Lief and I had organized relocations from the United States to Ireland then from Waterford to Paris. We knew how to do this. We notified the tenant of our rental apartment in Panama City that we wouldn't be renewing her lease. That set our clock. We had three months to engineer our move, which would take place early July. That would give Jackson a window of time to adjust before starting at his new school. Jackson is my son. He rolls with the punches. Still, I didn't want to take his resilience too much for granted. We found a property manager who assured us we'd have no trouble renting out our Paris apartment, which neither of us wanted to sell. All the pieces fell into place. We packed our bags and flew, July 4, from the City of Light to the Hub of the Americas.

Getting from Paris to Panama was easy. Starting two businesses at the same time was not. We had to compete for everything, including space. Our rental apartment in Panama City had one bedroom. Jackson slept on the couch. Lief was happy as a one-man show for his start-up phase, but I needed staff. I hired our daughter's boyfriend, Harry, to be my marketing assistant. It was an unexpected option, but no direct-marketing industry exists in Panama. I wasn't going to find anyone local who understood the business. Since finishing university, Harry had been a bartender in Annapolis, where Kaitlin was attending St. John's College. He was looking for an opportunity and said he was open to moving to Panama. It was a leap of faith, but Harry's open mind, curious nature, and strong work ethic gave me confidence enough to let him make it. We rented Harry a studio apartment a few blocks away. He'd arrive at our place by 8:00 o'clock each morning and boot up his laptop alongside mine at the single desk. Lief worked from the dining room table. It was tight quarters but we agreed not to take on unnecessary overheads because money was another thing we had only a limited amount of and needed to share.

Harry built us a website and helped me cobble together a mailing list, then I began writing a free daily e-letter showcasing opportunities for Americans interested in retiring overseas. It was the same plan I'd followed during my career at Agora. It generated income immediately, and I knew it would work long term because I'd made it work before, though I couldn't say exactly when revenues would exceed expenses. I was less certain about Los Islotes. So far, it was a zero-income operation that, though Lief had different ideas, I wasn't convinced would ever be anything more than a cash suck. I wanted to invest in list-building strategies.

BEYOND THE PATH OF PROGRESS
Chapter IV

Lief needed money for roads. We were burning through savings. Lief would check our bank balances online at the start of every week. One Monday morning as Harry and I were booting up our laptops, Lief looked up abruptly from his screen. "The Citizens account has fallen below my mark," he nearly shouted from across the room. "We've got Kaitlin's final tuition payment coming due. And you're talking about hiring another employee. What are we going to do when we run out of cash?" He said it all like an accusation, as though our entire predicament, being crammed together in a tiny apartment in a new country with negligible income and expanding financial obligations, was my fault. I wasn't the one who'd quit my job and then quit my wife's job for her. I understood that Lief was under pressure but so was I, and, while I didn't regret having left Agora, I objected to being held solely accountable for the consequences.

Harry kept his head down, intent on his laptop, pretending he hadn't heard. We had only been in Panama a few months. Harry hardly knew us. He had to be stressed by Lief's outburst and maybe, understandably, wondering if it had been a mistake to move to a foreign country to work for his girlfriend's mother's fledgling business. How long until we could no longer pay his salary? I wouldn't have blamed him if he'd reconsidered the whole situation. I didn't respond to Lief's flare-up. I couldn't think what I could say with Harry in the room. Really, I didn't know what to say period.

AT HOME AT LOS ISLOTES
Finding Our Way On This Veraguas Coast

The only thing I know to do when times are tough is to push ahead. For me, forward motion is the answer to all challenges. Harry never spoke of the scene he witnessed that morning. He only worked harder. Harry was new but no longer a question mark. He was the right man for the job and, more important, the right choice for my daughter.

Lief, Harry, and I had arrived in Panama at a pivotal time, less than a decade after the Americans had pulled out. Panama came to be because of the Canal and the Canal was thanks to Theodore Roosevelt. Roosevelt's presidential vision included a strong navy that could move quickly between the Atlantic and the Pacific. That required a waterway that didn't exist, so Roosevelt decided he'd build one. He made a straightforward deal with the Republic of Gran Colombia—cash for the rights to build a passageway between the oceans. But the Colombians got cold feet. They were only eight decades free of their Spanish conquerors. They didn't want to swap one overlord for another. If the Colombians don't want to cooperate, Roosevelt thought, maybe the Panamanians would.

Panama, like Colombia, had gained independence from Spain in 1821. The little isthmus feared that going it alone might leave the door open to re-colonization by the Spaniards so had grudgingly hitched its wagon to the new Colombian republic. Roosevelt suggested to the Panamanians that the United States might be okay with a Panamanian revolt against Colombia if the result-

BEYOND THE PATH OF PROGRESS
Chapter IV

ing nation would go along with his canal. Bolstered by that support, on November 3, 1903, Panamanian nationalists launched a revolution. It was a remarkably peaceful affair. Only five shots were fired and one man killed. Three days later, the United States recognized the Republic of Panama, and Roosevelt went to work on the construction of the Panama Canal not long after. Panamanians celebrate the anniversary of that revolt as a separation day. Panama's Independence Day is November 28. That's when they kicked Spain back across the Pond in this time a wholly bloodless revolt. Panamanians saw an opportunity when the Spanish governor left the country to march on a rebellious Ecuador. They simply declared themselves independent then quickly joined up with Gran Colombia. Panamanians don't think of themselves as former Colombians. They're former Spaniards.

You could say, and Panamanians would agree, that the United States became their next colonizer. Americans needed to manage the asset they'd built so they created the Canal Zone, a forty-mile-long, ten-mile-wide strip of land from the Atlantic to the Pacific bisecting the isthmus. It wasn't sovereign U.S. territory, but it may as well have been. The Americans controlled the Canal, and the disposable income of the GIs who worked and protected it made the Panamanian economy. In 1977, in response to growing resentment over U.S. control in the region, Jimmy Carter negotiated the Panama Canal Treaty. This called for the abolishment of the Panama Canal Zone in 1979 and for the Americans to turn

AT HOME AT LOS ISLOTES
Finding Our Way On This Veraguas Coast

the Canal itself over to the Panamanians on December 31, 1999. When the United States pulled out, Panama nearly collapsed. But, contrary to what most expected, the Panamanians turned things around. The United States had never operated the Canal for profit, but Panama did, and it began pouring the proceeds into infrastructure. When we showed up nine years later, the country was reinventing itself before our eyes.

Panama City had never been pretty, and it hadn't been planned. It was typical Third World sprawl. It was waterfront, but the water was putrid and stank. Masses of thick black electrical lines hung dangerously low along every street and over every intersection. The roads were potholed, the sewers clogged. People would steal manhole covers for the value of the metal, leaving open pits that people fell into all the time. When Panamanians finally took control of their destiny, they wanted to change all that. They conceived the Cinta Costera, a boulevard along the edge of the Bay of Panama. Previously, this stretch, known as Avenida Balboa, was three lanes in each direction. Now it'd be six lanes one way and four the other with a wide pedestrian zone, a park, and a bypass over the water around old town Casco Viejo. Cables would be taken underground and wastewater systems would be reengineered to clean up both the city and the bay. I'd spent enough time in the region to have no faith in any Central American government's assurances. Costa Rica had promised a new road to its Pacific coast for so long that, the story goes, cartographers began

BEYOND THE PATH OF PROGRESS
Chapter IV

including it on new maps. They figured it must have been built by now, right? The Panamanians restored my faith. Our apartment overlooks the bay. Each night after dinner, rather than turning on the television, we'd watch the construction outside our windows. It was like time-lapsed photography. Floodlights were erected so crews could work around the clock. First thing each morning we'd check to see what had been accomplished while we'd slept.

Then in 2009 Panama elected Ricardo Martinelli president. His first day in office Martinelli published a one-hundred-and-twenty-two-page Five-Year Plan in English. Everybody in these lands of bananas and *mañanas* has plans. Martinelli's was notable because Martinelli acted on it. He addressed the promises in his report as though he were working his way through a simple to-do list. He broke ground on a Metro across Panama City, extended the Cinta Costera, inaugurated tax-free investor zones, grew the international airports at Tocumen and David, started the Bay of Panama cleanup, and oversaw the US$5-billion expansion of the country's greatest asset. The Canal charges by the ton. The widened canal could passage bigger vessels in less time. The world's shippers were happy to pay more to get where they were going faster. Martinelli took office with unprecedented approval ratings. Eighteen months after the end of his five-year term, he was accused of having taken bribes from contractors bidding on his infrastructure projects. Martinelli was cleared of charges, but his two sons admitted to laundering money. They got three years

AT HOME AT LOS ISLOTES
Finding Our Way On This Veraguas Coast

apiece. Their dad later suggested he'd like to throw his hat in the ring again for president. That hasn't happened yet, but Martinelli's still alive and kicking. He's a take-no-prisoners kind of guy. No question, he has detractors. I wouldn't call him noble, but I sympathize with his predicament. The guy had a big agenda. It's hard to get things done in this part of the world. Martinelli found a way.

Six months in, my business began covering its costs. This took some of the pressure off, but Los Islotes remained a money pit. Before he could begin selling lots, Lief needed environmental impact approvals and zoning permits. We'd heard other developers on the Veraguas coast were flying under the radar. The region is so remote, they figured, who'd notice? They didn't worry about paperwork, which takes time and costs money, or, if they did, they looked for shortcuts. *Juega vivo.* It's how the game is played in Panama. Most foreign investors buy in. Lief and I keep on the straight and narrow. We don't pay bribes. It's not only an ethical choice. It's pragmatic. What do you do if the guy you slip a hundred bucks to fast-track your license approval doesn't? Do you complain to his boss? "Hey, that guy over there I paid a bribe to help me isn't!" File a grievance with the oversight authorities? There aren't any. No, you have no recourse. We chose to wait out the bureaucrats.

Segregating land isn't the same thing as selling lots. Lief is no salesman, and he knows it. He thinks most people are foolish,

BEYOND THE PATH OF PROGRESS
Chapter IV

and people can tell. When he began promoting opportunities at Los Islotes, interested buyers had questions that Lief found tedious, and his responses gave that away. Lief's attitude toward the human race wasn't going to change. He needed to get out of his own way. He found a woman willing to work as Los Islotes sales agent on a commission-only basis. Lief's marketing budget was small, but leads trickled in. Lourdes was capable, but her product had a big downside that even the world's best salesperson would have had trouble overcoming. The most important thing in real estate, they say, is location, location, location. In what we consider the most important ways, our location at Los Islotes is as good as it gets. The natural beauty is without peer. The levels of privacy and elbow room, likewise, would be hard to beat. On the other hand, the Veraguas coast is as far ahead of Panama's path of progress as you can get. Lief swears he can make the drive from Panama City in four hours. I've made it with him in five. Most people take six or seven, and if you hit weekend traffic leaving or returning to the city, there goes your entire day. Lourdes hosted tours for many potential buyers who bailed before reaching the property. Some didn't make it past Santiago. Frontier living isn't for everyone.

While Los Islotes continued to struggle, my publishing business expanded. Harry and I had hired an editor, a designer, and a webmaster, but we needed more support. Lief was the obvious choice. He'd helped me to build the *International Living* business

AT HOME AT LOS ISLOTES
Finding Our Way On This Veraguas Coast

in Ireland. He was more capable than anyone else I'd find, he had a vested interest, and his own business venture wasn't working out. Those were the same reasons he'd defaulted into the role of my right hand in Ireland. But working for his wife never sat well with him. In Ireland, he'd taken his dissatisfaction out on me, on staff, and especially on Agora management. "I'm just a slave to the man in Baltimore," became his constant refrain. When I left Agora and Lief found Los Islotes, he was reborn. During my retirement stage in Paris, he was more tender than he'd been since our first months together in Ireland. We were like newlyweds, taking late-night walks along the Seine and making time for dinners out just the two of us. Then I'd launched a business that was again overshadowing his. Bringing him on board could lead us right back where we'd ended up in Waterford. I wondered if we could survive that pressure a second time. The key to our happiness long term seemed to be making successes of both businesses. How could I help get Los Islotes off the ground? I filed that question away with all the others I pondered at 3:00 a.m.

Inevitably, though against my better judgment, I allowed myself to begin turning to Lief when I needed help that I knew he could provide. I'm technologically challenged and administratively handicapped. Those are Lief's strong suits. As the business grew, we needed more sophisticated systems. Lief started taking vendor calls with me and helping me compare their proposals. He'd scowl and huff in ways that reminded me of when I'd so-

BEYOND THE PATH OF PROGRESS
Chapter IV

licited his help downloading emails that morning in Dublin I'd met him for the first time. He wasn't happy about it, but he did what needed to be done. He wasn't going to sit idly by while I struggled. Within a few months, he was managing IT, order processing, and accounting. It wasn't long before we were both fully occupied with the publishing operation. Now Los Islotes was a bona fide stepchild. I suspected that Lief welcomed the distraction from his investment out in Veraguas but didn't ask. More and more we talked about Los Islotes less and less. It's hard to stay excited about something that's returning only grief, and we had children to support. Whenever I thought of Los Islotes, I remembered the joy it'd brought me during my first trip and other times, too. We'd made several weekend visits with Jackson and Harry. They were adventurers. They embraced what Los Islotes offered. They'd hike and body surf together in the ocean while Lief and I inspected road work and lot markers. We'd grill burgers and toast marshmallows over bonfires on the beach. Los Islotes made for memorable family getaways, but as a business it was giving nothing back.

Lourdes resigned. She needed to earn a living. Lief took over sales himself again, but his heart wasn't in it. He'd cancel tours to the property when he suspected, probably rightly, that the interested party was never going to buy. It would have been easy to move on from Los Islotes altogether, but I was surprised to find that the less engaged Lief became, the more committed I grew. I began participating in calls with the surveyors and meetings with the engineers. I offered to write copy for the website and the sales brochure. And I began considering the question Lief had leapt over and that I'd ignored to this point: What was our vision for this piece of property on the Pacific coast of Panama that we now owned? Lief's thinking hadn't moved past surveying the land and selling lots. I didn't think that'd get us far because the market for ultra-remote jungle house sites is limited. If we were doing this—and it seemed too late to imagine otherwise—we needed a grander plan that included things like a clubhouse, a restaurant, and a swimming pool.

That thought held my attention. I like to build things, and I enjoy taking big steps outside my comfort zone. Without discussion or transition, I assumed the role of Los Islotes' champion. We'd invested too much time, money, and sweat to walk away. I couldn't let Lief's dream die. It was our too big to fail. My publishing business was established. I'd delegate more, manage my day better, and carve out hours for Los Islotes. We rented a house twenty minutes from the property to save the hour-and-a-half drive down and then back up the peninsula to La Hacienda every visit, and I mandated that we make the trip out from Panama City at least twice a month.

My growing devotion to what could most kindly be described as an idea ahead of its time was more than a practical decision. From the start, Los Islotes captured my imagination. The place

Chapter IV

seemed almost sacred. The sense of joy I felt the day I'd seen it for the first time washed over me again every time we returned. When we made the turn south from the Pan-American Highway at Santiago, the money struggles and other stresses that continued to keep me up every night disappeared. My mind was soothed by the primitive scene outside the car window. By the time we reached the turnoff at Ponuga, I was entranced by the stillness of the jungle and the play of light and dark. Palm fronds and bougainvillea shimmered in the sunlight peeking through breaks between limbs and leaves to create kaleidoscope shadows on the asphalt. I felt protected and renewed. Doubts went the way of my worries, and by the time we reached our Los Islotes gate I again believed anything was possible. We could do this.

Los Islotes was a portal to a world I wouldn't have believed existed if I weren't engaging with it. How many spots on our globe remain wholly unspoiled? Across our planet, Nature has to compete with man. But here, without us humans to interfere, she's outdone herself. This Veraguas coast is an indictment and a promise. It reminds of the mess we've made across so much of the rest of the planet and it offers a glimpse of what the world could be without fast food, strip malls, and used car lots.

Coming and going and touring around when we allowed ourselves the time, we were slowly getting to know the place. People raised chickens and caught fish with wooden poles. Their children climbed trees rather than jungle gyms and hunted crayfish in the

AT HOME AT LOS ISLOTES
Finding Our Way On This Veraguas Coast

rivers in their underpants and bare feet. They'd climb up the banks, muddy, wet, and grinning as they held out fistfuls of crustaceans like hallowed offerings. Families of six and eight lived in two-room houses with dirt floors and slept altogether in cocoons, the little ones in their older siblings' arms. People got around on foot or horseback. They had cell phones but signal only at the highest points. Some had electricity, fewer access to the internet, almost none indoor plumbing. But those practical realities were incidental because the people of Veraguas were healthy and happy. They competed at rodeos and let loose at dances and festivals. They fell in love and had children and celebrated life's milestones. They were partners with the land they revered, feasting on its harvests but leaving it as they'd found it. The Veraguas coast was a bubble free from the daily news cycle and insulated from the world beyond. The more I knew of this world, the more I envied the people in it. I wanted to know them better, and I really wanted to know what they thought of us.

As much as I sometimes thought I wanted to, I couldn't tear myself away from this place Lief discovered. I was inexorably connected and that created a new problem. We'd come to Veraguas with the specific purpose of opening this coast to the world beyond. Now that I'd experienced what was here, I was having second thoughts about that agenda.

Lief bought a machete so we could cut hiking trails. I followed along behind him the day he hacked a path to the top of the point

Chapter IV

between our two beaches. Standing on that precipice for the first time, I was overwhelmed by the vista. The Pacific stretched before us to the horizon. Its surf pounded the rockface a hundred meters below. *When was the last time a human stood in this spot,* I wondered as I edged forward until the earth nearly ran out. In that moment, my position was clarified. It wasn't a question of segregating lots versus creating a full-amenity coastal community. It was that I didn't want to exploit this virgin outpost at all. I wanted to shelter it. The truth? I wasn't sure I wanted a single other outsider to know it.

V

Falling In Love With The New World

PANAMA CITY
2009

Lief held to his belief that we could make money from Los Islotes selling lots and building houses. I wasn't sure he was right. More important, I wasn't sure I wanted him to be right. But I was committed to backing my husband. My publishing business now had a staff of ten. I'd lean on that support, manage my day better, and carve out more hours for Los Islotes.

We had years of experience buying and selling property around the world, but developing a five-star resort community in the jungle isn't the same as amassing a portfolio of condo rentals. We needed help from experienced professionals. Lief found a U.S. land design company looking to internationalize, and a friend recommended a Panamanian architect. The bunch of us met in Panama City for a charrette. Ricardo, the architect, walked through the door carrying six oversized hardback books. "Would you like to take a look?" he asked as he sat down next to me. He

FALLING IN LOVE WITH THE NEW WORLD
Chapter V

held out his books to me as though sharing a treasure. I reached over to pick up the one on top. "Las Casas De Leon." Beneath it was "Haciendas De Cartagena." Ricardo had my attention. I had a shelf full of books like these myself. A light went on. *Now here's an idea I hadn't considered.* It was a thought so big that I almost didn't let myself acknowledge it.

Since that afternoon standing atop our rocky point, I'd been convinced that, in context, a Los Islotes property development, even a five-star one, seemed base. So what if we built something more noble? Something more lasting? What if we built a city? The notion was more worthy of the setting but so grandiose as to be delusional. It was also completely contrary to my developing instinct to safeguard this secret land we'd discovered. A city would invite the outside world not shield against it. This happens to me often, finding myself holding opposing views. Lief sees it as me constantly changing my mind. In fact, it's me being of two minds at the same time. I am okay continuing in that way until events unfold to the point that one perspective naturally overtakes the other or the two seemingly opposite ideas are somehow married. It drives Lief crazy.

Ricardo's seed landed on fertile ground. I'd been in love with Spanish-colonial cities since my first visit to Granada, Nicaragua, when I was twenty-three years old. In the decades since, I'd spent a lot of time in that and other New World cities that Spain built. I don't have to squint to imagine beyond the crumbling plaster,

AT HOME AT LOS ISLOTES
Finding Our Way On This Veraguas Coast

rusting iron, and rotting wood they've been reduced to by the passage of time. I see only how glorious these places must have been in their day. I prefer them to museums. When I visit the Louvre, I'm more interested in the architectural details of the palace than in the art it houses.

Spain's New World cities came to be at incalculable cost. When the Spanish arrived in the Americas and set about their colonizing, they imported not only a wicked agenda but also infectious disease. In the century-and-a-half after Columbus landed on the island of Hispaniola, the indigenous populations of the Americas fell by eighty percent. Those who didn't die of smallpox, measles, or scarlet fever were worked to death mining gold and silver for shipment back to the Crown. Realizing this was unsustainable, the Spanish began importing enslaved Africans to repopulate the diminishing workforces in their American colonies. It was a strategy that can only be described as soulless. The cultural and economic consequences plague the New World still today.

The sorrowful realities of how they came to be are hard to set aside, but the cities themselves are an architectural legacy. Spain's New World cities were built according to formal guidelines each around a central plaza anchored by a church. Classic Spanish-colonial design features soft arches, white stucco walls, red clay-tiled roofs, carved wooden doors, balconies, interior courtyards, and fountains. Why go to the trouble of building an arch when you could make the opening square? Why incorporate ornate iron-

FALLING IN LOVE WITH THE NEW WORLD
Chapter V

work? Because you can and because the resulting structure is more pleasing. Everyone who passes through benefits. Architecture is art, and great art boosts our spirits, lifts our souls, challenges our minds, and inspires our imaginations. We all can use as much of all that as we can get.

My first day in Granada, I walked to the square at dusk. The setting sun tinted the city's powder blue and apple red structures golden. Children ran and called to each other in play. Old men read the day's news. Old women shared the day's gossip. Young lovers sat close on wooden benches. Vendors offered warm tortillas and roasted corn. Guitarists serenaded. I returned the next night and the next to watch the show replay against the backdrop of edifices that'd stood that ground for five-hundred years. I appreciated the extraordinary beauty of the scene but even more the continuity of the experience. Generation after generation has played on this stage. Each picks up where their ancestors left off, adding their marks and further embellishing the set for the next in line. Resting in the shade of a lemonwood tree, studying the details of the grand buildings all around, I felt connected to the past of this rare place and a part of its future. Great architecture does that.

The Spanish started their development of the New World on the island where Columbus first set foot. In 1496, in what is today the Dominican Republic, Columbus' brother Bartholomew founded Santo Domingo, the capital of Spain's first colony in

AT HOME AT LOS ISLOTES
Finding Our Way On This Veraguas Coast

---

this part of the world. Calle Las Damas, the first street of the original city and the oldest paved street in the Americas, is lined with pale stone facades that have borne centuries of witness. Here the Columbuses built a customs house, a hospital, a cathedral, a university, and a library, everything required for a considered, comfortable, fulfilling life. The Spanish based their plan on the greatest cities of Spain and replicated it from Granada and Leon, Nicaragua, to Antigua, Guatemala, and Casco Viejo, Panama.

I left the Los Islotes charrette with a reading list from Ricardo and the start of my grander plan. We wouldn't just create a luxe-level coastal resort. We'd also build a city. My mind lit up at the thought. I'd been a classic architect enthusiast since, years before, when I was still living in Baltimore and traveling to Europe for business, my boss at Agora introduced me to a French architect. The three of us spent spare hours between meetings touring. Paris is many things but what mattered most for Frank were its buildings. He led us down cobblestoned alleyways and into hidden courtyards to introduce us to his favorite aspects of the City of Light and in the process awakened in me a latent interest. I was thrilled by every aspect of every structure Frank showed us. I felt physical pleasure listening to him detail seventeenth-century facades and eighteenth-century stairwells.

When I left Agora and suddenly found myself in Paris with free time on my hands, I picked up where Frank, Bill, and I had left off. I designed architectural walking tours for myself, cher-

FALLING IN LOVE WITH THE NEW WORLD
Chapter V

ry-picking sights from guidebooks. My favorite spot in the city became the center of the Tuileries. Standing in that garden lane, you have the Louvre on one side and Place de la Concorde and its obelisk on the other. Beyond Concorde is the Champs-Élysées and its triumphal arch. If you shift your head slightly, you can see the Eiffel Tower. The Tuileries are the work of Catherine de Medici, a wicked woman, mother to three French kings, famous for sacrificing her children, her country, and her principles for power. Alas, another contradiction in human history. I can't help but thank the monstrous woman for her part in the efforts that, over centuries, created the spot where I feel grateful to be alive every time I pass through. If I hadn't become a writer, I imagine I could have been an architect. Los Islotes presented a chance for me to indulge that smoldering passion.

Along the Veraguas coast Lief and I were pioneering, Nature seemed to extend a challenge. *Dear humans, could you make a place for yourself here that would do justice to the Eden I've provided, that marries the best you're capable of with my finest handiwork?* Perhaps we could try. I knew I couldn't create a new Paris in my lifetime, but I could lay a foundation. I could plan a city in the tradition of the cities the Spanish created but with an important difference. The people whose land the Spanish seized for their cities did not benefit. The Spanish understood how to install the infrastructure of good living—facilities for education, reading, and physical and spiritual care—but denied access to the people they'd forced to

AT HOME AT LOS ISLOTES
Finding Our Way On This Veraguas Coast

do the work. I'd engineer my city shoulder to shoulder with the people of Veraguas and for our collective benefit.

The notion was so embarrassingly lofty that I dared not admit it to anyone, not even Lief. I did, though, let myself make a suggestion to Lief's design team. "What if we incorporated a town center in the master plan?" I asked at our next meeting. Lief hemmed and hawed but finally went along because he'd begun to realize that we needed to set Los Islotes apart. Lots weren't flying off the shelf. A commercial space, as Lief relegated the idea, would make our situation at Los Islotes less isolated. I think Ricardo appreciated what I was really suggesting—not a spruced-up strip mall, as I feared Lief imagined, but a classic colonial town square—and he was delighted by the idea. I had an ally. It was a place to start.

Now, Los Islotes, which had seemed a burden, was an opportunity. This was my chance to create on a grand scale. If I embraced the dream to build something outstanding and lasting, the rest of my life would be determined. That decision would influence every choice to follow. I was okay with that. I had the sense that every decision I'd made before had led me to this point. I've always dreamed big, and I believe that key to making a dream come true is telling yourself that it can. The strategy had always served me well, though I'd never let my fantasies run this wild before.

I wasn't so taken with my fantasy that I lost sight of the fact that I had no reasonable reason to think I could pull it off. First,

FALLING IN LOVE WITH THE NEW WORLD
Chapter V

I'm a direct-response publisher. I have no business creating cities—no experience in urban planning, in pouring concrete, in designing bridges, or in figuring out how many public restrooms per capita. Second, Lief had made it clear he wasn't interested in building a city for the ages. He wanted to pull profits from Los Islotes and move on to a next project. Third, I had nothing like the funding required. We barely had the financial resources to build a resort community. Fourth, the Los Islotes labor pool was thin. Most in the villages around us hadn't been to school beyond the sixth grade. Many couldn't read. I doubted any of them had seen the kind of city I was imagining. Their houses had dirt floors and openings where the doors should have been. Even if I pulled off a miracle and wrangled my idea onto paper, found a source for unlimited funds, and got Lief on board, where would I source craftsmen to execute my grand plan? I wrestled with each of these hurdles before I closed my eyes every night, but I set the concerns aside each morning. Sunshine helps me to keep my worries at bay.

If I'd been honest with myself, I would have admitted that none of those practicalities was the real impediment. The real obstacle was the cultural divide. It didn't occur to me until we were too far along the path to retreat, but I was conceiving big changes for a place that'd never asked for any. I grew up taking for granted that development is a good thing, but that was before I knew a place as undeveloped as this one. Early in my career, an expat friend in Belize shared an insight. Mick had built a jungle lodge in Cayo.

AT HOME AT LOS ISLOTES
Finding Our Way On This Veraguas Coast

Travel + Leisure ranked it among the best hotels in the world. Mick had started from nothing. He'd bought a piece of land on a river in a place he'd never seen for US$300 from a guy he met in a bar in Belize City. Mick and his wife Lucy worked over decades to turn raw jungle into world-class luxury. "Our greatest challenge," Mick told me once, "has been the Belizeans. They're wonderful. Welcoming. Many have become great friends. We love being part of their country and their culture. But we've been living here fifteen years, and they still don't understand us. They'll never understand us. And we'll never understand them. That's just the reality." I wasn't able to fully apprehend Mick's perspective when he'd shared it, but I'd spent enough time in developing regions since to know he had a point.

To the people of Veraguas, we're aliens from outer space. I didn't want it to be true, but I feared that, no matter how hard we worked to integrate among them, we always would be. We and the people of this coast have nothing in common. Except, I'd begun to realize, a respect for the coast itself. The people of Quebro value the land of their ancestors more than anything else. Instinctively, I did, too. That was a commonality to build on. Still, I should have expected that some of the good folks of Quebro might not appreciate us outsiders showing up to show them how they could live better. I could have predicted but didn't that my hardest job wouldn't be building a city. My real trial would be avoiding a war.

VI

False Starts

PANAMA CITY
2010

At last Lief and I were both all in on Los Islotes. No matter that it was for very different reasons. We'd been building businesses together for a decade-and-a-half. I knew that when Lief and I row in the same direction we go places. However, we'd only get so far on our own.

We were coming and going from Veraguas sporadically. We needed a full-time supervisor on the ground we could trust to keep things moving forward when we weren't there. As with everything to do with Los Islotes, this proved a taller order than we ever could have imagined. Our first false start was Gary. After the 2008 real estate bust, Gary, an engineer with thirty years of experience building residential communities in North Carolina, was forced into early retirement he couldn't afford. That explained why the Southern Baptist who'd never traveled outside the United States and his stay-at-home wife Karen were open to

AT HOME AT LOS ISLOTES
Finding Our Way On This Veraguas Coast

walking away from their children and grandchildren to live in the Panamanian jungle. Gary spoke no Spanish. Almost no one in Quebro spoke English. Gary didn't mind using elaborate gestures to communicate. His pantomime was endearing but inefficient. Finally, he found a young woman to translate. None of the men Gary and Hermelinda interviewed had experience with the work we needed them to do. Two agreed their employment contracts by making their marks because they couldn't write their names. It was a motley crew, but Gary was a man of faith. We bought him a backhoe and a dump truck, and he showed his team how to cut a road. Each visit thereafter Lief and I were greeted by more dirt tracks over and around Los Islotes' rolling green hills. These pathways were critical. We couldn't do anything else until we had access across the property. At the same time, each cut brought angst. Who were we to make these marks on this virgin earth? I didn't share those thoughts, not even with Lief, nor let them interfere with our plans, but I couldn't make them go away either.

Gary's marching orders were to create a road system and to begin installing utilities. Lief and I wanted to operate by the book. Part of Gary's job his first year was figuring out what "by the book" meant. He learned, for example, speaking with government agencies in Panama City, that we'd need to file an impact assessment report with MiAmbiente, Panama's national environmental authority, every six months. They required that we plant a new tree for every one we cut down and update them on irrigation,

FALSE STARTS
Chapter VI

wells, sewage management, garbage collection, and construction within proximity of our mangroves. We didn't mind the attention. We'd seen the result across Central America of developers ignoring these kinds of things. We couldn't stay compliant on our own. Ricardo suggested we engage an engineer to help and put Gary in touch with a young woman named Madrigal.

Madrigal was my first female ally at Los Islotes. I knew we'd be friends as soon as Gary told me her story. Madrigal was born and raised in Santiago. After college she went to the States to look for work. "She managed to get a job," Gary said, "in Washington state running a department of engineers involved with the development of the port of Seattle. A young woman just out of school, Kathleen," he pointed out. "All thirty of her staff were men older than she was. Can you imagine?" Yes, I could. I'd been in the same situation at Agora.

In Seattle, Madrigal met and married an American. After their first child was born, Madrigal told her husband, David, that she wanted to move back to Panama. "I didn't want to raise my son in the United States," she admitted after she and I knew each other well enough to have the conversation. "I saw how kids there were growing up. They had cell phones by the time they were four years old. And they had little to do with their extended families. I wanted my children to grow up with their aunts and uncles and cousins all around. And I wanted their childhood years to be spent in nature, not a U.S. suburb." I'm not a fan of suburbia ei-

AT HOME AT LOS ISLOTES
Finding Our Way On This Veraguas Coast

ther. I appreciate great cities and uncharted frontiers. Suburbs are the not-so-interesting places in between. Paris has always been part of Lief and my long-term plan. Now we seemed to be pairing that with Los Islotes. That worked. It'd make for a life of stark contrast, something neither of us like to go too long without.

David resisted. How would he earn an income in Panama? He spoke little Spanish, and employment opportunities in Santiago were limited. When their second child was born, Madrigal insisted. "I couldn't bear that my son and daughter wouldn't know their grandparents the way I knew mine," she told me. "My favorite memories from when I was little are of Sunday mornings. My entire family would go to sunrise mass altogether. Then we'd walk to a restaurant where my mother and father have eaten since they were young. We'd have breakfast at the same table every week. We still do! Everyone in town knows my parents. They take turns stopping by to say hello and gossip. I wanted my children to be part of that world."

To Panamanians, family is everything, all around all the time. I'd left mine behind in Baltimore years before, and the longer I was away the more I missed them. Kaitlin had resented being torn from her grandmother and cousins when we moved to Ireland. I believe I made the right choice restarting our lives in Waterford. That put us on the path for Paris and then Panama and now Los Islotes. But I carry Kaitlin's pain from those years when she cried herself to sleep at night and begged me to let her return

FALSE STARTS
Chapter VI

"home," and I regret that Jackson never knew an extended family bond. We travel to Baltimore for Christmas and summer vacations when we can. I look for every opportunity to strengthen our family connections. In this regard, Los Islotes is an accidental do-over. Part of what Lief and I are creating on this coast is a future gathering place for our children, their children, and on and on. That vision has become an important motivating force for me.

Madrigal, David, and their two children moved into Madrigal's parents' home on the outskirts of Santiago with the mountains of Santa Fé on their doorstep. David opened a smoothie bar in town then a catering business. Neither lasted a year. Meantime, Madrigal had more business than she could handle. We put her on retainer so we wouldn't lose her. She'd drive down to Los Islotes from Santiago once a month. We'd tour the property together pointing out road, water, and other infrastructure work since her last visit. Madrigal would take photos and make notes in her log as support for her twice-annual filings with MiAmbiente. Madrigal knew her business and was well connected. She became our go-to resource. When we needed a surveyor, a well digger, or a permit to harvest river rocks, we asked Madrigal.

After two years of failing to make a living in Santiago, David told Madrigal he was returning to Seattle. Madrigal said she was staying in Santiago with their children. She was more certain than ever it was the right place for them. The couple didn't separate officially, only geographically. The years of conflict with her husband

AT HOME AT LOS ISLOTES
Finding Our Way On This Veraguas Coast

had taken a toll on Madrigal. Once she was on her own, the stress I'd watched build in her evaporated. Each time I saw her after David left, she seemed younger and brighter. Three months into this stage as a single working mom, Madrigal WhatsApp'd me a photo of her wearing white cowgirl boots with long white leather fringes. I wear cowgirl boots, too. They're good for hiking in the jungle and my imagined protection against snakebites. Most of my life, most of my friends have been male. Madrigal was the first girlfriend I'd made in a long time. Like me, she was focused on her business, but, also like me, she liked to take a minute now and then to discuss things like fancy footwear.

Gary needed a place to work and so did we when we were on site so our first attempt at vertical construction was a one-room office. The project became a metaphor for our situation overall. Lief wanted cheap, Gary wanted quick, and I wanted pretty. We built with concrete block, which was cheap and quick. I insisted on a pitched roof with red clay tiles for pretty. As an afterthought, Gary, a hobby woodworker, made us a sign. He cut individual letters in corotu to spell out "Los Islotes" on the wall beside the door. I brought a bottle of champagne our first visit after the structure was completed. We popped the cork and took photos alongside Gary's sign. It should have been a happy milestone, but, standing in the doorway of the little structure looking out at the acres of untamed jungle all around, I was overcome thinking of the years and dollars it'd taken to get us to this point. All that to create

FALSE STARTS
Chapter VI

forty square meters. What in the world were we thinking, imagining a resort development, and me beyond that a city? At the same time, I was still worried that we shouldn't be making any attempt in the first place. Every road cut cost me sleep. How was I going to make peace with a beach club and condos?

Now that we had an office, we promised Gary we'd be on site every four weeks. We'd drive out Friday and stay through Sunday morning. That'd give us one full day at Los Islotes monthly, a total of twelve days a year to develop three-hundred acres into a five-star destination. It was the best we could do. Even now that we were both fully engaged with Los Islotes, we couldn't take focus off the publishing business. It still paid for everything.

Gary was a friendly guy. He did his best to connect with his new neighbors. One day driving to work he passed a man and a woman he'd never seen before. They were laying concrete blocks to build the foundation of a small house just outside our entrance. Gary stopped to introduce himself.

"We need to report them to MiAmbiente," Lief said when Gary told us about Roberta and Mateo's construction project near our front gate. In Panama, it's illegal to build within twenty meters of a mangrove. MiAmbiente is the government agency charged with protecting the country's natural environment and therefore responsible for enforcing that law. This couple Roberta and Mateo had positioned their house less than a meter from the edge of the estuary that runs through Los Islotes. The estuary is fringed by mangroves.

AT HOME AT LOS ISLOTES
Finding Our Way On This Veraguas Coast

Roberta and Mateo were breaking another law, too. They didn't own the land where they'd decided to settle. Squatting might seem like a greater infraction than building in an environmentally sensitive location. But Dalys had helped us to understand that, as the people of Veraguas interpret things, it's not. The earliest inhabitants of this coast moved around. They set down roots where they wanted, hung around for a while, then continued on. Centuries later, the land up and down this coast has titled owners or is protected by the state. Still, the modern-day Indians of Veraguas, as they think of themselves proudly, share their ancestors' perspective. Land is for enjoying, not owning. We humans benefit from it while we're here then leave it to the next generation to do the same. We're stewards. The perspective resonated with me, and our attorneys agreed. Illegal tenancy was not the path to pursue. Roberta had no right to build a house where she'd chosen to build one, but we'd have a better chance of getting the government's help evicting her based on the mangrove-infringement charge.

"Do we need to rat them out?" I wondered aloud when Lief directed Gary to file a formal complaint. "Is it really any of our business?"

"Yes, it's our business," Lief replied wearily. Lief and I disagreed on almost every aspect of everything to do with Los Islotes from how to pave the roads to how much to spend on landscaping. It was exhausting. "Their eyesore of a house will interfere with our

FALSE STARTS
Chapter VI

ability to sell," Lief pointed out. "Their place will be the first thing potential buyers see as they approach."

"Well, we don't know that it will be an eyesore," I said. How optimistic. How naive.

Lief wasn't persuaded, but he agreed at my urging to let the situation percolate and reassess down the line.

Over the months to follow, we didn't keep our promise to Gary. We made the trip to Veraguas far less often than we should have. Jackson had school, and Lief and I were building a business. We'd moved out of our loft into a three-bedroom apartment. We were settled, comfortable, and busy, living like any family with a young child and two full-time working parents. We were up with the sun. Jackson would walk his dog Smokey along the Cinta Costera. I'd nag him to hurry up and eat the eggs I'd scrambled so he didn't miss his bus. Then, Jackson out the door, Lief and I were off for the worst part of my day—rush hour.

When we first moved to Panama City, we debated over buying a car. Taxis were everywhere and cheap. But relying on them for transportation came with challenges. They wouldn't always take you where you wanted to go. "*Dónde vas?*" They'd ask. Where are you going? If the answer to that question wasn't a direction they wanted to travel—because it would take them against traffic or too far from home near the end of a shift—they'd shake their heads. "*No voy*," they'd say. "I'm not going there." That response left us standing on street corners in the rain all the time. Taxis

AT HOME AT LOS ISLOTES
Finding Our Way On This Veraguas Coast

weren't metered, and some drivers would insist on US$5 for a trip that should cost a buck. Tourists didn't know and would pay the inflated rates, and the drivers didn't know we weren't tourists. We were constantly reduced to arguing with them over a few dollars. Ridiculous waste of time. Taxis were also often in need of repairs. One afternoon a driver handed Lief a pair of pliers to use to close his window when it started to rain because the window handle was broken. Lief applied the pliers and tried to turn the handle but no luck. The driver shouted over his shoulder that Lief was doing it wrong then leaned into the back seat while the taxi was still in motion to grab the pliers and turn the handle himself. Another day I hailed a taxi with Jackson. I hadn't thought to look down at the floor of the cab before getting in. As Jackson and I took our seats, I saw that we were in a Flintstones car. It had a hole in the floor big enough to put both my legs through.

After that incident, Lief and I decided to invest in a car of our own. In fact, we bought two—one for Lief and one for me—even though staff and friends warned us about traffic. How bad could it be, really, we wondered. We found out.

The International Monetary Fund reports on "convergence velocity." It's the rate at which one economy is catching up with another. Most countries don't measure up to the United States. Latin American economies often lose ground. That's "negative convergence." Recently, Chile and the Dominican Republic have been exceptions. They're gaining on the U.S. economy. Panama

FALSE STARTS
Chapter VI

is in a league of its own. It's catching up with the United States seventeen times faster than the average rate for the region. In 2000, Panama's GDP was US$12 billion. In 2023, it is US$63 billion. That's an existential increase. And the growth continues. It is expected that by 2030 Panama will no longer be a developing nation. It will have realized its goal of joining the First World.

One of the best measures of a country's development is its middle class. The middle class in Panama expanded from fifty-point-eight percent of the population in 2015 to fifty-six-point-nine percent in 2019. In 2023 the country has a relatively larger middle class than the United States. One distinguishing factor of a middle class is the money it has to spend.

Panama's exploding population in the middle has more to invest in housing than any previous generation in this country's history. When we arrived in the city, Avenida Balboa was being lined with new waterfront condo towers in real time, existing apartment buildings across Panama City were being refitted for higher-dollar buyers, and big swaths of land just outside the capital were being given over to housing developments targeting the middle-class demographic specifically. Thousands of houses appeared side-by-side on the landscape, each sold as a monthly payment. "Only US$200 Per Quincena." That's a pay period.

Panama's middle class has more money to spend on food, too. The first U.S.-style grocery store opened just before we made our move. It stocked, we were delighted to discover, Jif peanut but-

AT HOME AT LOS ISLOTES
Finding Our Way On This Veraguas Coast

---

ter, A.1. Sauce, U.S. steaks, French cheeses, and Argentine wines. Those were indulgences we wanted to consume, and we were okay spending twenty to fifty percent more to buy them than we would have in their countries of origin. We weren't alone. Panama City's middle class crowded the aisles of Riba Smith alongside us.

The growing monied segment of Panama's population could spend more to educate their children, meaning more private schools. They could afford to dress and furnish their homes better, explaining the appearance of Banana Republic, Hermès, Chanel, and Zara Home in shopping malls. And they could all buy cars.

At first they could drive them without learning how. No classes or test were required to get a license. Many didn't bother with a license anyway. All they needed, they figured, was the car key. Lief bought a Prado. Panama City's streets were built before SUVs existed. I chose a BMW. I figured its sedan footprint would make navigating the crowded, narrow roads easier and parking, too, which was also always a challenge. Jackson often kept me company in the kitchen while I was making dinner. One evening he looked out our kitchen window at the Avenida Balboa traffic below and started laughing. "These drivers seem to have trouble converging," he said. "I've seen three accidents in the few minutes I've been watching." From our fourteenth-floor perspective it was comedic. From street level, for me, it was terrifying. No one used turn signals. Right turn on red? These folks made left turns on red across three lanes of oncoming traffic. They cut you off. They

FALSE STARTS
Chapter VI

jumped the median. They drove on the sidewalks. We witnessed hit-and-runs as part of our day-to-day.

I reached my limit for Panama City drivers one night driving through the Avenida Balboa overpass in the pouring rain. Four lanes lead into the roundabout beneath two two-lane overpasses from each direction. Talk about trouble converging. It's a free-for-all. That particular stormy night, it felt like all those middle-class Panamanians in all their vehicles were competing for the space around me at the same time alongside the Diablos Rojos.

For decades, the United States has shipped old school buses to Central America. In Panama, they became an industry. Each is a private business. The owners paint them wildly, sometimes to tell a story like a graphic novel. Some have spokes on the wheels and long tassels flying from side mirrors. Others have giant exhaust pipes towering overhead like smoke stacks. These Diablos Rojos, as they're called, are a menace. They don't fit in the lanes, and their drivers don't care. The Panamanian department of transportation tried to take them off the road, but the plan wasn't thought through. The Red Devils are a key link in getting people to and from work. They were replaced in Panama City with modern buses imported from Europe, but people from Chorrera, Arraiján, and other nearby towns who commuted to Panama City each day couldn't connect. It was a miscalculation on the level of the new airport at Albrook, which had opened without air conditioning because the engineers forgot it.

AT HOME AT LOS ISLOTES
Finding Our Way On This Veraguas Coast

Just enough of the old school buses were put back into service to allow Panama City's workforce to get to work. That night I arrived at the Balboa roundabout, they surrounded me. I had one on either side and another speeding up behind. I couldn't change lanes and missed my turn. I finally made it home an hour later. That was the last time I got behind the wheel in Panama City. I told Lief I wanted to hire a driver.

Guillermo schooled me on the ways of Panama City's mean streets. "You've got to drive like a cowboy," he told me one morning after I'd told him he didn't need to cut back and forth from lane to lane. I wasn't in that great a hurry. "If I don't drive like this, Señora Kathleen, everyone will take advantage of us." It was a lesson in Panamanian drivers but also my introduction to *juega vivo*. Guillermo quit two months later. He moved his young family to Aguadulce. He'd had enough of playing the game of life in Panama City. He wanted to raise his children in the country. I didn't blame him.

Our second driver, Alberto, taught me about Carnavales. "Are you staying in the city next month?" he asked driving me to work one morning. It would be our first Carnival in Panama. Every previous year since our moved, we'd taken advantage of the holiday to schedule trips outside the country.

"We haven't decided yet," I said.

"If you're going to travel to the interior," Alberto said, "go early. Don't wait until the weekend before."

FALSE STARTS
Chapter VI

"The traffic will be bad?" I asked.

"You've never seen anything like it," Alberto said. "Nothing gets between a Panamanian and his Carnival." Alberto was Panamanian himself but he always set himself apart. "In November, we have our independence days," he said. "Then in December is Christmas," he continued. "That's all just the lead up to Carnavales. It is the most important event of the year. Every Panamanian who can afford it travels to the beach. If they can't afford it, they sell something so they can. People sell their cars, their furniture. I knew a man who sold his refrigerator. And another one who sold his business. It was a little cart. He pushed it along and sold empanadas that his wife made every morning. One year he didn't have money for Carnavales. So he sold his little cart."

Panama City's Carnival, which we decided to experience that year with Jackson, is tame compared with the stories Alberto and others told us about pre-Lenten celebrations elsewhere in the country. Las Tablas, on the other side of our peninsula south of Chitré, is famous for its Carnavales debauchery. Las Tablas has a population of ten thousand people. Ten times that many show up every Carnival season. Partiers fill the hotels and guest houses. When the indoor space runs out, the out-of-town revelers sleep on park benches and in people's front yards. If they sleep at all. Seco fuels an around-the-clock fiesta of throbbing music, exploding fireworks, and water. Kids spray each other with plastic pistols, and men hop atop water trucks called *culecos* to drench

AT HOME AT LOS ISLOTES
Finding Our Way On This Veraguas Coast

street dancers with fire hoses. Initially I'd wondered if the water elements had biblical connections, but they're practical. The water play isn't to purify souls. It's to cool down bodies. Frolicking for hours in the Panamanian sun works up a sweat. I've never experienced Carnavales in Las Tablas. I missed my window. It's something to try once when you're young.

It was three months before we were able to carve out time to return to Los Islotes. In that time, in one of his weekly update emails, Gary had written to tell us that Roberta had come to the Los Islotes office to say that she intended to operate a restaurant from her home when it was finished. Gary thought this was good news and so did I. Our men brought their lunches with them each day and sat on tree stumps to eat cold chicken and rice from plastic containers. Like Gary, I wanted to lend Roberta a helping hand because we could. More than that, I was impressed by this female entrepreneur. She'd noticed a market need and had stepped up to fill it. Backing her seemed the least I could do as a fellow businesswoman in a place where women don't count. Madrigal had taught me that. "I am an anomaly," she'd told me. "Women here don't run their own businesses or make their own money. They take care of the men in their lives."

Gary asked if he could donate bags of cement and labor to aid Roberta's effort. I told him yes before Lief could say no. "Why in the world did you agree to help that woman?" he wanted to know when he saw my email approving Gary's request. "You're just en-

FALSE STARTS
Chapter VI

couraging her!" Yes, I was. I thought it was the right thing to do. Lief and I agreed to disagree on the point. With aid from Gary and our crew, Roberta was able to open her restaurant in two months. She had no electricity meaning no refrigeration so Gary delivered meat each morning—chicken or pork—that Roberta used to prepare hot lunches for our guys.

Our first day back on site after our monthslong absence, Gary suggested we have lunch at Roberta's. Lief was reluctant. He didn't want to give the impression that he was okay with her presence because he definitely wasn't. On every previous visit we'd brought packed lunches, which we hadn't done this day, or driven back to Gary's house where Karen would prepare us a meal. "Roberta's restaurant is the easy choice," I told Lief who agreed begrudgingly. Roberta recognized us as soon as we appeared in her doorway. Gary had been telling her about Lief and me the way he'd been telling us about her. Her face lit up when she realized we'd come as customers. She was on the other side of a concrete counter, a tiny woman in a T-shirt stirring a giant pot of rice atop a two-burner stove. She sent her daughter Sophia to wipe down a table, drag it over to the window, then pull over three chairs. When Sophia had prepared a place for us, Roberta smiled in our direction and made a sweeping gesture with her arm as if to say, "Welcome, have a seat, make yourselves at home." "*Hola, mucho gusto,*" I called out loudly enough for her to hear from across the room. Roberta spooned rice, beans, and Gary's pork onto three

AT HOME AT LOS ISLOTES
Finding Our Way On This Veraguas Coast

plates. No vegetable. That's typical. Vegetables are luxuries. "She smokes the pork over an open fire out back," Gary told us. The smell of the meat cooking drifted in through the opening in the concrete block wall that served as a window. Sophia brought our food then three glasses she'd filled with water from an Igloo cooler. She was too nervous to make eye contact.

Other than Roberta and Sophia, I was the only woman in the room. I knew most of the men. They worked for us. "*Hola, hola!*" I'd offered with a smile and a wave to everyone assembled when we'd entered. No one had waved back. As Madrigal had helped me to understand, I'm an enigma to the men of Quebro. Their wives, girlfriends, and mothers are all at home, where these guys think women belong. They're okay with women serving them, the way Roberta and Sophia were doing, but here I was sitting down to lunch with the guys because I was managing the finca alongside my husband. The situation is extreme here in Veraguas, but it's been the same all my life. I've gotten used to men not knowing what to make of me. I don't mean to intimidate them, but I do.

On the wall alongside where Sophia had seated us was a framed photograph of a young boy in a military costume with medals pinned to his chest. He held a small Panamanian flag in one hand and a wooden baton in the other. His smile couldn't have been brighter. "That's Roberta's grandson," Gary said when he saw me staring. "He led the parade in town during last year's Independence Day celebrations." Roberta was a proud grandmother.

FALSE STARTS
Chapter VI

When we'd finished our food, Roberta came from behind her counter to collect our empty plates. "*Tu nieto es muy guapo,*" I offered, pointing up toward the photo. She beamed and nodded.

Later that afternoon, as the sun was beginning to set and Lief, Gary, and I were leaving Los Islotes to return to Gary's house for dinner, Roberta walked out from her restaurant and stood in the middle of the road. In each hand she held a big round gourd, the kind we find all around on the ground in summer. They fall from the calabash trees. These two had been painted. When we were alongside her, Gary stopped and rolled down his window. Roberta approached. "These are for you," she said in Spanish, looking at me in the back seat. "My granddaughter made them." Roberta gave the gourds to Gary who passed them back to me. One had been decorated with red and orange butterflies. The other showed the tiny yellow and white flowers that carpet our jungle floor. "*Muchas gracias,*" I said with enthusiasm. "*Son muy bonitas!*" I was touched by the gesture. The gourds seemed to have been made especially for us. The next day I placed Roberta's granddaughter's offerings on the shelf behind my desk in the office.

As our Los Islotes crew grew, so did Roberta's business. Lief and I would eat at her restaurant every day we were on the property. Some days we'd have to wait in line in the road for a table. I came to consider Roberta part of our team. I wouldn't say we became friends, but we'd ask after each other's children and she regularly gifted us watermelons and mangos. I knew that Lief

AT HOME AT LOS ISLOTES
Finding Our Way On This Veraguas Coast

still objected strongly to the situation, but he kept his reservations mostly to himself. I came to look forward to seeing Roberta each lunchtime the way I do the head waiter in the café on the corner down the street from our apartment in Paris where we go for dinner at least once a week. Familiar friendly faces.

Gary worked hard, but he got minimal direction from us and made limited progress. The problem was that neither Lief nor I had a clear plan. The more we got into Los Islotes, the more we realized that, in fact, we had no idea what we were doing. Gary gave us roads, gutters, and underground tubes for electrical lines. Now what?

The answer to that question was finally provided by an Italian friend in Panama City. With his chiseled features and full head of wavy white hair, Bruno could have been a 1940s movie star. He dressed in bespoke double-breasted suits and Italian loafers and you felt special when he smiled at you because it meant he'd noticed you. Bruno had been one of the first foreign developers in Panama, in the 1970s. When he found our publishing business online and got in touch, he was a successful developer in South Beach wanting to try Panama again. He believed Live And Invest Overseas could be the partner he needed to break into the American market and invited Lief and me to dinner.

After the Americans pulled out of the Canal Zone, Panama yearned for First World recognition. It invested the revenues generated by the Canal it now controlled into highways and hospi-

FALSE STARTS
Chapter VI

tals. The country's sustained commitment to infrastructure coupled with its zero corporate tax rate for income earned outside the country gave the Panamanians a leg up in the competition for global foreign investment. The world's biggest multinationals targeted Panama City for their regional headquarters then needed work forces in the thousands to staff them. Recognizing that his country couldn't meet that demand, President Martinelli had a genius idea. He issued an Executive Order making it easy and low-cost for a foreigner to become resident and get a work permit. This meant Nike, Estée Lauder, Dell, John Deere, etc., could import staff, especially managers. It was a game-changing move, and we were beneficiaries. We were able to complement our Live And Invest Overseas Panama team with Americans, Canadians, and Europeans with direct-marketing experience who helped train up our local labor. It was a win all the way around.

All the foreign executives relocating to Panama, including our own, wanted executive-worthy digs. Bruno was originally from Milan. His idea was to build a condo tower branded by the fashion designer Roberto Cavalli who would use the building as a venue to showcase lines exclusive to the Latin market. It was the business model that had established Bruno in Miami. I agreed that *yeyé* Panamanians would pay big premiums to own condos that came with access to private Italian fashion shows. The *yeyés*, the segment of the country's population that likes to hang out at the Union Club in Panama City telling each other how import-

AT HOME AT LOS ISLOTES
Finding Our Way On This Veraguas Coast

ant they are, are preoccupied with seeing and being seen. Panama is a tiny pond. The *yeyés* consider themselves the big fish. Bruno's business strategy would get their attention, for sure. It would also appeal to Venezuelans, Colombians, El Salvadorans, and others from the region spending time and stockpiling wealth in safe haven Panama. I was less certain of the appeal of a Cavalli-connected condo tower to our American readers, but Lief and I wanted to get to know Bruno better so we entertained the conversation. He became our Panama market mentor. When we admitted to him that our five years of effort at Los Islotes had netted us nothing more than dirt roads, ditches, and a one-room office, Bruno looked me in the eye and said, "You must build a house."

"People lack imagination," he continued. "They can't buy into your vision until you show it to them. Build a grand house in the style you intend so people can appreciate the opportunity in front of them." I knew instantly that Bruno was right. I was having trouble holding on to the picture I'd cultivated in my mind of what Los Islotes could be. How could we expect strangers to have any clue?

The timing was right. We'd sold a few dozen lots to owners who were now watching for a cue from Lief and me. They'd invested their money and their futures based on our plan to create the premier coastal community not only in Panama but in the region. It was an ambitious promise, and Lief and I both felt enor-

FALSE STARTS
Chapter VI

mous pressure to deliver. It was time for us to go all in. A personal building project would reconfirm our commitment, both to our buyers and to ourselves. But we'd need to find a new foreman for the project. Gary had given his notice. He was tired and ready to retire for real. We asked if he'd source us a builder before he and Karen returned to the States.

Steve Britman was a contractor running a construction crew in Boquete when Gary connected with him. We arranged to meet Britman in Panama City. It wasn't an interview exactly because we had no option. Gary had made it clear that it was this guy Britman or no house. He could find no other builder in Panama interested in taking on a job on our remote coast. Britman arrived late for the appointment and fell with a thump into the armchair across from my desk. He was sweating, out of breath, and dressed in short pants, flip-flops, and a faded floral shirt unbuttoned to reveal a bulging belly and a sunburned chest. I recognized this guy. In the twenty-five years I'd been scouting developing-world markets, he'd pulled his stool up next to mine dozens of times in bars from Belize to Nicaragua. Guys like him always have a story.

"I guess you've heard about what happened to me," Britman began. *Here we go*, I thought. "My accident was three years ago now, and still I'm suffering. But, hey, what are you going to do?"

"Ah, well, I'm sorry to hear that," I said, looking over at Lief because I didn't want to look at Britman, who was still sweating and now coughing. We didn't know about any accident.

AT HOME AT LOS ISLOTES
Finding Our Way On This Veraguas Coast

"A Mac truck drove over me," Britman continued. "On a job site. I broke twenty-seven bones and fractured three vertebrae. I'm in pain every day, but I'm on the mend. And I'm back to work." He paused and caught his breath. "So you want to build a house at your Los Islotes project on the Veraguas coast," he added, finally getting to the point. "I've got a partner out there. We're already building another house just north of your property. We could get started with you next week," he assured us with a smile that set off alarm bells. Were we really so desperate to push Los Islotes to a next stage that we'd hire this guy? It seemed we were. I brought the conversation to a close quickly because I didn't want to hear anymore of whatever Britman had to say. It didn't matter. We wanted a house. As soon as Bruno suggested the idea, I agreed it was the key next step to realizing the Los Islotes dream I'd let take hold. Britman said he could build us a house. He was who he was.

Lief had chosen the spot. Our house would sit on the side of a hill overlooking the ocean with mountain views behind. Ricardo designed a main house with two guest houses around a pool and patio in traditional Spanish-colonial style. Britman began pouring the foundations. Now that we were an active construction site, Lief and I relaxed a bit. We'd soon have something substantial to show for all our trouble. I cut out pictures from magazines and expanded my library of books showcasing details I wanted to incorporate not only in our house but in all the structures of the city

FALSE STARTS
Chapter VI

I fantasized about building eventually but still didn't talk about. This was before Pinterest. I filled plastic sleeves with images of balconies, courtyards, stairwells, floors, moldings, tiles, and on and on. Finally, we were getting to the fun stuff.

After we broke ground on the house, Lief and I were on site at Los Islotes even less often. The publishing business continued to grow and required more attention than ever. Lief began traveling again, as he'd done when we'd been running the *International Living* business, scouting new markets and business opportunities. Plus, of course, we were parents. Jackson had just started *quatriéme*, his final year before high school.

Before committing fully to Panama, Lief and I had made lists of the pluses and minuses. When Lief found Los Islotes, Panama defaulted into our next stop. It was a good choice for where to base my business, too, but we'd be making the move with four-year-old Jackson. Schooling options were a priority. Jackson had been in school in Paris since Pre-K. We were impressed with the French curriculum, and Jackson was thriving in it. Researching online, we found that the French education system is exported. These aren't schools where instruction is in French. These are French schools, administered by the French Ministry of Education, with all teachers and faculty imported from France, and Panama is one of the one-hundred-and-thirty-nine countries where you find them. That cinched the deal. From a going-to-school perspective at least, the move would be transparent for young Jackson.

AT HOME AT LOS ISLOTES
Finding Our Way On This Veraguas Coast

Jackson's first friend in Panama was Valerian. Like Lief and me, Valerian's parents, Muriel and Loic, had moved to Panama with entrepreneurial aspirations. They'd arrived from Paris the year before us and for years were our only non-work friends. I couldn't help Jackson with his homework. My French wasn't strong enough. But Muriel could. She and Loic let the boys work behind the counter at their Petit Paris restaurant. Valerian and Jackson took hapkido classes together and played catch with Lief and Harry in the street in front of our house. They became like brothers. When Muriel and Loic had to work late, as they did often, Valerian stayed with us. When Lief and I both needed to travel over school days, including to Los Islotes, Jackson stayed with Valerian's family. I took comfort from Muriel and Loic's support, but I didn't like Lief and me both being away from Jackson too often. So, while Lief came and went, I hunkered down in Panama City with Jackson and the team in the office.

We rationalized our continued extended absences from Los Islotes by reminding each other that soon we'd have a house. Our own home at Los Islotes would change everything for the better. It'd be something to show off to potential buyers, and it would mean we could stay on site. No more commuting from the house with the leaky kitchen sink, moldy air conditioners, and unreliable electricity we'd rented twenty minutes away.

Our year-end was busy with budget and planning meetings for the publishing business. Harry was fully fledged in his role as

FALSE STARTS
Chapter VI

---

my righthand man, and he and Kaitlin had made it through three long-distance years. The day after she graduated college, Kaitlin had moved to Panama so she and Harry could finally be together. She joined the Live And Invest Overseas team as managing editor, meaning the four of us got to see each other in the office every day. It was a blessing. Kaitlin and Harry created a well-rounded life for themselves. They rented an apartment overlooking the Bay of Panama, got a dog, joined expat groups, took Spanish lessons, rode their bikes on the Cinta Costera, and generally took great advantage of the entertainment and recreation opportunities all around them. Lief and I expected an engagement announcement any time. Our happy little family celebrated another good year for the business with a trip to Baltimore to spend the holidays with my mom and sister.

We returned to Panama mid-January. The soonest Lief and I were able to make time for a return trip to Los Islotes was early February. When we set out early Friday morning for the drive to Veraguas, it'd been more than four months since our last visit. I'd packed my plastic folders and books. I'd dog-eared pages to show Britman. It should be time to choose ceiling moldings and tile designs. I'd sketched floor patterns based on photos of historic haciendas in Granada, Nicaragua. I wanted to add niches to the wall of the breezeway and a pergola next to the pool. For more than five years, every Los Islotes discussion had had to do with wastewater treatment options and which grade of road tosca

AT HOME AT LOS ISLOTES
Finding Our Way On This Veraguas Coast

would hold up best during the worst of the rainy season. Finally we'd reached the point where we could talk about things I wanted to talk about.

We arrived at Los Islotes in the late afternoon and approached our build site as Britman and his crew were packing up for the day. Lief parked the car and turned off the engine. I stared out the window and couldn't move. I'd expected a house, but what I saw didn't resemble one. We'd been making progress payments as Britman had been requesting, so where was the progress? I got out of the car slowly. I didn't want to believe my eyes. Where the house should have been was only concrete and rebar, same as months before. I needed a minute to process.

The spot Lief had chosen for our house was surrounded by enormous black walnut trees. I noticed movement in one beside where we'd parked. Watching more closely, I counted twelve white-faced monkeys, including two babies. Most were nestled against the trunk but some dangled far out near the ends of long branches. They stared back, unbothered by the intrusion and as interested in me as I was in them. I wanted to call Lief over to share my discovery, but he was already speaking to Britman. I didn't want to join them. This was going to be bad. I could feel it. Couldn't I just hang out here with the monkeys? Did I have to go listen to whatever story Britman was going to spin? I knew the answers to those questions. "*Hasta luego, monos,*" I called out as I turned and headed reluctantly over to Lief.

FALSE STARTS
Chapter VI

Britman was rolling up a set of blueprints as I approached. He didn't look happy. "Steve," Lief was saying, "this is beyond disappointing. We expected much more. Given the money we've spent to date, we thought we'd have a house by now. You know, with rooms and a roof! What have you been doing all these months? Is there a problem we're not aware of?" Lief was showing remarkable restraint, speaking directly but not harshly. He was controlling his temper admirably. His questions were reasonable, his tone level. He was behaving much more calmly than I was feeling.

"Well, you guys haven't signed off on the foundations," Britman said. "I'm just waiting for you to give me the green light."

What? I'd reached the wooden table where Lief and Britman were standing together. I looked at Britman, a foot away. His eyes were smiling. He wasn't surprised by Lief's questions. He'd expected them. He'd set us up for this. I don't get angry often or easily, but my blood was boiling. We'd assured this guy every visit that everything looked good, and we'd asked on every visit and via emails in between about construction. It was always "about to commence." I knew I knew this guy that first day in my office. Now my worst fears were confirmed. Britman had been stringing things out, bilking us for payments. This two-bit conman had been taking our money under false pretenses for months. I bit my tongue. Lief and I needed to be smart. This house was a big investment. We had too much at stake to indulge an angry outburst. We toured the site with Britman, confirming that little had

AT HOME AT LOS ISLOTES
Finding Our Way On This Veraguas Coast

been accomplished in the months we'd been away. Then we told Britman, one more time, underscoring the point for the record, that everything looked good to us and he should start putting up walls. We exchanged painfully polite farewells as the sun was setting over the ocean beyond our mass of rusting rebar stakes and took our leave.

"Oh my God!" I said when Lief and I were in the car and pulling away from the job site. "Oh my God, oh my God, oh my God!"

"I know," Lief said calmly. We'd reversed roles. Normally, I was the one peeling Lief off the ceiling. "I don't ever want to see that crook again either, but I'm afraid we need to take some of the responsibility. We haven't managed this well. We haven't paid enough attention."

For months we'd been asking Britman to send accounting details. Instead we'd received more calls for cash with brief references to what it would be used for but never any reporting or receipts. "My accountant is on vacation," Britman had told us the first two months. Then his accountant was sick. Then she was visiting her sick mother in Chitré. Last month, she'd moved into a new office and hadn't been able to find the file with our paperwork. Lief was right. They were transparent excuses, and we should have seen through them. But we were distracted by the business and our lives in Panama City and so attached to the hope that Britman would come through with a show-stopper of

FALSE STARTS
Chapter VI

a house that we'd gone along. Some part of us had known for a long time that we were being played. Now we had no choice but to face grim realities.

When we got back to Panama City, Lief fired off an email. "Steve," he wrote, "we must have a complete financial report within one week." Two weeks passed. We didn't receive any accounting, but we did get another request for funds. When I read Britman's email asking for more money, I walked from my office to Lief's and shut the door. "Did you see?" I asked. "Yes, I saw," Lief said. "He's overplayed his hand. He's not getting another dime from us until we have a full accounting for every dollar we've sent him so far. This bozo thinks he can keep jerking us around? The guy's out of his mind."

"Agreed," I said. "And I don't think we should respond by email. I think we need to speak with Britman by phone. Right now. These shenanigans have been going on too long. I'll call him, okay?" As angry as I was, now Lief was angrier. I was worried he'd lose his cool. "I'll have a reasonable but serious conversation with him," I said.

I returned to my desk to make the call. When he picked up, I began, "Steve, we aren't going to be able to send any more money until we have a full accounting, including receipts, for everything that's been spent to date." There. Perfectly reasonable request. I would steer this ship back on course through force of will and rationality.

AT HOME AT LOS ISLOTES
Finding Our Way On This Veraguas Coast

"I'm already out of pocket," Britman replied sharply. "I can't carry you guys anymore. Yesterday I shut down the job site. We won't be able to go back to work until you reimburse me what I've advanced on your behalf. Then I'll need an additional US$50,000."

I'd been sitting back in my chair, looking out the glass doors of my office at our customer service team answering phones in the next room. When Britman told me he couldn't "carry us" anymore, I bolted upright. *Oh, my God,* was all I could think, again, over and over. My jaw hardened. I stood up and walked out of my office toward our back terrace. I stepped outside just as the guy made his US$50,000 demand. "You shut down the job site?" I asked, speaking loudly now that no one could hear. "You shut down the job site!" I repeated, nearly screaming. "Without telling us. Without even discussing the situation with us!"

"What choice did I have?" Britman replied, too calmly. "You're behind in payments. I can't work for free." I could hear him smiling. He was also lying. We weren't behind in payments. We'd responded quickly to every previous request, delivering cash as reliably as an ATM. Britman thought he had me. He expected that I'd run to Lief in a panic telling him to wire more funds immediately so work could resume. I don't respond well to extortion. If we never finish this house, I thought, that'll be okay with me. I wasn't rolling over for this hustler.

"You don't shut down the job site," I shouted back. "It's *our* job site. *We* shut it down. And that's what we're doing. As of today,

FALSE STARTS
Chapter VI

all work is halted. We will tell the security guard not to let you or your crew onto the property until you have presented a full accounting for all money spent to date and a complete budget for all costs remaining to finish construction. We also need a timeline. When will the house be completed? Until we have those things, work is stopped." I hung up. I was shaking.

I walked into Lief's office and relayed the conversation. "Yes, indeed," he said, coolly. He'd pushed through his anger to the state of steely calm I'd come to know well over the years. Britman didn't stand a chance. "As you told him, this is the end," Lief said. "He's not stepping foot back on our property until he's made this right." Lief picked up his phone and called our front-gate guard. "Go up to our house site to collect all the tools and equipment," Lief instructed him in Spanish. "Clear the place out. Lock up everything in the yard. Do not allow Steve Britman or any of his crew back inside the gate until further notice." Lief hung up and looked over at me. I was too worked up to sit down. I'd been pacing back and forth in front of his desk. "Britman gets his tools back when we get our accounting," Lief said with finality.

Britman didn't get his tools back. We never heard from him again. A dozen emails and phone calls later, we gave up trying for a response. I did what I always do in the face of big disappointment. I knuckled down. Live And Invest Overseas was not only my livelihood but also my refuge. It was my escape from the challenges of Los Islotes though sometimes I couldn't keep them

AT HOME AT LOS ISLOTES
Finding Our Way On This Veraguas Coast

from encroaching. In the weeks after the curtain was pulled back on Britman's funny business, I couldn't keep the worries at bay. *Good riddance to the scoundrel*, I thought as I sat at my desk a week later trying to work. I never have trouble focusing, but I couldn't. I turned in my chair to look at the photo of Lief and me standing atop the Los Islotes point looking out at the ocean. I'd placed it in my line of sight on the bookshelf across the room. It reminded me of what kept me connected to this place I thought of as both paradise and boondoggle. I felt foolish for having let Britman swindle us, but that wasn't the point. We'd tied the future of Los Islotes to the construction of our house. All we had to show for all the additional time and money invested was a foundation on a hillside at the edge of nowhere. Lief and I have known of dozens of failed property developments. Unfinished shells dot shorelines across Central America. Now we had a concrete and rebar ghost of our own.

Sometimes things don't work out. Sometimes you've got to cut your losses. Maybe Los Islotes wasn't our too big to fail. Maybe it was just too big a bite. Lief had gone silent like he does when circumstances become too much for him. I didn't know if I had it in me to pull him out of himself. I wasn't sure I could propel *myself* forward. And if I mustered the energy to get us both up off the mat, where did we go from here? I was so tired I almost didn't care.

VII

Dalys

LOS ISLOTES
2016

After Britman went AWOL, we downsized to a skeleton crew. With construction halted, we needed only security and groundskeepers. We didn't know for how long or what our next steps would be, but we put Los Islotes on autopilot. We didn't talk about it because we didn't need to. We were at a loss, and we both knew it. Los Islotes was a brain drain and a money pit. It would have been foolish not to focus our time and energy on the publishing business, so that's what we did, taking solace in its success. *We're not complete idiots*, I'd tell myself when I couldn't sleep.

We had a more important reason not to let the continuing struggles at Los Islotes get us too down. It was official. Kaitlin and Harry were getting married. Harry proposed in Central Park during a weekend getaway in New York. Kaitlin was over the moon. She asked if the wedding could be in France the following August. Kaitlin, Jackson, and I planned a driving tour to scout lo-

AT HOME AT LOS ISLOTES
Finding Our Way On This Veraguas Coast

cations. Kaitlin drove, Jackson navigated. I was Miss Daisy in the backseat delighting in the experience. How often does a mother get to eavesdrop on her children's conversations. Mine were mostly interested in discussing French rap (they're both fans) and the plan for the next meal (Kaitlin persuaded Jackson to try escargot but he refused the foie gras). Kaitlin chose a chateau an hour south of Paris and a wedding planner in the Marais.

Back in Panama, my mother-of-the-bride duties filled every non-Live And Invest Overseas hour. Busy as we both were, I began to wonder if Lief could be thinking what I was thinking. Maybe it was time to pull the plug on the property development plan and focus full time on the publishing business and our family. The stars seemed aligned against us out in Veraguas. I was afraid to ask because I feared that if I did and Lief wasn't thinking the same thing, he'd interpret the suggestion as betrayal.

So I grappled with the question privately for months. Should we pull out of Los Islotes or fight for our dream? Eventually my mind settled. *Failure is often giving up too soon.* The refrain played over and over in my head. It's what I tell my kids and my staff because I believe it. Lief and I had been tempted to give up many times in Ireland. No direct-response industry existed when we arrived in Waterford. This meant no relevant labor pool. We hired horse grooms and shop clerks and tried to teach them to market subscription services to Americans. We struggled to open a corporate bank account, to qualify for a company credit card, to negotiate employment contracts, even to rent office space because, it took us far too long to understand, doing business in Ireland is a never-ending dance of the seven veils. But we persevered and built a successful operation. Ireland put us on the path to Panama, and I wasn't ready for our Panama story to be over. My career has been built on helping people launch new lives in new countries. "At some point," I tell them, "you'll wonder what in the world possessed you to think that making a move overseas was a good idea. You'll doubt your decision, maybe your sanity. Wait it out," I say. "The new life you came in search of is just on the other side of that moment of panic." I decided to take my own advice.

In the wake of the Britman debacle, I remembered Ricardo. When Bruno recommended that we build a house, Ricardo had been my first call. "Do you know a builder who'd work out on our coast?" I'd asked him. "I don't make referrals to friends," he'd said. "I've lost too many friends that way." Now we were desperate. I decided to try Ricardo again. When I told him about Britman, he took pity. "I know a guy," he said. "A builder from Costa Rica who wants to diversify into Panama. His name is Alonso."

Alonso was the head contractor for Las Catalinas, a development on the Guanacaste coast where he had been building custom houses and installing infrastructure for six years. "Las Catalinas is very similar in vision and style to what you guys are trying to do at Los Islotes," Ricardo told me. "Alonso could be a perfect fit." If only Ricardo had told us about Alonso in the first place.

AT HOME AT LOS ISLOTES
Finding Our Way On This Veraguas Coast

But no matter. We were looking forward, not back. We got in touch with Alonso. The guy didn't waste time. He said he'd meet us at Los Islotes that weekend.

Our coast sees four tides each day, two high and two low. The swing is five-hundred meters. At its maximum reach, the ocean fills the cove of our swim beach. Waves wash the cliff face. Then, when the tide goes out, a land bridge is revealed. You can walk across it to the first of the three islands Los Islotes is named for. The islets divide the surf. At the spot where the three waves converge, the view to the horizon is like a portal to eternity. I make the twenty-minute walk as often as the timing of the tides allows. Most times, mine are the only footprints. When I get to the point directly facing the opening to the heavens, I pause and raise both arms above my head. I wave to the sky and to the sea. "*Hola!*" I call out to nothing and everything. At high tide, the spot is under water over my head. Standing in a place that in a few hours will be beneath the sea feels like hacking the universe.

When I reach the island, I find a rock to rest and reflect. I listen to the breeze in the trees and the surf on the sand. They tell me to take heart. *Stay the course, your path is true*, I hear over and over. Seated in this place, my vision for Los Islotes is clearer, my faith in our ability to pull it off renewed. I enjoy a certitude that I struggle to hold onto anywhere else. When despair overtakes me, I think of these moments. They sustain me. Lief and I could be doing anything at this stage of our lives. We could walk away from

DALYS
Chapter VII

Los Islotes and focus fully on the publishing business. We could start another business. Or we could retire. We've set aside enough of a nest egg. Some days the thought of retreating to our apartment in Paris and settling into the rhythms of life in the City of Light is almost irresistible. Fantasies of what our life could be if it weren't for Los Islotes have led both of us to threaten to abandon the project more than once but only to each other. Something keeps us here. Los Islotes has us like a yo-yo. Every time we come close to reaching our limit, it pulls us back. I wonder if we have any business being here, but the bond seems permanent. Setbacks don't finish us. They only adjust our way forward.

Alonso was the next step along the path. He was young and handsome with a thick dark beard and energy to spare. When he stepped out of his car and extended his hand for me to shake, I felt like I was reaching for a life rope. Alonso toured the property and inspected the house site. "This is quite a foundation," he told us. "These footers must go down three meters. This house will be standing on this hillside in three-hundred years." Britman was a scamster, but he'd done something right.

Alonso recognized the challenges he'd face at Los Islotes. We had no nearby source for materials or skilled labor. He'd have to build supply chains where none existed and import tradesmen. In the beginning, Lief and I had taken for granted that we'd hire locals. We intended to create an economy and wanted everyone around to benefit. Gary realized right away that wouldn't be pos-

AT HOME AT LOS ISLOTES
Finding Our Way On This Veraguas Coast

sible. No one living anywhere around was capable of doing the work we needed done. They had no experience with construction. Most had never had a job of any kind. They survive off the land like their ancestors. Britman had echoed the complaint. Alonso was undaunted. He said he'd find able-bodied men in the Quebro area then bring over members of his crews from Costa Rica to train them. He'd build a small workers' camp where they could all live together, one month on then a week off. "I'll need thirty guys to start," he told us. "I'll build teams for woodworking, plastering, tile work, etc. I've got five-hundred men working for me in Guanacaste. I started from nothing there, too. I know how to do this."

If you accomplish nothing, I thought, *just having you in the conversation could rescue us.* His positive spirit was contagious.

"Now, I'll be making a big investment to get up and running," Alonso continued. "And it'd make a lot more sense for me if I could spread that cost around a little. If I were working on, say, three houses at the same time, I'd benefit from economies of scale and so would you."

Since the disaster with Britman, I'd been ready to give up on construction. Heck, I was close to giving up on Los Islotes altogether. Now, we were not only preparing to resume work on our house but also considering committing to building two more. There was something about Alonso that gave me confidence it could be done. Alonso showed us photos and maps from Las

Chapter VII

Catalinas. Climbing the hill behind the beach were winding cobblestoned streets, squares with shade trees and fountains, a whitewashed church with a bell tower, and townhouses with powder blue shutters. It was like a small town in Provence. Ricardo was right. The developers at Las Catalinas shared our architectural priorities. Alonso could be our guy. The more time we spent with him, the more like myself I felt. By the end of our first weekend together, my perspective had been reset, and Lief was reviving, too. Maybe Alonso couldn't pull off what he was proposing, but I believed he'd give it all he had, and showing up and making an effort are often enough.

"So what do you guys think?" Alonso asked when we regrouped Monday morning before his return flight to Costa Rica. "Are we going into the construction business together?" Lief and I looked at each other and relaxed for the first time since Britman. I nodded slightly to let Lief know I was on board again if he was. "Yes," Lief said reaching out to shake Alonso's hand. "Let's build some houses."

Alonso was an optimist but not a fool. He realized that, while he knew how to manage crews and construction, he didn't know Veraguas. His first hire, Emanuel, was nineteen-years-old, thin but able, clever, funny, and well-connected. His second day on the job, Emanuel brought his cousin with him. Lief and I were at our desks in the office, heads in our laptops. I heard the door open and glanced up. I would have gone straight back to my

AT HOME AT LOS ISLOTES
Finding Our Way On This Veraguas Coast

work, but the young woman entering the room with Emanuel held my attention.

The girl closed the door behind her then stood beside her cousin with her arms at her side like a soldier reporting for duty. She was average height and build, but you felt her presence in the room. Her brown eyes were wide and bright. She smiled straight at me through a giant mass of dark curly hair. She seemed near bursting, like she wanted to speak but was holding herself back. *Who is this girl*, I thought.

Finally, the young woman could contain herself no more. "I can carry a bag of *cemento* and use a machete as good as any man," she blurted out, still smiling in my direction. "I am qualified to join your crew." I almost giggled. How was this young lady so unself-conscious presenting herself unannounced to two foreign strangers many years her senior?

I looked over at Lief. He was smiling, too. Neither of us knew how to respond. Emanuel saved us. "Señor Lief, Señora Kathleen, *buenos días*," he said. "This is my cousin, Dalys. When I told her last night that Alonso is hiring more crew, she asked if she could come with me today. She would like to work here, too."

Alonso was at our house site. Emanuel went to ask if he would join us in the office. When he did, Alonso, Lief, and I sat down with Dalys around our small meeting table. "I can work," Dalys said again unprompted. "I am a woman, but I am abnormally strong. I can show you." I thought she might leap out of her seat

DALYS
Chapter VII

and start doing push-ups. I've hired hundreds of people. Experience helps, but a can-do spirit outweighs everything in my book. Dalys won me over instantly.

"I believe you could work alongside my men," Alonso told Dalys after she'd made her case. "But I do not want to hire you to build houses. You speak English and your cousin has told me that you can use a computer. If Lief and Kathleen agree, I want you in the office. You'll be the one managing the crews, the boss lady. You'll be my assistant when I'm here and the one in charge when I'm not. You'll earn more money than any of the men." It was a big, spur-of-the-moment offer, and if Alonso hadn't made it, I would have. I had no doubt the girl across the table from us could do what Alonso was suggesting she could do. Dalys didn't hesitate. "Okay, sounds good," she said. In the years to follow, I came to count on that simple, confident refrain from her. She started work that afternoon.

I understood the culture of Quebro well enough to recognize the temerity Dalys showed accepting Alonso's offer. She agreed without a second thought to become responsible for the efforts of dozens of men, most older than she was, men who she knew expected women to cook their dinner, wash their shirts, and keep any ideas to themselves. Dalys understood that men in Veraguas don't work for women, but she was smart and strong enough not to turn down a chance she'd likely never get again.

Lief and I left Los Islotes two days after Alonso hired Dalys.

AT HOME AT LOS ISLOTES
Finding Our Way On This Veraguas Coast

We'd be away at least three months. When we were in the office in Panama City, we were distracted by concerns over what was or wasn't going on out in Veraguas, but when we were at Los Islotes, we noticed incremental degradation in the office in Panama City. The publishing business continued to finance both our lives and our investment at Los Islotes, so it remained the priority. We needed to be present for it. Alonso promised to send real-time construction updates on the three houses. He'd also expand the office and develop plans for ocean-view condos and a community pool. "*No hay problema,*" he told us during our final meeting before our departure. If he could do what he said he could do, he'd accomplish more in a few months than we had in more than five years. I'm predisposed to believe things will get better and work out. Since Britman, I'd been waiting for a way to let myself dream again. Alonso gave it to me.

Lief and I spent six weeks in planning and budgeting meetings with our staff in Panama City, hosted a conference in Belize, then enjoyed the Christmas holidays with our kids in Paris. We had weekly calls with Alonso and Dalys to review to-do lists and were in daily contact by email. All reports were positive. We couldn't wait to get back to see the progress for ourselves. We'd be making the trip just after the New Year, the start of Panama's summer. The rains on our coast end mid-December but their benefits continue through January, when hillsides are lush and every shade of green. You could imagine yourself in Ireland if not

DALYS
Chapter VII

for the tropical temperatures and brilliantly sunny skies. January through March, children are off school and all Panama escapes to the beach every chance it gets. We'd celebrate our return with a barbecue on the beach.

But first things first. We arrived back at Los Islotes late Friday afternoon and drove through the gate, past the office, and straight up the hill. Alonso had reported that our house was finished save the punch list. He'd be waiting, he'd written the day before, to greet us at our new home. As we pulled up, my heart soared. The view from the front was everything I'd hoped for, white stucco structures punctuated with arches and oversized windows all topped with red clay tiles. Simple, traditional, elegant. We took our time following the winding white-stone path from the driveway to the front door. Alonso had been watching from inside the house. He opened the door as I reached for the knob and ushered us in formally. To the left was the great room with its vaulted ceiling and thick beams made from wood harvested on the property. Three sets of French doors opened to a balcony overlooking the ocean. The floor was laid with hand-painted tiles in the Spanish-colonial pattern I'd seen in Granada creating a wall-to-wall ceramic carpet in an explosion of red, green, and yellow. To the right was the master suite. We'd get to all that, but for the moment I couldn't look away from the view directly in front of where we were standing. Through the glass-paned doors on the other side of the vestibule we could

AT HOME AT LOS ISLOTES
Finding Our Way On This Veraguas Coast

see a wide staircase leading down to the pool and patio. The sun was beginning its descent over the sparkling sea beyond. The sky was ablaze.

Lief moved on to our bedroom. I joined him on our private balcony. Because the house is positioned on the side of a mountain, our room sits above the others. Standing on the balcony we looked out onto the clay-tiled roofs of the guest rooms. It was a sea of red above the ink blue Pacific. The sun tinged the scene golden like it does when it sets in Granada. I slid my arm through Lief's. We stood there together for a long moment, not speaking. We'd worked hard for this. We wanted to soak it in.

When we were able to pull ourselves away from the sunset, we toured the living room with its built-in bookcases and the kitchen with its hardwood countertops and bar. On the wall above the stove were tiles we'd brought back from a recent trip to Portugal. Fitted together they formed a lemon tree. The kids' rooms had their own balconies with their own ocean views. A covered breezeway connected the patio to the garage, and a series of arches behind the pool led to an outdoor bar. Alonso had prepared surprises. He'd collected small black stones from our beach, polished smooth by the surf, to create a mosaic on the floor of the bathroom by the pool. He had used bamboo, also from the property, to cane beneath roof overhangs, and he'd connected garden areas with herringboned-patterned brick pathways. We had a generator to ensure uninterrupted electricity and Wi-Fi

DALYS
Chapter VII

everywhere. In less time than Britman had spent messing around with foundations, Alonso's crew had built us a house worthy of *Architectural Digest*.

I had the fun of furnishing to look forward to, but we'd had the foresight to send out a bed for our room. Alonso had positioned it in place, and Dalys had fitted it with new sheets so we could spend the night in our new home. I embraced Alonso and kissed him on both cheeks, and Lief hugged him, too. In that moment, he was our hero. Alonso took his leave, promising to return the next day for the beach party. Lief and I had brought snacks and champagne. We sat up late on our balcony, again not speaking. Words couldn't do the moment justice so we held hands and listened to the monkeys.

The next morning dawned clear and bright, a perfect day for a cookout. We would hold it at Panama Jack's. The open-air tiki bar had been Alonso's other project during our absence. He'd used teak logs for the posts and had covered the high-pitched roof with red clay tiles. We'd made these a trademark of the project. Every structure at Los Islotes would have them. The bar was positioned just back from the sand, near enough to the ocean to catch the spray when the surf is high. To the right is the rocky cliff separating our two beaches, my favorite spot on the property. I sneak off every chance to climb to the top of the point between the two beaches. The view from the edge of the cliff is exalting. Standing at that precipice, with the Pacific crashing a hundred

AT HOME AT LOS ISLOTES
Finding Our Way On This Veraguas Coast

meters below, I feel the same high I experienced the day I saw this coast for the first time.

Seated on our new Panama Jack's deck that Saturday, I leaned back in my beach chair to give myself a chance to appreciate the scene. What we'd come through to get to this point. "Imagine when we'll be able to hang out at the beach in style," Lief and I had comforted each other for years. Now here we were. No more hauling umbrellas, chairs, and coolers back and forth. Our day-at-the-beach scene was permanently set. Ceiling fans stirred the air overhead, and Jimmy Buffet crooned island-style in the background. Lief mixed himself a mojito at the bar.

Alonso had invited the entire crew for the welcome back cookout. Since we'd been away, he and Dalys had hired forty guys we'd never met. This was our chance to introduce ourselves. As I got up from my chair to join Lief at the bar, I saw Dalys approaching. Dalys and I had barely met, but watching her coming down the dirt lane was like sighting a trusted friend you've been away from for too long. "Señora Kathleen, Señor Lief!" Dalys called out. She was in cut-offs and a flouncy blouse covered with red and yellow butterflies. The breeze off the ocean had her great mass of long curly black hair swirling wildly. Her wide eyes were bright. She was flanked by two young women.

"I am very happy to see you at Los Islotes again," Dalys said. "This is my sister, the baby of the family, and this is my cousin who for me is like another sister," she added, introducing the two

DALYS
Chapter VII

young women she'd brought with her. "I'm sorry we are late. My mother wanted to go to a friend's party today so we had to manage lunch at her *fonda*. We just finished. The *fonda* is hard work."

"What would you know about hard work in the *fonda*?" her sister said in Spanish with a smirk and a playful shove in Dalys' direction. "You're at Los Islotes. I'm the one at the *fonda* with mom every day." *Ah, ha*, I thought, *Dalys' sister is envious*. At last a clue to what the people of Quebro thought of Los Islotes. I'd been wondering about their impressions of us since our first visit but we'd been so preoccupied trying to get this train on its tracks that I hadn't had time to get close enough to anyone to gauge their opinions.

"I'm so excited to be part of Los Islotes," Dalys said, ignoring her sister. "This is my neighborhood. When I was a little girl, my friends and I, we rode our horses through this jungle to get to the beach. We played in the ocean and the river and chased the monkeys in the trees. When it was time for the turtles to lay their eggs, we snuck out at night to watch. I have wonderful memories of this place. And now I am working here."

"Alonso is helping me to see your vision for Los Islotes," Dalys continued. "You are building something special that will continue for a very long time. All four of my grandparents are still alive. They all live within a short walk of the house where I have lived with my mother and father my whole life. I see my grandparents every week. Family is the most important thing to me. And I believe that what I'm part of here at Los Islotes is the future for my

AT HOME AT LOS ISLOTES
Finding Our Way On This Veraguas Coast

family. I believe it's the future for all Quebro. And I am not the only one. People around, they are very happy you are here."

We'd come to Panama to build a business, taking for granted that growing an economy is a good thing. The people who were now our neighbors fished, they raised chickens, they got by. We assumed they'd want more. But really we had no idea. It was a relief to hear Dalys confirming that at least some of the people who called this place where we'd settled uninvited home saw value in the future we were engineering. I'd let myself embrace my vision for marrying this natural Eden with a city of light, but what about the people who had lived there their whole lives? I hadn't considered the possibility but needed to: What if my fellow residents didn't care?

"Thank you, Dalys," I said. "I can't tell you what it means to hear you say that. Yes, we have big plans, and we know we can't follow through without a lot of help. Please, bring chairs over for you and your sister and your cousin. Can I get you all some beers?"

"You don't know me well, Señora Kathleen, or you wouldn't ask. I'll always take a beer."

"Dalys," I said impulsively, "I'm going to Santiago next week. I have a long list of errands. Would you be available to come with me?"

"Yes, of course, Señora Kathleen," she said with another big smile. "If you need me, I am there." In that moment I was more optimistic about our chances for success at Los Islotes than I'd ever been.

VIII

Ancestors

SANTIAGO
2016

I'd invited Dalys to join me for my shopping trip to Santiago because I wanted to get to know her better and because I could use the help. Supplying our home, office, and construction operations at Los Islotes had become about keeping lists. I carried them everywhere so I could add to them in real time. From fresh produce and food for our two dogs (we'd gotten a second rescue puppy who we called Dora to keep Smokey company) to wood screws and door hinges, from lightbulbs and light fixtures to sandpaper and wood polish, and from paint and tile grout to cooking gas and antibiotics, it all went on the list. I kept separate track of errands. Twice a month I'd travel to Santiago to spend the day crossing things off. Whatever I forgot or couldn't find we did without. These were marathon days. I figured having a local guide like Dalys would make this one less arduous.

But Wednesday morning when I saw Dalys pull up in our

AT HOME AT LOS ISLOTES
Finding Our Way On This Veraguas Coast

driveway shortly after sunrise to collect me, I had a flash of dread. Small talk is a torturous waste of time yet I'd signed on for a full day of it with an employee. Dalys had impressed me from our first meeting, but the truth was I hardly knew her. I'd begun to think of her as crucial to our success, but I was projecting, like I do. I set expectations too high too quickly, and often things don't play out as I'd hoped. It's another behavior of mine that drives Lief crazy. I hadn't told him I'd begun imagining a big role Dalys could play for Los Islotes long term. I didn't need to hear his "You're doing it again!"

"We've got a lot to accomplish today, Dalys," I said as she drove us down the hill from our house toward the front gate. "In addition to a full grocery shop, we need to find leather to replace the seats on our Panama Jack's barstools. We need to renew the license plates for two of the Los Islotes pick-up trucks that require my signature. And I'd like to stop at the bank to replenish petty cash."

"Okay, sounds good, Señora Kathleen. I have lists, too. Alonso needs some tools. I think we'll have to visit two or three different *ferreterías* to find it all. And he wants me to see if the compactor is repaired. If it is, we can bring it back with us today. I put ropes in the back to tie it down." This young woman continued to win me over. While I revolt at chit-chat, I'm always ready to talk business.

We waved to the guard as Dalys drove through the gate then past Roberta's compound. She was in her yard, chasing a chicken. I waved, but she didn't see me. Roberta was adding on to her

ANCESTORS
Chapter VIII

restaurant. I worried about the expanding footprint. Roberta was creating a barrio. Lief had gotten more vocal about wanting to file a complaint. "She should be evicted," he'd said many times. Every time Lief brought it up, I urged him to hold off. We're the outsiders. It's not our place to question our neighbors' choices. I didn't want to start a feud. Plus, I continued to admire Roberta's entrepreneurial spirit. No one else had had the wherewithal to open a restaurant to feed our crew. But I realized we'd have to address the situation sooner rather than later. We couldn't have a slum outside our entrance. Maybe we could plant a tall hedge along our boundary or build a wall for camouflage. I'd been meaning to ask the land planners for their thoughts. I also wondered about Dalys' perspective.

"Dalys, do you know the woman who lives in the house here?" I asked.

"Oh, sure, Señora Kathleen. Roberta. Everyone knows Roberta."

"Lief and I are a little concerned about the situation. We don't want to cause any trouble, but we're afraid that what she's creating here distracts from our entrance. Do you see what I mean?"

"Oh, yes, I understand," Dalys said. "It's kind of a mess, isn't it?"

"Yes, Dalys," I said chuckling. "It's kind of a mess. Let's consider ways we could shield it from view for people traveling down our road here."

"Okay, sounds good, Señora Kathleen. I will think about it." I didn't imagine that most people in Quebro would have appreciated the point I was making, but Dalys, I was realizing, was not like most people in Quebro.

We followed the bend in the road past the estuary. Then the jungle enveloped us. I lowered my window so I could experience it directly. I savor this part of the drive. It's as though nothing exists beyond this spot. It'd rained overnight. I breathed in the soggy earth. We passed the grove of yellow bamboo, and I heard the waterfall. Lief and I had picnicked there the Sunday before on Dalys' suggestion. The dense growth hides the cascade from view though it's only a few meters from the road. Light can't penetrate the canopy along this stretch, and the only sound was water falling into a rock pool. The dark stillness belies the reality. The jungle is alive. Hidden amidst the forty-meter corotu and ceiba trees are snakes and lizards, gato solos and coyotes, monkeys and toucans, butterflies and bees, all oblivious to our presence. They don't know to fear us. *This land is as it has always been,* I thought, as I did every time I passed through. *And perhaps as it should remain.* The realization ran directly contrary to our very existence here and to every idea for change we had brought with us. I kept putting off facing the conflict because I didn't know how. I still couldn't articulate my concern to Lief. I was afraid it'd freak him out even more than my city-building agenda, which I had finally worked up the courage to tell him about.

The week before, as we were preparing for our return to Los Islotes after having been away so long, we'd gone for dinner at a

ANCESTORS
Chapter VIII

new restaurant in Casco Viejo. Panama City's old town was undergoing a renaissance. Its centuries-old colonial structures were being renovated into private homes, hotels, and dance clubs. Lief and I rarely have time for a night out. But Jackson was at Valerian's to work on a science project so we took the advice of staff and made a reservation at Las Bóvedas—"the vaults." Part of the city's original fortifications, the eighteenth-century structure had been built as a dungeon. Legend has it that prisoners were put into cells here at low tide and left to drown when the sea came back in. Now the place was a wine bar. I was excited to see inside this structure with such a gruesome past. It didn't disappoint. The low-ceilinged vaulted stone rooms were creepy and cozy at the same time.

"So, now that we're refocusing on Los Islotes," I started as the waiter uncorked the bottle of Malbec Lief had chosen, "I want to share an idea I've had for a while."

"Another idea?" Lief said, after he'd tasted the wine and nodded for the waiter to fill our glasses. "That's always trouble. And usually expensive."

"Ha, ha." *He thinks my day-to-day ideas are costly*, I thought. *Wait until he hears what I've dreamt up now.* I nearly reconsidered. It wasn't like I imagined we'd start work on my New World city of light anytime soon. It was a long-term plan. Still, it wouldn't hurt to plant the seed.

"I was thinking of asking Ricardo to meet with me and the land planners to talk about evolving the town center," I said.

AT HOME AT LOS ISLOTES
Finding Our Way On This Veraguas Coast

"What do you mean 'evolving'?"

"Well, since our charette, you know, where we met Ricardo and he showed us his books on the great Spanish-colonial cities, I've been thinking that we should think grander."

"Grander?"

"No one builds classic anymore. We talk about the crassness of modern-day architecture all the time." When we moved to Waterford and began shopping for a house, Lief and I joked that the Irish must have banished their architects. How else to explain the dull, lifeless, every-one-the-same housing estates going up across the country. From 1998, when we arrived, until 2005, when we departed Waterford, five-hundred-and-forty-eight-thousand new houses appeared across the Emerald Isle. That was thirty-four percent of the total housing stock. For every Irish Georgian home of character now there were hundreds of ticky-tacky just-builts, a blight on the glorious ancient landscape.

"Yes, agreed," Lief said. "I prefer old buildings, too. That's why the building covenants for Los Islotes are so strict. We want a community of traditional-style houses like ours. But I'm thinking that's not what you're thinking."

"Well, I'm thinking that but also more. Right, we've agreed that all home construction will incorporate traditional Spanish-colonial elements. But I'd like to anchor that community around a proper city, built according to the parameters the Spanish followed when creating cities like Santo Domingo and Granada."

ANCESTORS
Chapter VIII

"You want to build an actual city? Why would we do that?"

Lief was getting right to the heart of the matter, wasn't he. I'd been trying to answer that question for myself for some time.

"The Veraguas coast you discovered is special," I began. "It deserves better than to be developed in the way that coasts in this part of the world are typically developed. It shouldn't be littered with cookie-cutter condos and strip mall eateries. That coast is one of Nature's most impressive canvases. It should be beset with a jewel of a city." *Or left completely untouched*, I couldn't keep myself from adding, but only to myself.

"I don't know about all that," Lief said. "Maybe someone should build an eternal city on our hills, but what in the world makes you think that someone should be us? Where in the world would the money come from? I know you don't think much about budgets, but I do. Ours is nothing like what would be required to do what you're suggesting. Nothing like. We'll build the small town square that the land planners have designed. That makes sense to me. It's all we need."

Lief's response was more favorable than I'd expected. I'd been prepared for a dramatic, "That's insane!" Instead, he'd simply pointed out that we don't have the resources required for such a big idea. He wasn't wrong. He was also right that I don't let budget worries get in my way. I'd return the city idea to the back of my mind, but I wouldn't give up on it. Lief's relatively low-key response buoyed me.

AT HOME AT LOS ISLOTES
Finding Our Way On This Veraguas Coast

However, I'd continue to keep any thoughts that we shouldn't attempt to remake this coast at all to myself. The depth of that conflict would set Lief spinning. I embrace uncertainty and can hold two opposing thoughts in my mind at the same time, formulating and even progressing plans for both objectives, no matter how disparate. Lief likes things simple. He processes the world in black and white. I'd learned to choose my battles with him, and I certainly couldn't reveal my misgivings to anyone else. We needed to preserve a consistent face for the marketplace. As far as the world was concerned, we were here to install infrastructure and sell lots. I pushed ahead believing that the resolution to my mental tug-of-war would present itself in time. I rely on the strategy often. It almost always works out.

I stared out into the forest. From my first visit, I'd felt that the land here had a truth it wanted me to know. I listened again now, as hard as I could, wanting to hear what the earth had to say because I suspected that was where the resolutions to my internal conflicts would come from. It remained beyond me. I closed my eyes. In the tranquil womb of this wilderness, I felt closer to the God I'd never been sure I believed in than I ever had anywhere else. My mind settled, and my heart knew peace. I felt a blessed part of a great whole.

The jungle gave way to rice fields. Quebro's cash crop. The road is public, but Hector, the biggest rice farmer in Quebro, raised and paved it and his men maintain it. Otherwise, the mega-trucks they

ANCESTORS
Chapter VIII

send from Santiago to carry their tons of rice each season would never make it out. From the road's edge, the land falls several inches, below sea level. This time of year, the fields are fallow. The rice was harvested in November and will be seeded again in May. In season, this view is a sea of tall slender grass bent by the breeze to the horizon. Now it was a dry swamp. Without the jungle canopy, the sun was bright. Dalys turned at the cross, onto the coastal road, and we were northbound to Santiago. I closed my window. The spell was broken.

"My father is from here in Quebro," Dalys said, interrupting the silence as we drove through town. We passed the mayor's office on the left, then the police station next door. Behind those concrete block buildings, down a dirt road that runs alongside the Rio Quebro, I knew, was the rest of the town—the school, the health center, and the church. Quebro is ten minutes from our front gate. Every time I pass, I try to imagine what it must be like to grow up here, but I struggle. I was raised upper middle class. My father had his own successful engineering firm. My childhood home was a large house in the country that my dad designed himself. My three siblings and I had every comfort. In Quebro, extended families live together in one-room concrete-block structures with dirt floors and outhouses. Panama isn't far from the Equator. The length of day is constant twelve months a year. The sun appears every morning at 5:00 a.m. Dinner is at 5:00 p.m., as the sun begins to set. People rarely venture beyond their homes

AT HOME AT LOS ISLOTES
Finding Our Way On This Veraguas Coast

after dark. Dalys told me she was ten when electricity was brought to her family's house and fifteen when the coastal road from Santiago was paved for the first time. Before then, visits to the city were a rare treat. Each family in Quebro is its own world. It's both idyllic and despairing. Most people don't have jobs and most kids go to school only sometimes. The socio-economic factors are troubling, but I also wonder about the tedium. Once you'd secured food for the day, what would you do with yourself? I asked myself the question often, realizing that it was a product of my perspective. Maybe ennui is a First World problem.

"My mother's family comes from Morrillo," Dalys continued. Normally I would have preferred to be left alone with my thoughts. Long drives are good chances to revise business objectives and consider current challenges. But I'd wanted a look inside the world of Veraguas for a long time. It seemed that today I was finally going to get one.

"Morrillo is ten kilometers up the coast," Dalys explained. "My mother, Elizabeth, she had relatives in Quebro. When she was growing up, she and her brothers would travel to visit their aunts and uncles down here in Quebro once every year. They'd come in summertime, before the rains. One year, when my mother was twenty-two, she and her brother Mauricio left their home in Morrillo early on a Saturday. My mother has told me this story a thousand times, Señora Kathleen," Dalys said laughing to herself. "It is the story of me. I want you to know it."

ANCESTORS
Chapter VIII

I made a point of catching Dalys' eye and smiling encouragingly. Few people have opened up to me as quickly as this young woman was doing. She spoke without agenda and unconcerned that I might judge her. What a risk she was taking. She didn't know me any better than I knew her. I hoped my response would reassure. I wanted to hear her story as much as she seemed to want to share it with me.

"So, this Saturday, my mother and her brother took off south on horseback for the ride to the home of their father's sister. This was their dearest aunt. The trip took a whole day. They wanted to visit with their Tía Juanita, of course, but they'd also planned the trip in time for *la pista de lazo*. That's the rodeo we have in these parts every summer. The rodeo was Sunday. My mother stood off to the side of the dirt arena where the cowboys show off on their horses, watching. Soon enough, she saw a young man on the back of a very strong horse. He bolted from the chute swinging a lasso above his head and racing fast toward a calf. She caught her breath and knew in that moment that this young man would be important in her life."

A *coup de coeur*, the French call it. I'd had one myself the day I saw Lief in that hayloft in Sligo.

"As soon as the rodeo was over, my mother and her brother set off north again, as they'd promised their parents they would do, but my mother kept looking back over her shoulder. She was hoping the boy she'd seen in the rodeo would follow. And sure enough,

AT HOME AT LOS ISLOTES
Finding Our Way On This Veraguas Coast

---

he did. Peter was his name. At first he kept a distance behind but then he couldn't help himself. He caught up to my mother so he could ask her questions. He wanted to know everything about her life, her family, her plans."

We were following the same road those three young people would have traveled that day and passing people on horseback. I wondered where each one was headed. It'd be hard going in a saddle beneath this sun.

"My mother was working as a maid in Panama City," Dalys said. "The boy from the rodeo, Peter, he was only seventeen. He was still in high school in Santiago. But, after that Sunday in Quebro, my mother and this boy looked for every chance to be together. My mother would take the bus back and forth from Panama City as often as she could."

"That wouldn't have been an easy trip back then," I said. "And the cost of the bus fare would have been significant for your mother, wouldn't it?"

"Ah, yes, Señora Kathleen, yes, it was. But my mother, she was in love."

"The crazy things we women do for love, right, Dalys?"

"You said it, Señora Kathleen. I am a romantic. Which means I am a sucker."

This is a girl after my own heart, I thought. She's open and direct, and she doesn't take herself too seriously.

"In September, my mother realized she was pregnant," Dalys

ANCESTORS
Chapter VIII

continued. "She was happy for the child she would have, but she didn't imagine she'd stay with Peter. She was sure he was too young to take on the responsibilities of a family. She thought that when the baby came, she would go home to her family in Morrillo. My mother had her baby in Santiago. That was me, Señora Kathleen. My parents weren't married. In fact, they've never married. Not in the way you would think of it with a ceremony and a judge or something. People in these parts, they don't get married in that way. Sometimes, though, they stay together. My parents have stayed together all these years. That is the important thing to me."

"People here don't get married? Not ever?" I knew many married Panamanian couples in Panama City, but now that Dalys made the point, I couldn't say the same for Veraguas.

"Well, no, almost never. Getting married costs money. You have to go to Santiago for the license, and that is hard for people. Our ancestors didn't marry, and we don't either. A man takes up with a woman. They have children. Then the man moves to another woman, and they have children. The men swap around. It is like that. Most women here have their first baby by the time they are fifteen or sixteen. Then they might have three or four more babies with different men."

"Isn't that difficult for the women?"

"Oh, yes, Señora Kathleen, it is horrible for the women, but it is the way. When a man leaves a woman, all the woman can think is that she must find another man. Women here do not think about

AT HOME AT LOS ISLOTES
Finding Our Way On This Veraguas Coast

going to school or getting a job. They think only about keeping a man." I'd always wanted a committed partner in life and a family, but I'd often seconded those desires to ambition. I've also always wanted to make a mark. My parents supported my aspirations when I was young. I grew up taking for granted that I would have a career. I wished the girls in this world could know that kind of backing.

"But not you, Dalys? You don't care about keeping a man."

"No, not me. That has never been the way for me. I've always wanted to be my own woman. Why do I need a man? When I was young, I wanted to study marine biology. After I graduated high school, I registered at the university in Santiago. When I showed up for the first day of class, they told me they didn't have a marine biology teacher. They said I would have to choose another program. I couldn't think of anything else I wanted to study. So, instead of starting college, I went to Panama City. I got a job at the movie theater. It had just opened. It was the first one in the country. I sold the tickets. I was happy to be making my own way in life, but I got lonely. I missed my mom and my dad and my little sister. I came back to Quebro because I wanted to be with them, but I was sad. I felt like I was giving up on my future. I never imagined I could have a big life or be an independent woman with a career, not in Quebro. But two days after I returned home, my cousin told me about his new job at Los Islotes. When he told me I could come with him the next day to ask for work, I knew it was

ANCESTORS
Chapter VIII

my big chance. When you and Señor Lief and Alonso hired me as office manager that day, it made a change for me. It showed me that I didn't have to leave my home to have my dream. Like I said, I am a romantic. I believe that Los Islotes is my meant-to-be."

"Wow, Dalys, that's a lot of pressure for Los Islotes. We'll try not to disappoint you!"

"Oh, no, Señora Kathleen," you could never disappoint me. Los Islotes is the path to the life I was meant to have. I am sure of it."

A lot of certainty for a twenty-four-year-old. I was the same way, full of big ideas from an early age. When I was Dalys' age, I was on a fast career track at Agora. It didn't lead where I was sure it would. The publishing business, yes. That was always my secret dream, to have my own publishing house. But that ambitious twenty-four-year-old me never could have imagined she'd be developing three-hundred acres on the coast of Panama three decades later. The unexpected detour had led to a new private dream. Maybe my city plan wasn't completely crazy. I'd dismissed the publishing business as pie in the sky for decades, but it had come to pass. Live And Invest Overseas was alive and kicking and paying all the bills.

"So you were born in Santiago? When did your mother and father come to Quebro?"

"After I was born, my father would visit my mother and me every day after school. Soon he began spending the night. My mother is very funny about this. She talks about these kinds of things, about sex and things, very openly. She is not like most

AT HOME AT LOS ISLOTES
Finding Our Way On This Veraguas Coast

mothers. She does not get embarrassed. In time, my father's commitment persuaded my mom. The day after my father graduated from high school, we left Santiago altogether, along with my grandmother, my father's mother, on a boat. That boat was called *La Fortuna*. I think that is a good name for the boat that was the start of my way in life, don't you?"

I nodded. "And your good fortune is our good fortune because it led you to Los Islotes. But why did you make the trip to Quebro by boat? Didn't this road exist?"

"It was just a trail then. Okay for horses but not for cars. Back then boats used to travel back and forth from Montijo—that's the port near to Santiago—to Quebro like buses. On the way north to Santiago, they'd carry rice from here in Quebro. That has always been a big business for us. From Santiago, that rice was sent all across the country. We are proud of that. Quebro helps to feed everyone in Panama.

"When the boats returned, they carried fuel, food that we can't grow in Quebro, and other things that we don't have here. The boats also transported people. My mother, my father, my grandmother, and I, we shared *La Fortuna* with eight other people. Everyone else sat up through the night on wooden benches. But the captain said my mother and I should have the bed in his cabin. We arrived in Puerto Nance before sunrise. You know where that is, Señora Kathleen? It's just down the road behind Roberta's place. When we came to shore, a tractor was waiting to take us home.

ANCESTORS
Chapter VIII

That is how I came to be in Quebro. My mother says that we had help from our ancestors. They made the way easy for us. I was seven months old." I'd seen the boats Dalys was talking about. They have no head, no galley. I imagined Dalys' mother making the overnight voyage with her baby on a small boat like that, even in the captain's quarters, and then bouncing over rutted dirt roads on the back of a tractor. It didn't sound like an easy trip to me. Compared with the women of Quebro, I'm higher maintenance than I like to admit.

"The other way to get to Quebro from Santiago back then was by plane," Dalys added. "There were small landing strips all around. My father's father, Silverio, he was friends with Torrijos. His planes landed in our fields all the time. Do you know who that is, Señora Kathleen? Omar Torrijos?"

"Yes, Dalys, I know of Torrijos."

From 1968 to 1989, Panama was controlled by a military junta. The leader of the junta, Omar Torrijos, nominated a series of presidents, eleven altogether. The position was a revolving door and just for show. Torrijos was the guy in charge. Torrijos attended the United States' military school in the Canal Zone. The curriculum focused on torture, execution, and blackmail techniques. When he graduated, he became a spy for the CIA. But, after the 1968 coup against President Arias, when Torrijos came to power, he showed himself to be a nationalist. His priority agenda became wresting control of the Canal from the Americans. He was successful. In

AT HOME AT LOS ISLOTES
Finding Our Way On This Veraguas Coast

response to pressure from Torrijos and across the globe, President Jimmy Carter signed the Torrijos-Carter Treaty on September 7, 1977, handing control of the canal to the Panamanians. It was a violence-free coup for Torrijos.

"To Americans Omar Torrijos was a typical Central American puppet dictator who went rogue," I said. "He was in bed with the cartels and generally bad news. At least that's how we remember the guy. Is that how Panamanians think of him, too?"

"He was maybe a good man to start, Señora Kathleen," Dalys said. "Maybe he had good thoughts in the beginning. Most Panamanians would say that. Some remember him as a hero." Torrijos' legacy remained intact among enough Panamanians twenty years later that they elected the guy's son president. "But to me, Señora Kathleen, Torrijos was a murderer. He killed many people, including children and even a priest in San Francisco. That is the most horrible story."

"Do you know why he had those people killed, Dalys?"

"I do not know about the children. Two students were killed in Mariato, for example. No one knows for sure what they did to make Torrijos go after them. But Torrijos killed anyone who said anything bad about him. It was like that. I know that is what happened to the priest. He was a very good man, Señora Kathleen. Very well known. He began speaking out against Torrijos. He wanted to help people fight back. So Torrijos killed him, too. To this day, Señora Kathleen, no one has found that priest's body.

ANCESTORS
Chapter VIII

It is said that Torrijos and his people had secret places where they put bodies so no one would ever find them. A lot of people disappeared in that time."

"What was the underlying conflict, Dalys? What was the priest trying to help people fight against?"

"Torrijos said he was trying to help the poor people. That was what he talked about all the time. It was his political line, you know. And he did some good things. He started many schools. That was good. We needed more schools. Even today we need more schools. Torrijos started our school in Quebro. His mother was from Veraguas. That's how he knew my grandfather. But Torrijos also stole land. He would come to a place and say he was claiming it for the poor people. But the poor people never got the land. Torrijos kept it for himself. He stole land and he killed people. That is the truth about Torrijos no matter what others might say."

Torrijos' Chief of Military Intelligence was Manuel Noriega. After Torrijos died in a plane crash, Noriega became Panama's de facto ruler. Noriega, like Torrijos, ran guns and drugs and worked for the CIA until he'd outlived his usefulness and the United States invaded Panama to remove him. I hadn't expected to discover a connection to this notorious period in Panama's history out here in sleepy Quebro.

"Torrijos and his people weren't the only ones to fly around these parts," Dalys was saying. "Planes landed along this coast every day from Santiago and Panama City. The plane ride from Quebro to

AT HOME AT LOS ISLOTES
Finding Our Way On This Veraguas Coast

Santiago was US$5. That was a lot of money but not so much, you know. People could afford that when they needed to. Then, after the Americans came, you know, after Noriega was gone, things changed. Everything became much more expensive, especially gas. The plane ride to Santiago went from US$5 to US$50. The people here, they couldn't afford that. That's when boats like *La Fortuna* became so important."

Panama has a love-hate relationship with Americans. We are familiar, a longstanding part of the landscape thanks to the Canal. Panama woos American retirees and investors. It also celebrates two national days of mourning. One commemorates the 1964 anti-American riots over sovereignty of the Panama Canal Zone. The second remembers the Panamanians who died during the 1989 U.S. invasion to take out Noriega. No one has ever expressed any animosity, but it's hard on those days to feel completely welcome.

We'd reached my favorite part of the drive. The Veraguas coast is breathtakingly beautiful but mostly hidden as you travel the coastal road. It finally appears as you approach Torio. The road follows the edge of the cliff. As you come around the bend in the mountain, it's like you're soaring above the Pacific. The indigo sea stretches out all around to the horizon, frothy and churning a hundred meters below. For an instant, you think you might launch over it. You feel nearly airborne, alongside the gulls and pelicans. Then, too soon, the road turns back into the hills.

This is the part of the drive I dread. First, to the right, on the

ANCESTORS
Chapter VIII

side of the road opposite the ocean, is the home of a Dutchwoman who breeds horses. The woman and her boyfriend designed and built the house themselves. It looks like an airplane hangar. At the next intersection is the round house on stilts that some other expat painted pink. Behind it, up the hill, are three concrete block structures in a huddle. One is a seafood restaurant. One serves Italian. The third advertises tapas. Lief and I had been excited when we'd first noticed the road signs. The more amenities in the area the better for us developers. We'd stopped by one day for lunch. We walked from one to the other to decide which place to try. Dogs wandered with us at our feet, licking scraps from the concrete floors. We settled on seafood. The ocean is right there. That had to be the best choice, right? But our shrimp were cold and limp, the garlic sauce they'd been cooked in flavorless. The foreigners on this Veraguas coast are either running from something or chasing freedom. Lief and I appreciate the lack of oversight, too, but with no one to insist otherwise, it's tempting to cut corners. Lief and I wonder if we're fools for following the rules when no one else does. Then I remember Torio. It's proof, when I need it, that rules matter. Without intention and attention to detail, order and beauty are lost. Along with hope of a decent meal.

Across from this sad restaurant row, an American placed a rusty shipping container at the side of the road out of which he runs his real estate business. He tried to dress up the container with bamboo shingles, but no amount of bamboo could hide the metal

AT HOME AT LOS ISLOTES
Finding Our Way On This Veraguas Coast

eyesore. The sign in front invites passersby to come inside to speak about cheap beachfront lots. When that sign went up, I knew Torio was lost. Soon these oceanfront hills would be covered with many more random, crappy structures. Seeing that sign reinforced the mission formulating in my head. I had to keep Quebro from falling next. So far, thankfully, Lief and I were the only developers along our stretch of this coast. But what made us any different from the gringo peddling lots from a rusty shipping container in Torio?

I've made a career of scouting the globe to identify interesting places for people to spend time and money. I've shared my discoveries from the platforms of *International Living* and now Live And Invest Overseas. My first recommendation was Costa Rica, in the mid-1980s, followed by Belize, Nicaragua, then Honduras. In 1996 I sent my property scout Bob Fordi to Panama City. "This place is shaping up to become the greatest investment opportunity of our lifetimes," he reported. "And right now it's a screaming bargain."

I visited for the first time later that year. Over the decades to follow, I put Panama on the map for global retirees and investors. I started by covering the sale of former U.S. military housing. After the turnover of the Canal, Panama owned this inventory. They put officers' homes in Clayton and Albrook on the market for US$20,000. Today these sell for a million dollars and more.

After Lief joined the conversation, he and I targeted Avenida

ANCESTORS
Chapter VIII

Balboa in Panama City, then Coronado and the City Beaches, Panama Pacífico, and Costa del Este. Homes and condos we recommended in those spots two decades ago are worth multiples more now.

I toured Boquete with U.S. developer Sam Taliaferro in 2000. He showed me the valley he intended to purchase to create the world's first expat retiree community. I reported on Valle Escondido in real time and named Boquete the world's best place to retire overseas in 2001. The AARP claimed the same of this flower-covered valley of eternal spring in 2010.

From the capital city, the nearby beaches, and the central highlands, Lief expanded our search to the east coast of the Azuero Peninsula. We told readers in the market for a comfortable, affordable retirement and investors shopping for an undervalued beach property play to look at Pedasí, Las Tablas, and Chitré. We predicted each of these markets was set to boom, and they did.

Then, in 2008, Lief identified the next big thing in Panama— the other side of the Azuero Peninsula, our Veraguas coast. When he shared it with readers, he heralded this discovery as the biggest of his career and then he put all his money where his mouth was at Los Islotes.

I've watched the effects over decades of the recommendations I've made in these places and dozens of others. In some cases, the impact has been insignificant. In big markets like Fortaleza, Buenos Aires, and Montevideo, the bump in demand is a drop in a

AT HOME AT LOS ISLOTES
Finding Our Way On This Veraguas Coast

bucket. Even in a relatively small locales like Punta del Este, Uruguay, one of South America's premier beach resorts, the hundred or so added buyers are unnoticed among the thousands of annual property transactions and hundreds of thousands of yearly visitors.

In some hot spots, the influx benefits both the local community and expats. In Quito, Ecuador, for example, readers who took my advice were the only market for the dilapidated, abandoned buildings in the historic city center. Today these colonial structures have been beautifully restored into homes, apartments, restaurants, and boutique hotels. Everyone agrees that everyone won.

The dilemma arises in places where the influx of expats changes the character of the destination. On this list I'd put Roatán, Honduras, Vilcabamba, Ecuador, Granada, Nicaragua, and Boquete. Whether the effects are good or bad depends on your perspective.

A few years after I recommended Vilcabamba, an expat contacted me and demanded that I never write another article about the valley. I'd ruin it by encouraging more people to come. She was the most recent foreign arrival in the Ecuadorian mountain village, and she was having a common reaction. Many who find their way to paradise want to close the door behind them. It's understandable. We all would like to keep a place just as it was when we fell in love with it, before all the newcomers arrived. Of course, we were the newcomers once. And what we can fail to appreciate is that the current newcomers are falling in love with the new version of the destination. Otherwise, they wouldn't keep coming.

ANCESTORS
Chapter VIII

Out-of-the-way places appeal to risk-takers. As more expats settle, the destination gains broader appeal. The way has been paved. The first expats to take me up on my recommendation to retire in Cuenca, Ecuador, loved that there were virtually no other expats in town. For them, that was the appeal. Today's residents appreciate the fine dining, art events, and energetic expat community that exist only because more expats followed the first expats. Today, Cuenca is a much easier place for a North American to settle. Some like it less, but many like it better.

Foreign retirees and investors can change the landscape of a place fundamentally. In a small market, they can also drive property prices up significantly. I've not heard anyone who bought early and sold for a profit complain. And I've known many local property owners who have benefited selling into new markets expats create. On the other hand, do the foreign investors price locals out of their own market?

I'd considered this debate for decades. I'd adopted the position that everyone deserves a chance at paradise. Who am I, who is anyone to decide who gets in and who doesn't? Then came Los Islotes. My experience on this coast has led me to reconsider many things, including the idea that it's not reasonable to want to keep others out because, once I got to know the Veraguas coast, that's what I wanted to do. I've struggled to balance that protective instinct against my realization that even if Los Islotes is an exception and so special that it should be kept secret, the aim's not re-

AT HOME AT LOS ISLOTES
Finding Our Way On This Veraguas Coast

alistic. We can't hide a place like Los Islotes, and we shouldn't try. Beauty is to be shared.

I'd never bought into a profit agenda at Los Islotes, and I'd been working for years to help Lief adjust his perspective. He was finally less confident that Los Islotes would be his road to riches. Certainly he'd had to admit that it was not a get-rich-quick strategy. But if Lief and I aren't on this coast to make money, what are we doing here? The gringo salesguy was clear in his agenda. It was time for me to clarify mine.

Just up the road from Torio's property agent in a tin can are Sammy's cabanas. Sammy was the first American we met in Veraguas. The gate to his property was open as Dalys and I drove by. Lief and I had stayed in Sammy's one-room thatched-roofed bungalows our first years on this coast. It was a trade-off. Hot water, air conditioning, a restaurant, and a two-hour drive to the property if we stayed at La Hacienda in Santiago or none of those creature comforts but only a twenty-minute commute to Los Islotes to and from Sammy's. The best part of staying at Sammy's cabanas was Sammy's stories.

We'd heard that Sammy wasn't Sammy's real name and that Sammy never gave a last name because he was on the lam. I'd heard wild rumors about who might be after him, but no one knew for certain. Sammy had developed his piece of oceanfront paradise to include a muddy pond where he kept a pet caiman. After his girlfriend gave birth to their son, she complained about

ANCESTORS
Chapter VIII

the caiman. It could swallow her baby whole, she pointed out. One night, Sammy and his girlfriend's brothers got drunk and agreed they'd had enough of the nagging. They lured the caiman from the pond and managed to get it into the bed of Sammy's pick-up truck. Then they drove it south and released it into a river. Either they didn't drive south far enough and it found its way back home or maybe another enterprising caiman saw an opportunity, but two days later Sammy's pond was again inhabited by a caiman.

The worst part of Jorgen's place down the road from Sammy was Jorgen. Jorgen had migrated to Panama from Amsterdam a decade before us and purchased hundreds of acres, making him the gran daddy foreign land owner on the coast. Jorgen has a restaurant and he's built houses that he rents out. He needs cooks, waitresses, and maids. Rumor has it that local fathers don't want their daughters working for him. He manages, though, to find girlfriends. Something happened to one of them. I shouldn't say more because I'd be repeating gossip, and Panama enforces strict slander laws with scary punishments. It's a vestige of the country's time under dictatorship when politicians wanted to control what people said. You still need to be careful what you put on the record.

After whatever happened to Jorgen happened, he disappeared. A month later, he supposedly turned up in photos on social media, face bruised and swollen, with a message saying he was being held in Panama City and needed help getting back to Veraguas. No one

AT HOME AT LOS ISLOTES
Finding Our Way On This Veraguas Coast

tells the story openly, only in hushed tones after too many beers. If you visit this coast, don't bring it up.

Sammy, Jorgen, the Dutchwoman, whoever had thought it a good idea to paint a house the color of Pepto Bismol, and the real estate agent in a tin box. Those are our peers on this Veraguas coast. We've made expat friends over the years, but we've never felt at home in expat enclaves like Torio. In the two-and-a-half decades Lief and I have been outside the States, in Ireland, Paris, and now Panama, we've preferred living among the locals. Too often, the expats, especially in remote locations like Veraguas, didn't make their moves to embrace discovery and adventure. They ran away from their homes. I've observed that whatever you've run from chases you no matter how far you go.

"My favorite memories of growing up," Dalys said, returning my attention to less knotty thoughts, "are of reading with my mother. She always had books around. I didn't realize how special that was or how much trouble it must have been for her to find books for me. We don't have many books here in these parts, Señora Kathleen. We don't even have enough books in the schools. And not everyone can read. But my mother taught me to read before I was five."

This didn't surprise me. Gary had been the first to tell me about the lack of books on our coast. Each teacher has one or two textbooks to work from. Lief and I began bringing boxes of books with us every visit. Gary would distribute them among the four nearby

ANCESTORS
Chapter VIII

elementary schools. It wasn't near enough. I wanted to make a bigger impact. I couldn't stand the thought of kids growing up without access to books. My city, if I build it, will feature a library. It'll be part of a Learning Center that'll also offer a computer lab and language lessons. Kids will be able to come to read, to study, and to access the internet. Most don't have it in their homes.

"When I was seventeen, my mother told me it was time for me to learn English," Dalys said. "This was a big deal, Señora Kathleen. Even bigger than learning to read. My mother and father didn't speak English. No one around spoke English. But one day my mother came to me and said, 'Dalys, our world is going to change.' She knew, Señora Kathleen. She knew about Los Islotes. She showed me a brochure. 'If you learn English,' she said, 'you can be a part of this.'"

"If no one around spoke English, Dalys, how did you learn?" I asked.

"I like American music. In my room at school in Santiago, I had a radio. You know, the kind with a battery. I would listen every night to a station in Panama City that played American pop music. I learned the words to songs by Madonna and Michael Jackson. You know, that kind of thing. That was the start of my English."

Over the years, others in this part of the world have told me they've learned to speak English by watching American music videos or television. I find this amazing. I struggle with languages. I've spent decades in Latin America and years in France, but I

AT HOME AT LOS ISLOTES
Finding Our Way On This Veraguas Coast

don't speak Spanish or French fluently. Jackson is embarrassed to go out with me in Paris. "Tell me what you want to say, Mom," he instructs when we leave the apartment together, "and I'll say it for you." I've tried immersion programs, Berlitz, and Duolingo, all with limited success. How does someone learn a language by watching TV or listening to the radio? Maybe it's a cop-out, but I've decided it's beyond me. Like playing music.

Normally the rutted road made the trip to Santiago a slow and painful two-and-a-half hours. Listening to Dalys' stories, I hadn't noticed the time passing. I'd been engrossed by the insider view of the place Lief and I had tied our future to. Dalys' stories deepened my connection to her Veraguas. I felt more committed than ever to my dual agenda. I wanted both to protect this place and to put it on the world map. *I wonder*, I thought, *if maybe those two objectives aren't really completely at odds.* I'd have to come back to that question. When I looked up from my musings, I saw that we'd already passed the Ponuga turnoff. Santiago was just ten minutes away.

IX

Santiago

SANTIAGO
2016

When we reached the end of the coastal road from Quebro, Dalys turned left. For a few minutes we traveled the well-paved four-lane Pan-American Highway with its median and wide shoulders. Then, a few hundred meters past the Mykonos Hotel, Dalys turned left again, and we were in a different world. This is Panama. Cutting-edge twenty-first century infrastructure alongside developing world chaos. Each street we turned down was narrower than the one we'd just left. Reggaeton music blasted from car stereos. Motorbikes passed on both sides spewing exhaust and cutting through gaps between vehicles I was sure were too tight but somehow they made it.

"We'll start with the barstools," Dalys said as she navigated the pandemonium. "Better to take care of our business in this part of town early. In another hour, these roads will be unpassable. This is old Santiago," she added. "Do you know it, Señora Kathleen?"

AT HOME AT LOS ISLOTES
Finding Our Way On This Veraguas Coast

"No, I've never been here before," I told her. I trusted Dalys. If she said the congestion would get worse, I believed her, but the scene outside my window looked like gridlock already. Lining the road were crumbling one-story adobe structures showing traces of the yellows, blues, greens, and reds they'd once been painted. I looked inside the open doors as we passed. One housed a restaurant. I rolled down my window and was rewarded with the smell of freshly fried empanadas. Outside the door of the next structure were piles of bamboo baskets. In front of the little house adjoining were stacks of sneakers. Up ahead I saw rocking chairs and saddles. "That's where we'll go for the leather," Dalys said, pointing.

People wandered from shop to shop without aid of sidewalks or concern for traffic. In the countryside around Quebro men sometimes tied T-shirts over their heads for protection against the sun. Here in town all the men had hats. It was practical but also stylish. Typical footwear in Quebro for men and women is leather sandals or flip-flops. Here the women passing wore pumps. They'd dressed to go to town. I appreciated the effort. It couldn't be easy to navigate this partially paved and very rutted landscape, jockeying for position amidst the vehicles and other pedestrians, in heels.

We were barely moving. Dalys stopped the pick-up and put it in park. "Should we leave the car here like this?" I asked. "No one will be able to pass." Drivers behind us were honking their horns and shouting. "It's okay, Señora Kathleen. Everyone does it.

SANTIAGO
Chapter IX

People can get by if they really want to, and we won't be long." I followed Dalys through the maze of traffic, shoppers, and wares. "I know this man," Dalys said as we approached the leather shop. "He should give us a good price." Every previous trip, Lief and I had been on our own to find the best places to accomplish all the things on our lists. Lief's Spanish skills are stronger than mine. On my own, communication is painful. It was a relief to have a local guide.

The old man greeted us with a big smile as we walked through his door. "*Buenos días*," he said as he came from behind his wooden counter. He had to move stools and saddlery out of the way to cover the small distance between us. "*Hola, hola, Joseito*," Dalys replied, using the diminutive at the end of her friend's name as Panamanians do to show affection. She gave the old man a hug then explained what we were looking for. Dalys and I had no choice but to huddle close in the tiny, crowded, un-air-conditioned shop as the man rummaged around his shelves. "What do you think, Señora Kathleen?" Dalys asked after Jose had laid out three pieces of leather for my consideration. "Let's go with this piece," I said. "It has a good weight. Would you please ask your friend, Dalys, if he has it in a darker brown. And ask how many meters he thinks we'll need to cover twelve of these." I showed Dalys a photo of one of our barstools on my phone. The man had the leather in the color I wanted and quoted a price then reduced it twenty percent without us having to ask. Wow. At this rate,

AT HOME AT LOS ISLOTES
Finding Our Way On This Veraguas Coast

we'd accomplish everything on our lists in no time. No exchange was ever so easy when I was alone.

"Would you like to try somewhere else?" Dalys wondered. "There are many leather shops along here. Don't feel like you must buy from my friend."

"I appreciate that, Dalys," I said, "but don't worry. Your friend has what we need, and I trust his price." I paid the gentle old man, and Dalys and I returned to the bedlam of the street. "Where next?" I asked Dalys, thrilled not to have to answer that question for myself.

Santiago was the fastest-growing city in Panama when we arrived in Veraguas. When the Spanish landed on this coast, it didn't exist. The town was founded in the early seventeenth century by Indians from Montijo, the port village *La Fortuna* set out from centuries later to voyage Dalys and her family to their first home in Quebro. The colonizers aggrandized the place, adding churches, squares, and parks. Like all cities in this part of the world, Santiago wasn't conceived for growth. The Spanish planners couldn't have imagined the infrastructure challenges a booming twenty-first-century middle class would create. By the time we discovered Santiago, its old town had long since outgrown itself. Developers targeted land on either side of the Pan-American Highway for expansion. You couldn't ask for better access.

The anchor for new Santiago was the Mykonos Hotel. Santiago's main economy is cattle. One wealthy rancher decided to

SANTIAGO
Chapter IX

build an alternative to the only other decent hotel at the time, La Hacienda, with more capacity and convention space. We welcomed the Mykonos. We'd use it as a stopover, for ourselves and the tour groups we intended to bring. The wife of the Panamanian businessman behind the Mykonos dreamt of holidays in Greece. The Aegean blue and white structure was out of place in this Central American cow town, but it was still the best choice for business meetings.

A year after the hotel opened in 2012, Santiago's first shopping mall broke ground next door. Two years after that, on the other side of the Mykonos, a PriceSmart appeared. I'd cheered the news. Hard to beat PriceSmart for convenience. It became a regular stop on our twice-monthly Santiago tours.

I like clothes, and I redecorate for fun. I've invested many Saturday afternoons in retail therapy and am known among friends for my impulse buys. But connecting with commerce-limited living on our Veraguas coast was shifting my perspective. I'd begun to deliberate over every purchase. I knew I didn't need another little black dress. The conflict was greater than that. I began considering the real cost of a thing. Someone had made it. Others had packaged it then shipped it then stocked it. Now, if I bought the thing and took it home to Los Islotes, it'd take up space in my closet or our bodega. Its wrappings would fill our trash can. When the thing became worn out, broken, or out of favor, I'd toss it away. Between now and then, what use would I get from it really?

AT HOME AT LOS ISLOTES
Finding Our Way On This Veraguas Coast

Likely, I could live without it. More and more I bought less and less. I became especially uncomfortable shopping at PriceSmart where we bought things like boxes of a hundred fifty-five-gallon garbage bags. The purchase suggested, rightly, that eventually we'd fill them. Where did all that waste go? I've always abhorred wasting time, but now I was becoming sensitive to consumption. If Los Islotes were built out according to Lief's plan, we'd have hundreds of addresses and thousands of residents. We needed a garbage management plan, but wasn't a better strategy not to buy so much in the first place? The big-footprint shopping I'd once welcomed as support for building a comfortable community at Los Islotes now seemed offensive. Still, I was a regular customer at PriceSmart. I couldn't resist the temptation of convenience and that bothered me even more. Every time I entered the warehouse ode to twenty-first century priorities, I felt complicit.

"Next we'll go to the *ferretería* I like," Dalys said as we climbed back into the pick-up. We weren't the only ones who'd left our vehicle in the middle of the street. Dalys had been right. Drivers were weaving among all the parked cars. They proceeded by inches from every angle. Dalys pushed forward until she was able to turn right at the corner. In a few minutes, we were back on the Pan-American Highway. We traveled along briefly at sixty kilometers an hour over the smooth pavement then cut back into old Santiago. We continued like that, venturing into the old world to find what we needed then retreating for a comfortable mo-

SANTIAGO
Chapter IX

ment to the modern one that existed just alongside, until nearly 1:00 o'clock.

"Time for lunch, Dalys," I said. "I don't want to keep Madrigal and her father waiting."

I'd scheduled lunch with Madrigal so she, Dalys, and I could get to know each other better. Dalys and Madrigal had both become important for Los Islotes, and I was trying to build a team. More than that, they were the closest things to girlfriends I'd made in years. I liked the idea of the three of us hanging out together. Madrigal had asked if she could bring her father. "I want you to meet him," she'd said. "He's the most important person in my life." It was a show of respect, to want to introduce me to her family.

Madrigal and her dad were already seated in the Mykonos Hotel restaurant when Dalys and I arrived. Señor Hernandez stood up as we approached. The eighty-eight-year-old was tall and thin. He held on to the back of his chair for support but extended his hand to shake mine then Dalys' when we reached the table. Madrigal's father was the picture of a traditional Panamanian gentleman in his white guayabera shirt and straw hat. Not the Panama hat tourists know. Those come from Ecuador. They're stiffer and have just one thick black band around the brim. The real Panamanian hat has many thin black patterns woven into soft white reeds. Madrigal's father removed his when Dalys and I sat down. You don't see *caballeros* like Señor Hernandez in Panama

AT HOME AT LOS ISLOTES
Finding Our Way On This Veraguas Coast

City anymore, but you find them still in Santiago. They represent the best of old Panama.

"Kathleen, Dalys, I'd like to introduce my father," Madrigal said in Spanish for her dad's benefit. Then, "Papa, these are the ladies from Los Islotes I've been telling you about."

"*Mucho gusto*," I offered smiling. "Madrigal has told me that you were a university professor."

"In fact," Madrigal said, "Dad is still teaching. He's giving a class this semester in the history of Veraguas. That's his passion."

"Ah, ha!" I said. "Madrigal, I'll bet your father is just the man I've been wanting to speak with. Everywhere around—in Santiago, in Mariato, in Quebro—I've seen the image of an Indian. Mostly on government buildings but also in banks and other places. He's always holding a machete and an axe. I keep meaning to ask about him. Do you know who I mean?"

"Yes, of course," Dalys spoke up enthusiastically. "That is Urracá. He is our national hero."

"Yes," Madrigal agreed. "Urracá is a very important figure in the history of Panama, especially for those of us from Veraguas."

"We Veraguenses," Dalys said, "we call ourselves Indios de Veraguas, like Urracá, and with pride. Urracá was a warrior. He had real courage and a determination to fight no matter how great the enemy." I'd never heard of him. My time living outside the States has shown me that we all know little about each other's histories. It's one of the things that makes it hard for us all to connect.

SANTIAGO
Chapter IX

"My father is something of a Urracá expert," Madrigal added. "Dad," she said, in Spanish, "Kathleen is asking about Urracá." The old man sat up straight and his face brightened. "Maybe you could tell her the story," Madrigal encouraged.

After a long pause, Señor Hernandez spoke slowly, like he was revealing a secret. "The only recorded history of this part of Panama was written by the Spanish," he said softly and in Spanish. I had to lean in to follow. "The Indians only told their stories. Still today the Indians of this coast have no written tradition. They keep their ancestors alive through the spoken word. What the Spanish have written of their arrival on our shores is not the true story. I will tell you the true story." First I'd been treated to Dalys' tales of life on this Veraguas coast, now I'd hear a Panamanian's perspective on its history. I was learning more about this place Lief and I had adopted in one day than I had in eight years.

"His name was Maniá Tigrí," Madrigal's father continued. "He was called '*ubarraga.*' That is the Indian word for 'leader.' The Spanish heard it as '*urraca.*' There were many *urracas*, many chiefs, but the man we know as Urracá was special."

I wished my Spanish was stronger. I had to interrupt Señor Hernandez every few sentences so Madrigal and Dalys could translate. I didn't want to miss any of the story.

"When the Spanish discovered this isthmus and claimed it, they placed Pedrarias Dávila as governor," Señor Hernandez continued. "Pedrarias established a base at Nuestra Señora de la

AT HOME AT LOS ISLOTES
Finding Our Way On This Veraguas Coast

Asunción de Panama. Today this is Panama City. Spain gave Pedrarias simple orders. He was to capture land, to extract gold, and to enslave the Indians. This Veraguas region was known for its fertile earth and its great stores of gold. Pedrarias dispatched his soldiers to our coast. When those Spanish invaders came ashore at the Gulf of Montijo, they found something they didn't expect. The Indians of Veraguas had always fought among themselves. Splintered, they were no threat. But Urracá had united the tribes to create the biggest army there has ever been in this land, then or since. Urracá's forces pushed the Spanish back to Castilla de Oro, nearly all the way back to the capital. And the Indians held them there. They kept Pedrarias' men from Veraguas for nine years." I was listening so intently to Señor Hernandez's tale that it wasn't until Dalys giggled that I realized she and Madrigal were watching me. "Your eyes are so big, Señora Kathleen."

I laughed with her. "I've never heard any of this before. An Indian chief who amassed the biggest army in the history of Panama? An army that managed to keep the Spanish attackers at bay for nine years? How did I not know this?"

"Few people outside Panama know about Urracá," Madrigal said. "He is not a part of the story the Spanish wanted remembered." How much history is lost because only the winners' tales are preserved.

"The Spanish were desperate," Madrigal's father continued. "They considered retreat. Finally, they decided they would set a

Chapter IX

trap. They invited Urracá to a meeting. They told him they would discuss a truce. Urracá showed up in good faith. But there was no meeting. The Spanish captured Urracá and put him on a slave ship with other Indians being sent to Spain." Incredible. One man armed with a machete and an axe had led the Spanish on a yearslong manhunt. And he was caught only because he made the mistake of trusting the invaders. "Urracá escaped and swam many days," Señor Hernandez continued. "He finally returned to our shore, but it was too late. The course of history had turned. Without Urracá to lead them, the tribes that he had banded together dispersed. Urracá saw that his story was finished. He went alone into the mountains of Santa Fé. He was never seen again."

Could this man really have escaped a Spanish galleon and swum for days to get back to shore? The story of Urracá is part legend, no doubt, but it must have been based in truth. I'd never known of any indigenous group that'd put up a real fight against the colonizers. The Spanish came and they conquered, simple as that. Once they'd targeted these Veraguas shores, the conquest was inevitable. But Urracá made them work for it. And he kept their mark small. The Spanish established no base in this part of the country.

"It is said that when he withdrew into the hills Urracá took his gold with him and buried it," Madrigal said. "All the Indian chiefs of the time are believed to have done the same. They hid their treasure all around Santiago."

AT HOME AT LOS ISLOTES
Finding Our Way On This Veraguas Coast

"It is not what is believed," Madrigal's father interrupted his daughter to insist. "It is fact. Urracá and his people had great wealth. When they died, it was buried in *huacas*."

"A *huaca* is a giant burial hole," Dalys explained for my benefit. "Many of these hiding places have been uncovered all around Veraguas."

"When I was a boy," Señor Hernandez continued in Spanish, "I knew other boys who wore gold plates on their calves and chests and thick gold bracelets on their arms. These were treasures of the Indians found on their family's land. This is not legend. I saw this with my own eyes."

"What my father says is true," Madrigal agreed. "It's how some of the richest families in Santiago got that way. They unearthed Indian *huacas* on their property. Urracá's *huaca* has not been discovered. People say it is buried on the banks of the Santa Maria River. In the center of Santa Fé."

"In all this time, no one has found it? Has anyone searched?" I asked.

"Yes," Madrigal said. "Many people have tried to unearth it, but Urracá's treasure remains lost."

We finished our lunch. I embraced Señor Hernandez and thanked him for his stories. Madrigal agreed she'd come to Los Islotes the following Saturday for dinner. Dalys and I went next door to PriceSmart to finish our errands. It was dark by the time we started back down the coast. Neither of us spoke. It'd been a

SANTIAGO
Chapter IX

long day, and I was distracted. As we drove, the story I'd just heard played over in my mind. I couldn't help but draw comparisons between the Spanish conquerors and Lief and my modern-day invasion of Veraguas. "Pedrarias sent his army to rape our coast." That's how Madrigal's father had put it. And they were successful only because the people they were assaulting let their guard down. It helped to explain why the people of Veraguas are reluctant to open up to strangers. Madrigal and Dalys stand out as exceptions.

The isthmus between the Americas has been colonized in series. First came the Spanish who found the place by accident and decided they'd have it. They were also the first to have the idea of carving a water passageway from one coast to the other. It would have made their plundering and pillaging easier. The French arrived four-hundred years later. They'd just completed a canal from the Mediterranean to the Red Sea and thought creating another from the Pacific to the Atlantic would be a piece of cake. They were forced to admit defeat after nine years. They'd underestimated the costs and the challenges, key among them the non-cooperative position of the Colombian government. Next came the Americans. They puppeteered a coup to take Colombia out of the conversation and establish control of this small piece of land critical to both Roosevelt's presidential ambitions and global trade routes. Now the country was seeing another wave of foreign invaders—developers like Lief and me. The motivation in every case has been greed. We've all wanted to reshape this bit of earth

AT HOME AT LOS ISLOTES
Finding Our Way On This Veraguas Coast

for financial gain. I'd never heard one say it, but Panamanians must feel manipulated because they have been, again and again.

My day out with Dalys, Madrigal, and Señor Hernandez set off a chain reaction in my mind. Dots began to connect. Dalys had said Los Islotes was her meant to be. Perhaps it was mine, as well. Until Los Islotes, I thought I'd leave my mark with my writing, but now I saw that I was in a unique position. I'd fallen in love with this extraordinary world at a turning point. This coast was again under attack from outside forces. I could protect it because I understood the threat. I *was* the threat. Urracá had kept back the Spanish. In similar David and Goliath fashion, Lief and I would do our best to stand up to the opportunists. I wasn't sure what that would look like, but I was certain it was part of the reason Lief and I had found our way to Los Islotes.

That part of my position was clearer, but I was still torn. This place with such extraordinary history deserved more than preservation. Urracá should be known. Could we put Veraguas on the world map. Could we reshape its most valuable asset—the land—in a way that protected it while also setting a stage for a glorious future. Could we build a modern-day city of light in the New World? The seed Ricardo had planted was taking root.

"Not too much longer, Señora Kathleen," Dalys said interrupting my daydreaming. "Soon we'll be back in our beloved Quebro."

"Yes, indeed, Dalys," I said. "It will be good to get home. We have work to do."

X

Martin

LOS ISLOTES
2017

It was too soon to return to my city of light idea with Lief. My husband had made his position clear. We'd undertaken dozens of property projects as a couple—buying, building, renovating, and selling—over two decades and across two-dozen countries. I'd learned that if I push, Lief rebels. His first thought is always of the purse strings, but, beneath his accountant façade, his agenda is the same as mine.

Since the purchase of the two-hundred-year-old Irish Georgian country house we renovated as newlyweds in Waterford, we've been trying to create legacy. Our focus has been real estate because we believe land and what we humans can forge upon it are the only true stores of value. Lief and I have been slowly amassing a property portfolio around the world that generates cash flow and provides home bases, but none of it is for us. The pleasure for me is in the doing and the building. My hope is that

AT HOME AT LOS ISLOTES
Finding Our Way On This Veraguas Coast

my children, grandchildren, and descendants beyond will appreciate the access to our big beautiful world that these properties Lief and I have chosen create and benefit from the no-borders lifestyle that the investment approach we have pursued supports.

Los Islotes is the climax of this plan. In typical fashion, Lief and I stumbled into it, but it turns out to be our summit. We aren't in Veraguas to segregate and sell building lots. We'll do that, but as part of a bigger plan. Our real purpose on this coast is nothing to do with money. In the weeks following Dalys and my trip to Santiago, my thinking solidified. We have a dual mission. First, we are here to help preserve a sanctuary on the edge of extinction. Why us? Because the choices we've made over decades have brought us here and the experiences we've had along the way have armed us for the fight. Lief would see it, too, in his own time. Until then, his focus on infrastructure would pave the way for the grand scheme taking hold in my mind.

Our second aim is to glorify this place with a city worthy of the setting. The Spanish built great cities on these shores to awe, humble, and control. We'll create ours to hearten, elevate, and embolden. Now that I'd let all that settle in, I needed reinforcement. In the months after our first day out together in Santiago, Dalys and I met every afternoon. Our road trip had broken the ice. I decided I'd let her in on my secret.

"Dalys," I began slowly, "I have a big idea."

"Oh, no, Señora Kathleen. You know what Señor Lief thinks

MARTIN
Chapter X

about your big ideas."

"Yes, indeed, I do," I said laughing. "This one is no different. In fact, this one is so big that Lief could be right. It could be quixotic. Do you know that word, Dalys?"

"Yes, Señora Kathleen, I know Don Quixote and his *hombre de la mancha*. My mother gave me that book to read when I was young."

"Well, I've imagined a mission for us, Dalys, like Don Quixote. A vision for what we're building here at Los Islotes that would change the course of this coast's history."

"That sounds very exciting."

"I believe it is. You told me once that you went to Panama City to try to find a career path but came home because you missed your family even though you wanted a big life and you didn't believe you could have a big life in Quebro."

"Yes, that's right, Señora Kathleen. But I have found my true path here at Los Islotes."

"Yes, I believe you have, Dalys. And I believe it is bigger than you've imagined. When Madrigal's father told me the story of Urracá and his army protecting their homeland, I was inspired. Lief and I came here at first, you know, to build a resort community. But now I believe the real reason we're here is to help fight off twenty first-century invaders the way Urracá fought off the Spanish. Does that make any sense to you?"

"Yes, of course, Señora Kathleen. We see what has happened in

AT HOME AT LOS ISLOTES
Finding Our Way On This Veraguas Coast

Torio. Developers building things there don't respect the land or the people either. Torio for me is sad."

"It is sad for me, too, Dalys, and I'd like to do what we can to keep the Torio Effect from reaching Quebro."

"Sounds good to me, Señora Kathleen. You just tell me how I can help." I knew I could count on Dalys.

"But there's more, Dalys. A second part of the idea I've got."

"Yes? Tell me."

"I'd like to build a city here. A classic colonial-style city."

"You mean like Casco Viejo?"

"Yes, like Casco Viejo and Granada and Santo Domingo. Do you know those cities?"

"Yes. Sometimes I come into your office when you're not here and look through your books. I hope you don't mind. I like the big books that show pictures of those cities. They're beautiful."

"Yes, they are, Dalys. And, no, I don't mind. You're welcome to look at my books anytime."

"So when will we start on our city?" she asked with a serious tone. Dalys wasn't concerned about why, only when. Or perhaps she already understood why better than I did. After all, she was seeing the invasion from the other side.

"Not for some time, Dalys. I imagine this will be a project that extends over the rest of my life. We will push ahead and get as far as we can together, then, when I'm gone, I'll need your help to carry the dream forward."

MARTIN
Chapter X

"Yes, I understand," Dalys said. "We are each a point along the path."

"We'll need to get Señor Lief on board."

"Well, he always comes around eventually, doesn't he, Señora Kathleen?"

"Yes, he does. So we won't push. Our city plan will be our secret for now."

"Got it, Señora Kathleen, sounds good. We can do a lot of thinking in the meantime. We will need lots of things to build a great city, won't we?"

"Yes, we'll need lots of things. I don't know yet how we'll get them, but we won't worry about that today."

"No, of course not," Dalys said. "Today we should talk about our gardens. Have you seen the tamarindo trees that Danillo has planted all around the office? The place is looking really great, don't you think?"

"Yes, I've seen the trees. They're lovely. And, yes, our gardens all around are a delight. Please tell Danillo thank you." More than any other force in my life, Dalys helped me to keep things in perspective. I needed to get better at appreciating what I had rather than constantly pushing for more.

I'd been counting on Alonso for my city plan. His work at Las Catalinas showed that he could create the structures I envisioned. After he finished our house, though, he visited Los Islotes less and less, and his enthusiasm waned. Finally, he came to Lief and

AT HOME AT LOS ISLOTES
Finding Our Way On This Veraguas Coast

---

me to say that the costs of importing craftsmen, materials, and supplies to our edge-of-the-world outpost had proven greater than he'd figured. Los Islotes was his attempt at diversification, but it wasn't working out as he'd hoped. He was losing tens of thousands of dollars a month. He appreciated what we were trying to create at Los Islotes, but he was tired. He'd been traveling back and forth between Panama and Costa Rica every other week for a year-and-a-half. He'd appear in a rush and could never stay longer than two days. While at Los Islotes, he was constantly on his phone with the crews in Costa Rica. The business in Guanacaste was his livelihood, as Live And Invest Overseas was ours. When Alonso announced he was pulling out, we understood and thanked him. One step forward, one-half step back. That's how Los Islotes worked.

Alonso rescued us from the Britman fiasco. He delivered us a Spanish-colonial home that was the first incarnation of my Los Islotes dream. He showed us how to manage work crews. He trained Dalys. And, finally though hardly least, he connected us with Martin.

Martin was a young Costa Rican who had been working for Alonso at Las Catalinas for five years when Alonso diversified into Panama. Martin was the first man Alonso placed on the ground at Los Islotes. Martin was Alonso's second but, in many ways, Alonso's better. With his green-blue eyes and movie star smile, he was also the best-looking man I'd met in real life. I

MARTIN
Chapter X

wasn't sure Martin realized he was beautiful. If he did, he didn't care. Martin cared about getting things done. He was a naturally gifted craftsman across trades and he understood pretty. We can train men to lay clay roof tiles and install crown moldings, but they either appreciate beauty or they don't. My vision for Los Islotes is based on layering the best we humans can muster atop the extraordinarily beautiful canvas Mother Nature provides along our Veraguas coast. I need people like Martin.

One evening driving back from Mariato, I noticed a white pick-up truck with a green Los Islotes logo parked in front of Roberta's compound. "What was our truck doing outside Roberta's place last night?" I asked Dalys the next morning.

"Martin has been going there every day after work since he and Roberta's daughter got together," she said. Oh.

I was happy Martin had found companionship, but of all the girls in Quebro why did he have to choose Roberta's daughter? Lief had begun to insist regularly that we should have the woman evicted. Our architect had designed a formal entrance including a wall along the road in front of Roberta's place. Nothing moves quickly in Panama so we had time, but eventually our attorneys would have to have a sit-down with Roberta. I dreaded it.

When he heard that Alonso would be folding his operations at Los Islotes, Martin asked to meet with Lief and me. "Would you keep me on?" he wanted to know. He was enjoying his work, he told us, and happy with the new life he'd begun. If we'd known

AT HOME AT LOS ISLOTES
Finding Our Way On This Veraguas Coast

Martin better, we would have made him the man in charge, but we worried he was too young. We told Martin we were thrilled he wanted to remain at Los Islotes, but, instead of promoting him, we imported one more false start to be his boss.

The year before we'd invested in an apartment in Medellín, Colombia. We had business in that city and were bullish on its property market. The rental had needed a complete renovation. We'd found a local contractor named Carlos to perform the work. When Alonso gave us his notice, we thought of Carlos. He was a decade older than Martin and getting divorced. Carlos needed a new start. When we got in touch, he jumped at the chance to relocate to Panama. Betting on Carlos was another misstep, but it taught us one more important lesson.

We'd been frustrated by the lack of progress under Gary. Britman had taken the wind out of us, nearly for good. And we were disappointed when Alonso quit. But we were running a relay. Each leg had made us less unqualified to have undertaken the transubstantiation of the cattle ranch known as Los Islotes into a world-class destination in the first place. We hadn't been ready to go further until we were. We were getting the big failures out of the way while the stakes were still relatively small, I'd tell myself when I couldn't sleep at night, and each one left us stronger and wiser.

I'd worked with Ricardo to design a town square anchored by a church, a school, and a library. Lief was okay with our modest

MARTIN
Chapter X

plan, and I liked it because it incorporated the cornerstones of a great city and gave me something to build on. Carlos appreciated the vision but couldn't progress it. It wasn't entirely the Colombian's fault. Panama's economy is more robust than Colombia's, and Panamanians resent that Colombians migrate to Panama for jobs. Colombians think Panamanians are backward. Colombian cities have art galleries and opera houses. Panama's operating budget has increased significantly since it took over management of the Panama Canal, but the cash goes into highways and bridges. Panamanians like nicknames. Carlos' was Colombia. "Colombia, go home," our guys would taunt.

It wasn't Carlos' fault that Panamanians don't like Colombians, but the main reason Carlos failed was his approach. One area of our work yard is set up for heavy machinery repairs. Something is always broken. One day I looked out the window of the office as Carlos approached one of our crew working on an excavator. He walked up to the guy with a look of contempt. He said something. The worker said something. Then Carlos grabbed the wrench out of the guy's hand and pushed the guy aside. I couldn't hear the exchange, but the message was clear. Carlos didn't trust the guy. Another time Lief and I were meeting with Carlos when he got a call over the radio. "Carlos? Carlos? Can you come to help, please?" Eric asked. Carlos got the same look of disdain he'd had that day in the yard. "Go ahead, Carlos," I said. "We can take a break while you find out what Eric needs." "No," Carlos

AT HOME AT LOS ISLOTES
Finding Our Way On This Veraguas Coast

---

said too quickly. "*No es necesario. Es algo tonto. Como siempre.*" He wasn't going to respond because he was sure it was something stupid, like always. Then he turned off his radio. Carlos didn't work alongside our guys, showing them new and maybe better ways to do things. He told them the way they did things was wrong. He didn't respect them so they didn't respect him.

Carlos chose Los Islotes, but he was unhappy with the situation from the start and it showed. Lief and I were relieved when he threw in the towel. Now we had a chance to remedy one of our mistakes. We put Martin in the leadership role. Then we watched as, at last, after a decade of effort, Los Islotes found its footing. No one wanted the Costa Rican to go home. Under Martin's direction, our guys were learning and having fun. Maybe, with Martin, we could begin to develop the talent I'd need for my city. I extended a challenge.

Lief and I had decided to build a second office. We wanted to spend more time on site and needed more work space. Dalys and Martin would take over the office Gary had built. In the designs for the new structure, I included parquet floors. Martin was experienced in all aspects of construction, but wood was his true love. I wanted to find out how capable a carpenter he was. The day after we'd agreed the parquet plan with him, as we were driving down the hill to the beach, Lief and I noticed Martin and two of our crew in the jungle. Lief pulled over to wait for them. "What are you doing?" he asked when the trio popped out of the bush. "*La*

MARTIN
Chapter X

casa de madera," Martin grinned. He was hunting wood, scouting the material he'd need to make the floors I wanted. He raised his machete over his head, tipped it in Lief's direction like a salute, then pointed the blade to the left as he reentered the forest. His men followed. That was Martin. A natural-born leader.

After they'd harvested enough corotu, Martin showed Rayito and Arnoldo how to cut the logs into boards and then into the shapes required for the parquet. Three weeks later, the bodega alongside their workshop was filled with tall stacks of wooden hexagons, squares, and rectangles. Then, over the weeks to follow, Martin knelt alongside Rayito and Arnoldo to lay the shapes one by one to create our new lobby floor. When one of his apprentice's fits wasn't to Martin's standard, Martin quietly explained why and watched patiently as his student tried again. The finished product was as precise as the parquet in our apartment in Paris, and those three-hundred-year-old floors had been laid by masters.

Our white pick-up became a fixture in front of Martin's girlfriend's mother's house. He invested his evenings and weekends helping his not-quite mother-in-law develop her property. A third room appeared, then a small porch. Martin's efforts were well intentioned, but they didn't hide the garbage. The bigger the footprint grew, the more Lief and I worried about how it reflected on us. Lief continued to insist we enlist professional help to remove the squatters before their structures encroached all the way to our gate. Now, in addition to my natural aversion to conflict and

AT HOME AT LOS ISLOTES
Finding Our Way On This Veraguas Coast

my instinct to support a fellow female entrepreneur, I had another reason to leave Roberta be. I didn't want to risk offending Martin. In a short time, he had shown himself to be more valuable to Los Islotes than Gary, Carlos, or Alonso. Lief and I respected Martin and enjoyed his company, and I counted on his energy. I didn't want to cause friction between him and his girlfriend's family, and I wasn't sure he'd understand the problem. Martin appreciated pretty, but did he recognize how much Roberta's compound interfered with our plan? I enlisted Dalys' help. "Would you mind asking Martin," I said one day as we drove past Roberta's, "if he'd plant some trees along the road here? I'd like to create a screen," I said, looking at Dalys' face to gauge her response.

"Yes, of course, Señora Kathleen. Good idea," she said. "Don't worry about Martin," she added after a pause, confirming she understood the intent behind my question. "He is with Los Islotes. We are his family in Panama. He has told me this many times. And he tells Roberta, too. He and Sophia have found a way to set the troubles between us and Roberta aside. Martin says Roberta never speaks to him about Los Islotes. Mateo tries. He shouts at Martin sometimes and tells Martin he must leave Los Islotes, but Martin walks away. He doesn't let Mateo draw him into the argument. Martin is happy. And he is loyal to Los Islotes. Don't worry." The next week, small trees and shrubs appeared between our road and Roberta's restaurant. They didn't hide the blot on the landscape behind them, but it was an improvement.

MARTIN
Chapter X

Martin had been staying in a small house nearby our gate. We rented him a bigger place twenty minutes away so he and Sophia could live alone together removed from her family. Our day at Los Islotes starts at 7:00 a.m. Some of our crew have bicycles or horses, but most walk to work. When Martin began commuting through town, he offered to collect any worker who wanted a ride. Still, the guys have to get to the police station in Quebro or to the cross in the road by 6:30 each morning. For some, that means leaving home before 5:00 a.m. They hop in the back of Martin's pick-up as he passes the meeting points and dismount when he pulls into our work yard. Martin and Dalys confirm the day's assignments. Then our men sign out the tools they'll need from the bodegas and disperse into vehicles to be deposited around the property. Everyone is in position to be hard at it by 7:00. I leave our house for the three-minute drive down the hill to the office about that time every morning. I wave to the workers I pass and call *"Buenos días"* from my open window. I make an effort to be cheerful because I'm humbled. I work hard, but these guys have eight hours under our tropical sun ahead and some are long into their day already.

Our new office features a wide covered porch framed by three big white arches across the front and two more on each side. The day Martin and his men finished construction, Dalys appeared at quitting time with coolers of beer. It was a bright, breezy afternoon. "Is it okay if I turn on some music, Señora Kathleen?"

AT HOME AT LOS ISLOTES
Finding Our Way On This Veraguas Coast

Dalys asked. "Yes, of course," I told her. We'd hired Dalys an assistant to manage inventories and purchasing. Fernanda was the first to start swaying. Joaquin our surveyor joined her then Eric who oversees the warehouse and Bonilla who manages road work. Soon everyone was dancing. "*Gracias a todos!*" I shouted above the music. "*Gracias a* Martin!" I said raising my beer in his direction. "*Gracias,* Martin!" the group responded in unison.

By the time our new office was finished, Lief and I had spent great amounts of time and money at Los Islotes, but no one would have guessed. Most of the investment had been underground. We needed more vertical construction. My city plans were never far from my thoughts, but we were years from acting on them. I still had no idea where the funding would come from. I put that existential question out of my mind and focused on the projects next on the list for Martin and his men, starting with the stables.

Our kids have been enthusiastic riders since Ireland. I keep a photo on my desk of Kaitlin with her arms around two-year-old Jackson on her pony Chesapeake in the forever muddy back garden of our home in Waterford. Kaitlin and Jackson belonged to riding clubs there and in France and Panama City, too. An equestrian center was always part of the Los Islotes plan. Carlos had grown up with horses in Colombia and helped introduce them to the property. "A rancher in Cocoa has some fine horses, Señora Kathleen," he came to me to say one day out of the blue. "He's interested in selling some of them. Horses would be nice here at

MARTIN
Chapter X

Los Islotes, don't you think? I could help to take care of them."

Cocoa is a pueblo south of Quebro known for its horse farms. The following Saturday, Carlos drove me there to meet the rancher he'd gotten to know. We settled on three mares. Two were pregnant when we bought them though no one realized. All three gave birth the next year and all three foaled again a year-and-a-half after that. Señora Cortez gave birth a third time eighteen months later. "I think Carlos found us the most fertile horses in all Veraguas," Dalys joked.

The stables were well under way when, one afternoon not long after we'd inaugurated our new office, Dalys came to me with a city of light idea I hadn't thought of that we could pursue immediately. She walked in holding a big formed stone in one hand and a smaller one in the other. "Señora Kathleen, *mira!*" she called out. "Look at what I've found. It's a *metate!*" she said as she laid the two pieces on our conference table. "Our ancestors used these for cooking. They would put grains or spices on this small table here. See? Then they would grind the things with a rock."

"Wow, Dalys," I said, picking up the two pieces to feel their weight then holding them next to each other. They fit together perfectly. "This is very cool. Where did these pieces come from?"

"From our beach, Señora Kathleen," she said. "I just found them. At the swim beach, behind the old fish trap. I was walking down the hill, looking all around thinking how nice it is down there now that Danillo has planted more flowers. Then I saw

AT HOME AT LOS ISLOTES
Finding Our Way On This Veraguas Coast

something sticking out from the dirt that didn't look like an ordinary rock. I dug out the big piece then saw the other piece was there, too. Can you believe it? It is broken, but it's still good. You can see what it was."

I wasn't entirely surprised by the discovery. The day after we hired Dalys, we toured the property with her to review plans and to-do lists. We arrived at the swim beach at low tide. I'd stood in that spot before when the tide was out but hadn't studied it. Our coast is rock cliffs. Boulders extend into the sea. When the tide is out, they create a moonscape in the sand. In one area the stones appeared intentionally placed. "It's as though someone positioned those rocks in a giant circle deliberately, Dalys," I said. "Look over there."

"Yes, that's right, Señora Kathleen," Dalys replied. "Those rocks were put there long ago. That was how our ancestors caught fish. The tide comes in over the stones. Then, when it goes back out, water remains inside the stone circle. That water is full of fish. The Indians could come back at just the right moment and scoop out their dinner."

That our ancient fish trap remained fully formed centuries after it'd been built also got the attention of Panama's Ministry of the Interior. When their representative visited with Madrigal as part of our permitting processes, he told her we should preserve the rock formation. "He also made the point," Madrigal relayed after the inspection, "that the fish trap suggests the spot was a

MARTIN
Chapter X

settlement. Just up the hill behind it is another circle of bigger stones. That would have been the fire pit. You could find artifacts all around that area. If you do find something, we're meant to notify the ministry."

A year later, one of our bulldozer operators uncovered two old clay pots. We pulled them from the earth, placed them carefully in a box, and called the number the government agent had left with Madrigal. Another agent came a few weeks later to collect our find. We asked for a receipt, but he said he didn't give receipts. We never learned what became of our artifacts. We called several times to ask after our pots. Each time, the person who answered the phone told us they didn't know what we were talking about. Lief and I decided that if we found any more artifacts, we'd keep them to ourselves. "Maybe we'll build a museum," I'd mused. This was before the idea to build a city had struck.

"What do you think we should do with it, Señora Kathleen?" Dalys asked. "Madrigal says we are supposed to call the government, but I don't want to call the government. I don't want them to take our *metate*."

"I agree, Dalys," I said. "We can preserve it ourselves. In our own museum."

"Museum" was a generous description. My idea was simply to display artifacts. We realized that the treasures weren't ours. They belonged to this place and to these people. I wanted to protect and showcase them. I'd been burned too many times by the Pana-

AT HOME AT LOS ISLOTES
Finding Our Way On This Veraguas Coast

manian government to trust them with the treasures. We'd create a site where we could keep them secure so that generations to come could know them, too. They were a key to understanding this Veraguas coast.

Dalys and I met with Luis, our in-house architect. We conceived a Welcome Center alongside the guardhouse at our front gate. One side would be a visitors' bathroom. The other our *museo*. It'd be open, no charge, to anyone who wanted to stop in for a look.

"I'd like to show a timeline in pictures on the walls, Dalys," I said after we'd finalized the plans. "Do you know someone who could paint scenes of the history of Veraguas?"

"I know just the guy," Dalys said. "El Tigre."

"El Tigre?"

"His name is Jose, but everyone knows him as El Tigre. He paints all the *fondas* around. He's very good, considering."

"Considering what, Dalys?"

"Well, he only has one eye. And also he drinks. Sometimes a lot. When he drinks too much, then he can't paint so well. But if we keep him away from the seco, I think he could be great." El Tigre's penchant for the local firewater didn't bother me. Every artist has his process.

"He'll need to stay on the property," Dalys said. "If he agrees to do the work, he'll need a place to sleep and to cook."

"No problem. He can stay in the worker camp that Alonso built."

MARTIN
Chapter X

El Tigre took the job. He wasn't able to start on the date originally agreed because when Dalys went to pick him up that morning he was too drunk to get into her pick-up. She told him to go home and sleep it off. She'd come back for him the next day. After Dalys told me why the work had to be delayed, I got a little nervous. Worst case, I told myself, if what the guy produces is ridiculous, we'll cover over it. I was used to things going wrong. A painter too on the sauce to paint hardly registered.

Dalys was as excited for our timeline mural as I was. I'd emailed her photos of the scenes I wanted to illustrate. We'd start with the Pliocene Epoch. That's when the isthmus today known as Panama was formed. For the first time, animals were able to migrate between North and South America. Then we'd show the Indians of pre-Columbian Veraguas followed by Columbus' arrival on our coast in 1502 and the founding of Panama City in 1519. I wanted a painting of Urracá and his army defending their homeland, as well as panels depicting the opening of the Panama Railway and the Panama Canal. Finally we'd represent the Miami-like skyline of modern-day Panama City. Now that I knew the limitations of our artist, the plan seemed ambitious. After lunch on his first day, I went to check on El Tigre's progress.

Jose hadn't drawn anything on the walls. He'd looked at the photos on Dalys' phone and picked up a brush. By mid-afternoon, he'd painted the continents of North and South America overlaid with a dozen animals. Apes, big cats, dinosaurs, giant sloths,

AT HOME AT LOS ISLOTES
Finding Our Way On This Veraguas Coast

armadillos, porcupines, and enormous rodents were on the move across his map. I was encouraged. "*Bonita*, El Tigre!" I told him. "*Perfecta. Gracias!*"

Each day after that, I made a habit of stopping by. El Tigre's freehand paintings were naive but full of life. Urracá stood tall against the Spanish invaders. The oversized engine of the Panama Railway appeared to roar from the wall straight at you. Two weeks after Jose had begun his work, Dalys came to me to say that he'd asked if he could go home to his family for the weekend. He'd return Monday. He needed only three or four more days to finish. "That sounds fine to me, Dalys," I said. "I'm sure it's lonely for Jose, living alone in our worker camp." "Yes, maybe, Señora, Kathleen," Dalys said, "but I'm going to tell him no. He needs to stay until the work is complete. If he goes home now, we might not see him for weeks. We've paid him half already. That money will buy a lot of seco."

"Okay, Dalys, sounds good," I laughed. "I'll leave it to you."

Jose finished our illustrated timeline the following week. Martin's crew installed wooden shelves. I wrote text for a label that Fernanda had printed and laminated in Santiago. We placed our first artifact on the ledge beneath El Tigre's painting of the Indians of Veraguas at work in their cornfields. "Metate," the label read. "Found at Los Islotes."

The next week, one of our front gate guards stopped me in the road. He wanted to show me something on his phone. "These

MARTIN
Chapter X

are from here, too," he said in Spanish holding out a photo of stone spearheads and clay pots. "These things are from the beach over there," Juhenio explained, pointing. "These are your things?" I asked. "Yes," he said. "Would you like them for the museum?"

We purchased Juhenio's pieces. Our museum collection had increased sixfold. Fernanda made more labels. Two weeks later, Dalys rushed into my office holding out her phone. "Look, Señora Kathleen," she said. "Look at this." The image showed three big wooden tables covered with clay bowls, urns, grinding stones, and axe heads.

"What is all that, Dalys?"

"It's from the *huaquero* in Chitré," she said. "He has all these things. He has spent his whole life finding them and saving them. They come from all around. From here around Quebro, from Nata, from Coclé. These things are real treasures, Señora Kathleen. Very old. The *huaquero*, Miguel, he heard about our museum and wants to know if we would like more things to put in it."

"A *huaquero*, Dalys? I don't know that word."

"I am not sure how you would say it in English, Señora Kathleen. For us it is someone who takes old things from graves."

I told Dalys I'd like to meet the *huaquero* and see his treasures. Lief and I could travel to Chitré over the weekend if Miguel were available. Dalys returned to her office to arrange a meeting. I sat at my laptop to google the word she'd used. A *huaquero*, I discovered, collects treasures from archeological sites. I didn't want to

AT HOME AT LOS ISLOTES
Finding Our Way On This Veraguas Coast

get involved in clandestine activity, but I was intrigued. Miguel said he could meet Saturday morning. The Live And Invest Overseas business was scaling up to a next level. Lief and I had been working long days for months. A road trip to meet a modern-day tomb raider would be our reward.

The peninsula known as Azuero sits midway along Panama's Pacific coast. Los Islotes is near the bottom of its western half. Chitré is at the top on the other side. The repaving of our coastal road had been finally completed the month before. For years, we'd dreaded the drive to and from Santiago. Now the way had been remade. The trip was as painless as we remembered from our earliest days making it. At the top of the peninsula, Lief turned right to the other side of Azuero rather than left to Santiago. Ten minutes later, we turned right again, to head back down the peninsula. The road on this eastern coast is two wide lanes each direction with shoulders and a median. It's smooth-going all the way to Pedasí.

"Imagine if we had a road like this on our coast," Lief said. Our road was like new but still only one narrow lane each way with no room for miscalculation. Residents of our coast get where they're going on foot. They have no choice but to walk in the road. Kids play soccer in the road, too. Chickens cross and cows pass from pasture to pasture. On this eastern Azuero coast, we saw no pedestrians or farm animals. This was a modern highway.

"Yes," I said ruefully. "Imagine how much easier it'd be for peo-

MARTIN
Chapter X

ple to get to Los Islotes. Imagine how much more construction there'd be." On the drive up our side of the peninsula, we'd passed the start of work for a new gas station north of Mariato. Another sign of the world's approach. "Imagine the people. Imagine the traffic. Imagine how our coast would be remade. Just like this one has been. It'd be awful," I said. "I'm very happy with our current road. It's easy to travel but not too easy."

"You recognize how perverse that thinking is, right?" Lief chuckled. "Given why we came to Veraguas in the first place?"

"I do," I said. "But do you disagree?"

"No," Lief said, no longer laughing. "I really don't. Not anymore." Lief's perspective continued to shift, as I'd hoped it would.

Chitré is a traditional place, like America's Midwest. November's Fiestas Patrias—Panamanians' series of independence days remembering their breaks from Colombia and Spain—are celebrated enthusiastically. The rest of the year the town is quiet and easygoing. All Panama is growing, including Chitré. With its U.S.-style grocery store, home remodeling centers, and strip malls, Chitré offers convenient small-town living. As a result, its population is expanding quickly. I appreciate Chitré, but am glad it's on the other side of our peninsula.

Dalys had WhatsApp'd us a google pin to guide us to Miguel's house. The big, friendly Panamanian met us at his gate and welcomed us into his home. He introduced us to his wife and his mother. They were sitting on the back porch with Miguel's three

AT HOME AT LOS ISLOTES
Finding Our Way On This Veraguas Coast

children enjoying the peaceful Saturday morning. Each child stood in turn to greet us and shake our hands. Then we followed Miguel through his backyard to a covered terrace. Here were the tables Dalys had shown us. Miguel had unpacked more treasures since the photos he'd sent her had been taken. Now six tables and as many chairs displayed clay, stone, and shell artifacts. Beneath the tables were boxes with more. "These are from Veraguas," Miguel said in Spanish, indicating the table in the center. "Those over there are from Coclé."

"I guess Dalys told you about what we're doing at Los Islotes?" Lief asked.

"*Sí, sí,*" Miguel smiled. "Dalys explained that you have a museum. I had heard about this."

"Yes," Lief said. "We want to preserve the history of this region."

"That is a good thing," Miguel said. "No one knows about us Indians of Veraguas. Our ancestors were very clever. They had many skills, many talents. They knew many things that have been forgotten. Too much of their knowledge has been lost."

"Look at this," Miguel said, to make his point. "This was used to hold wax." The clay object he picked up by its handles had four small cups on a carved, footed base. "This made light for ceremonies. This was used in rituals, too," he said, picking up a chalice with black markings around the lip. "This was for making medicine," he said, holding up an urn. Its bulbous bottom had been blackened by fire. "This pot contained corn seeds when we

MARTIN
Chapter X

found it," Miguel said. "This had corn seeds inside, too," he added. "It made music like a maraca. These small pots were for painting. The Indians filled them with dye. This whistle was to call to each other from very far away," he said, blowing into the clay piece. The high-pitched sound set his dog barking. "And this is a pectoral, worn by a chief," he said proudly holding out a carved conch shell.

"Can I ask how did you come to have all these remarkable things?" I said.

"I have become well known," Miguel explained. "When someone finds an artifact on his land, he calls me. I go to the place and search around. Whatever I uncover, I bring here. I sell the things and I share the money with the owner of the land where they were found."

"Who buys from you?" Lief asked.

"I have sold to the new hotel in Chitré. They wanted to make a museum, like you. I have sold to schools in Panama City. And I sell to people who hear about me. Wait," Miguel interrupted himself. "Wait here. I will be right back. I have something special to show you." Miguel went inside his house.

"How many pieces do you think we should buy?" Lief asked.

"You know me," I said. "I want to ask him how much for all of it."

"Let's not get ahead of ourselves," Lief said. "Let's choose one or two of each thing. We can always come back for more."

Miguel returned and motioned for me to hold out my hands.

AT HOME AT LOS ISLOTES
Finding Our Way On This Veraguas Coast

Then he placed four small smooth objects in them, one by one. "This is the papa," he said. "This is the mama. And this is the baby." The three jaguarundi had been carved from black stone. "And here is the alligator chasing them!" he said, dropping the fourth piece into my hands in a flash. We all laughed.

"A man from Panama City says he is coming next week to buy these," Miguel said. "But I would rather for you to have them. The man says he will sell these stones at auction in London. He is right. They have great value. But I want them to stay here. I want people from these parts to see them and I want people from beyond these parts to come to see them, too. I want people to know about our Indians."

Lief and I chose forty pieces, including the carved stones. Miguel handed his phone to Lief. "Here, maybe you would like to watch this video while I pack your things," he said. "It shows the day I found these pots here," he pointed. "These came from near to Los Islotes." The video showed Miguel pulling himself through a muddy hole in the ground to land in a cavern. On the cave floor were two of the pots we'd chosen for our museum. The video showed Miguel lifting the lid from one to reveal the carved stones the guy from Panama City had wanted to buy to sell at auction in the U.K. Miguel wrapped our treasures in newspaper and placed them in boxes. He and his son carried the cartons to our car and positioned them securely in back. "We'll send you photos after we've placed the pieces in our museum," I said. "Or, better," I cor-

MARTIN
Chapter X

rected myself, "you should see for yourself. Please come visit us at Los Islotes. You are welcome anytime."

"*Sí, sí, Señora,*" Miguel said. "I would like to do that. I would like to see these things on display. I will tell everyone about your museum so they can see these things, too."

I had the start of my city.

XI

Quebro Township

LOS ISLOTES
2019

Our accidental museum was a turning point. After a decade of frustrated dreams and one struggle after another, we'd created something worthwhile. It was a small step, but it inspired us all to engage anew. Everyone was delighted the first time someone arrived at the gate asking about it. Our guard welcomed our inaugural visitor and told the story of the provenance of each piece proudly.

Dalys introduced a daily meeting. At 8:00 a.m., after work crews had been positioned, she and Martin met in their office with Fernanda, Joaquin, and Luis. Dalys asked for white boards. Martin hung them on the wall behind her desk, one for current projects, the other for future projects. Then Dalys asked for a weekly meeting with Lief and me. We three would confer then Dalys would translate our ideas into to-do lists that she prioritized on her white boards. She ordered uniforms. Work shirts

QUEBRO TOWNSHIP
Chapter XI

for the crew, white polos for the office staff. The morning they arrived, everyone gathered to change into their new duds. Fernanda came out of the bathroom like a runway model, posing and smiling. We laughed and applauded. Finally, we were building something greater than a property development. We all felt it. Our team was working hard and enjoying the rewards. Three of our guys bought motorcycles. Fernanda was able to afford a used car. Dalys invested in her first ever washer-dryer. It was too big to fit inside her house so she built a roof over her back porch and installed it there. "After I plugged it in, I spent two days washing things," she told me. "I washed everything I own and then I washed everything again."

For years Lief and I had had to force ourselves to make the trip to Los Islotes. We'd dreaded meetings with Gary and Britman. Now when we were elsewhere we counted down until our return, and once in residence we didn't want to leave. Finally, we weren't transients. Living in Paris, we'd learned that that city operates according to centuries-old cycles. You have the new wine each fall. Then Christmas when the city is festooned with white lights. Next come the tulips and cherry blossoms of spring. Every August, all Paris decamps to the countryside or the beach. Then the city is reborn each September with *la rentrée*, the annual return to work and a new school year. When we stuck around long enough to see beneath the surface, we found that Quebro, like Paris, has annual rhythms.

AT HOME AT LOS ISLOTES
Finding Our Way On This Veraguas Coast

"How much longer will you and Señor Lief be here at Los Islotes?" Dalys asked one early October morning. "I'm not sure, Dalys," I said. "We'll go to Paris for Christmas." After their wedding, Kaitlin and Harry had returned to Panama for three years. When the business reached the point where a satellite operation in Europe made sense, they'd asked if they could reposition to Paris. Kaitlin had always wanted to return. Lief and I spoke with them every day for business, and we traveled to Paris at least twice a year, at Christmas and again each summer. But it wasn't enough. I felt their absence. Jackson was a sophomore at NYU. We saw him less.

"Otherwise, our schedules are flexible," I added. "Why do you ask?"

"Well, it is time for the turtles, Señora Kathleen. The babies will start hatching later this month. My friend Lea at the Turtle Foundation invited you and Señor Lief to come to watch one morning if you would like." Our coast is a turtle nesting site. Locals scoop up the eggs. It's appalling in current context, but turtle eggs were a delicacy for the Indians of Veraguas, and they are for their descendants, too. Groups like the one run by Dalys' friend patrol the beaches during turtle season to keep predators away, human and otherwise. Every morning at 3:00 a.m., volunteers set out in search of mama turtles laying. When they come upon a nest, they transfer the eggs to a protected area back from the surf near the edge of the jungle. Then, at sunrise every morning

QUEBRO TOWNSHIP
Chapter XI

to follow, they check every nest until, about forty-five days later, they detect movement.

"We would love to watch a hatching," I told Dalys. "Just let us know when."

Before dawn two Saturdays later, Dalys sent a text. "The first nest hatched overnight," she said. "At least two-hundred-and-fifty babies. Can you make it to the beach at Mata Oscura by 7:00 o'clock?" "See you then," I replied with an enthusiastic thumb's up.

Lea was waiting for us at the gate on the sand. "*Buenos días,*" she said quickly. "We need to work fast. We must release all the hatchlings before the sun rises too high in the sky. The light distracts them, and they lose their way. Here, would you like to put these on?" Lea held out plastic gloves. "The baby turtles have bacteria that can harm us, and the bacteria on our hands can make them sick."

Lea led us to the far end of the fenced-off area. "There," she pointed. "It's that nest there that hatched overnight." Lea lifted the cover from a giant plastic tub. Inside, a mass of tiny turtles writhed and wriggled all over each other in a giant heap. None remained king of the mountain long. "Go ahead," Lea said. "You can pick one up if you'd like. Hold it like this." Lea separated one from his siblings and held the little guy by the edges of his shell between her thumb and forefinger. I reached into the bin as she had done. I extended my arm so my little guy faced me. His legs were pinwheels twirling so fast I thought they might spin off.

AT HOME AT LOS ISLOTES
Finding Our Way On This Veraguas Coast

"*Hola*, little *tortuga*," I said. "I'm very pleased to meet you. It's time for your odyssey now. *Buena suerte*. I'll be rooting for you." I put the turtle back in the tub atop his fellows.

"This is the best part of my job," Lea said as she picked up the container and headed toward the ocean.

"Do you set them down one by one?" I asked.

"No, we release them all at once!" Lea nearly shouted back at me over her shoulder with glee. Then she tipped the bin on its side. Suddenly two-hundred-and-fifty baby turtles were scurrying across the sand, making the most important journey of their lives. Some took the lead. Others hung back. One wandered toward me, away from the sea. I bent down to help the little fellow.

"Please don't," Lea said. "I know it's hard, but we can't interfere. They have to make this trip on their own. Nature must run its course. The turtles not strong or smart enough to make it into the sea must be allowed to go their separate ways."

Herons appeared overhead. One swooped toward the beach. The turtle he'd targeted escaped and darted into the sea. Lief began waving his arms to scare the birds away. "Please don't do that either," Lea said. "We have to stay out of this. Each turtle has his destiny."

Lief let his arms fall to his side. We stood together watching as one by one the turtles disappeared into the waves. Some were washed back to shore but rallied to try again. In twenty minutes, nearly all of our babies had realized their destinies. Two had wan-

QUEBRO TOWNSHIP
Chapter XI

dered into the jungle. Three had been snatched by seagulls. "Not a bad attrition rate," I said to Dalys. "Yes" she said. "We lost just five out of two-hundred-and-fifty. But I am sad for those five."

"Me, too," I said. "But it's the circle of life, I guess. Every path plays a role."

Monday morning, Dalys came into my office to extend another invitation. "Next week is November 3," she said. "The start of our Fiestas Patrias. It is my favorite day of the year."

"Yes, Dalys? Why is that?"

"Because, on this day," she said, "we Panamanians forget everything negative. This is the one day when we set aside all differences and troubles and simply feel pride in our homeland. It's a very emotional day for us."

"What will Quebro do to celebrate?" I asked.

"What else?" Dalys replied. "We will throw a party! In fact, we will have two parties. We celebrate our independence from Colombia on November 3. Then, on November 4, we have the Día de la Bandera. Flag Day. Both days, the events will begin at the Quebro school. Children with the best grades have the right to wear our red, white, and blue country ribbon over their uniforms. It is an honor. Each day, we will sing the national anthem while we raise our flag. Then the children will compete in games and races. We are lucky because our Quebro school has a small band. On November 3, the band members will lead the parade through town. The highlight of the celebrations is the crowning of our

AT HOME AT LOS ISLOTES
Finding Our Way On This Veraguas Coast

---

queen. Then we all follow along behind as she is driven through the village in a wagon. It's a day of real joy. I would like you and Señor Lief to come to see for yourselves. What do you think?"

"Count us in, Dalys," I said.

For too long we'd ignored Quebro. We'd naively or arrogantly dismissed the town on our doorstep as irrelevant to what we were building on the other side of our gate. Dalys had become our bridge. First she told me stories of life in Quebro. Now she was getting Lief and me out of our bubble so we could experience it ourselves.

As Dalys had promised, all Quebro township—some four-hundred souls—turned out for the November 3 celebrations. Months earlier, the town had named its queen. The young lady sat atop a flower-covered ox cart in her white *pollera* smiling and waving to her adoring townsfolk. Every city and village across Panama, from Panama City to tiny Quebro, would have elected a queen of their own to lead their parade this day, and each queen would wear the traditional dress. Families save for months so their daughters can have the finest *pollera* possible. The most elaborate, with layers of lace and intricate embroidery, take a year to make and cost thousands of dollars. Other than the one she wears on her wedding day, her *pollera*, if she's lucky enough to have one, is the most important dress in a girl's life.

Drummers led the way. Boys and girls sashayed to the beat. Women carried fans and parasols. Men carried open bottles of

QUEBRO TOWNSHIP
Chapter XI

seco, some with backups in their back pockets. They tipped their hats to me with their free hands as I passed. We progressed slowly along the dirt lane. No one was in a hurry. Where better to be this blue-sky afternoon than right where we were? *"Buenos días!"* one *caballero* called out. *"Un abrazo?"* I worried he'd fall from his horse when he leaned down from his saddle, extended his arm, and hung there, waiting for my response. It was the seco talking but I appreciated being addressed as a friend. I stood on tip-toes to return the embrace and kissed this man I'd never met before on his cheek.

We reached the center of town. The drummers sat down on a log to continue playing. Now everyone was dancing around the young queen's carriage. Lief and I lingered in the shade. I didn't want the day to end. "We could take a drive down the coast to Flores after this," I suggested.

"Okay," Lief said. He was enjoying himself as much as I was. "On the way back we can stop at the bramador for dinner."

I steel myself for the drive to Santiago. I can't enjoy what comes before Torio because I know Torio is up ahead, and I can't enjoy what comes after because I'm recovering from having come face-to-face again with my greatest fears about the future of this coast writ large. Every trip from Quebro north brings despair.

The drive from Quebro south to the bottom of the peninsula is a meditation. The sea is never visible. The road is inland. It winds through the rolling hills of a broad valley. Mountain ranges rise on

AT HOME AT LOS ISLOTES
Finding Our Way On This Veraguas Coast

two sides. This is the view from the edge of the clifftop between our two beaches at Los Islotes. Standing in that elevated position studying this forgotten land from a distance steadies my mind. Passing through it grounds my soul. No outsiders have ventured this far south yet. The world of the ancestors is undisturbed.

The road ends at Flores. Beyond is the national park. In all these years, we'd never visited. We're always too pressed for time. In the past we've turned around without venturing into the village. "Let's drive through," I said. Lief turned left. Tidy Flores was laid out before us. Small houses along both sides of the road faced each other. They'd been built so close together that a resident could reach from his front steps to hold the hand of a neighbor on the porch next-door. Front doors were open to the late-afternoon breeze. Children swayed in hammocks. Their parents chatted from rocking chairs. They looked up as we passed, surprised for visitors they didn't recognize, but they waved and smiled. *This would be a nice place to call home*, I thought as I waved to a little girl eating a mango.

We headed back up the coast to the bramador. Before Gary retired, Hector Moreno started construction of the Plaza El Bramador. He sighted his red brick compound at the cross. We watched as a hotel, restaurant, and bar appeared then a convenience store, rancher's feed and supply, and gas station. It was the Veraguas equivalent of a Walmart Supercenter. We considered it a blessing when it opened. Before the bramador, the nearest chino was for-

QUEBRO TOWNSHIP
Chapter XI

ty-five minutes away in Mariato. The nearest U.S.-style grocery store was in Santiago. "It's like we're living in a whole different town," Dalys told me the day the bramador opened. Having a place to go for a loaf of bread, a tank of gas, or a dinner out ten minutes from the Los Islotes gate was a game-changer.

Every stool at the bar was taken when Lief and I walked in. I recognized some of the men. They'd been at the parade with us earlier. We took a table and ordered the special, garlic shrimp. As the sun set, a party erupted around us. Lief and I ate slowly, feeling like locals and happy to be part of the scene. Back home later we still didn't want this day to be done. We sat together on our bedroom balcony. Our black walnut trees hid us from view, but privacy wasn't a concern. We were alone with Los Islotes. The moon was full. It reflected on the ocean before us. "All these years we've imagined sitting like this someday," I said.

"Yes," Lief said. "Now here we are. I'd say this is about as good as life gets."

"No argument here," I said. "But now what? If we continue trying to do what we came here to do, this place will be changed forever. And I don't think for the better. Imagine Torio duplicated over and over all the way down this coast. I'm afraid that's what's coming. The thought makes me sick to my stomach."

"I don't disagree, and I believe that's why what we're trying to do matters as much as it does." Lief said. "We hope to profit from our development plan, building homes, etc., but the locals will

AT HOME AT LOS ISLOTES
Finding Our Way On This Veraguas Coast

benefit and the land, too, because we respect what's here already. You could argue that what we intend to create will be a net benefit to Quebro."

"So you've come over from the dark side," I teased. "This is no longer just about the money for you?"

"Ha, ha," Lief said. "I agree that we don't want Quebro to develop like Torio. We want to control how our coast is changed and preserve as much of its natural beauty as we can. I want to keep the character of this place, but I also want to make it more comfortable and more accessible. Are you going to say we shouldn't have built this big house? That you'd rather we didn't have five bathrooms, air conditioning, and fiber-optic internet?"

"No, no, not at all. I appreciate all the creature comforts," I said. "And I realize it's hypocritical to want to close the gate to the rest of the world behind us. Why should we alone benefit from this extraordinary place?"

"Well, when you put it like that, I'm of a different mind entirely," Lief countered. My husband could always be counted on to take the contrary position to whatever point of view I suggested. I'd learned not to take it personally. I'm a contrarian, too. Our instincts always to consider the alternative perspective can be exhausting. They make the going painful, but I count on the push and pull to get us where we need to be.

"Why should we benefit?" Lief said. "Because we're the pioneers. We've struggled and persevered. We've earned our position

QUEBRO TOWNSHIP
Chapter XI

here. Everyone who comes behind us will have an easier job of it. Eventually it'll be too easy to make your way here. Like it is over in Chitré. So, right, when you frame the question that way, I take your position. Let's shut down operations. We've got everything we need. Let's stop work now and keep Los Islotes all to ourselves."

We sat in silence for a while listening to the cicadas and the waves pounding a hundred meters below. "Don't worry," Lief said. "I don't expect a response. We're not going to answer these big questions tonight. I'm tired. I'm going to bed."

"I'll be in shortly," I said. Lief went inside. I stayed alone in the moonlight. I didn't want to halt development. My city of light idea was firmly in place in my mind. Dalys was on board. We were building a team. We had a starter-city plan. How would I get from where we were to where I envisioned? And how would I both protect this land and put it on the world map at the same time? Like Lief said, I wasn't going to know the answers to those questions tonight, and I didn't need to. Tomorrow was another day. Time for sleep.

XII

Ariadne

PARIS
2019

Lief and I joined the kids in Paris for Christmas then returned to Panama mid-January. We spent two weeks in the city finalizing new year budgets and agendas for the publishing business. We returned to Los Islotes February 1.

Dalys came into my office first thing our first morning back. I'd missed seeing her. Her bright eyes and ready smile boost my spirits and bolster my resolve. I need regular doses of Dalys.

"How long will you stay this time, Señora Kathleen?" she wanted to know.

"We're here for the duration," I told her. Lief and I were in no hurry to leave.

"I am glad to hear that," Dalys said. "That means you will be here for our big rodeo. Do you remember me telling you about it? It's where my mom met my dad when they were young. It is in March. You and Señor Lief had such a good time at the inde-

ARIADNE
Chapter XII

pendence day parade last year. I thought you might like to see the rodeo, too. It is a very important day. People come from all across Veraguas and even from farther away. People who have moved to other parts of the country, who are away from their families, they all come home just for the rodeo."

Ah, ha, I thought, *very good idea, Dalys.* Quebro's rodeo could be an opportunity to reconnect all the way around. Lief and I continually reconsider nearly all agendas to do with Los Islotes, but more than a decade in we agree on one thing. This is a family affair. Whatever we ultimately accomplish on this Veraguas coast won't be for us. Lief and I will do the best we can with the time we've got, but we won't reach the finish line. Dalys is our succession plan on the ground, but we are counting on our children to take up the torch alongside her when we are gone. We want them to feel part of what we're building.

We arranged a two-week visit. It would be the kids' first time at Los Islotes since Alonso had finished our house. Every previous visit we'd stayed with them at the cabanas in Torio or Mykonos in Santiago. Finally we were in a position to receive our family properly. Jackson asked if he could bring three friends.

It was a full house. Normally, I like order, but with the whole family and more visiting, we had chaos, and I loved it. The kids kayaked in the estuary, surfed at Panama Jack's, rode horses on the beach, and fished for corvina in the river. Jackson and his friends borrowed my Jeep to run to the bramador for snacks and to shoot

AT HOME AT LOS ISLOTES
Finding Our Way On This Veraguas Coast

---

darts in the bar. "All that's missing are the swinging saloon doors," Jackson told me after he'd seen the place for the first time. He was a cowboy, like his dad.

"It's so great to see them going around town," Dalys said. "Everyone in Quebro is talking about them. People want to know who they are and how long they will be here."

On Dalys' suggestion, we'd sponsored Quebro's rodeo team. She'd had more shirts made. Our *caballeros* wore white chambray with the Los Islotes logo embroidered on the back in green. We arrived at the arena Sunday morning as the guys were mounting up. The eight of them formed a semi-circle on horseback. Lief and I stood in front then called Kaitlin, Harry, Jackson, and Dalys over for a family photo. The raised platforms around the arena had been covered with fresh thatch. Each team had been assigned a viewing stand. "Our area is just over there," Dalys pointed. A couple dozen people were settled on the platform, including Dalys' family. "We're up next," Dalys said.

I knew Dalys' mother, sister, and cousin but hadn't met her grandmother. It was her father's mother who'd traveled with baby Dalys from Santiago to Quebro on *La Fortuna*. The tiny white-haired lady was delicate but animated. She was dressed for the special day in a blue and green checkered cotton dress and seemed thrilled to meet us. A wide-brimmed hat kept the sun off her smiling face. Looking beneath it, I saw where Dalys got the twinkle in her eyes. Dalys' grandmother opened her arms wide in

ARIADNE
Chapter XII

welcome and pulled me in for a kiss. "You stay right here, next to me," she told me in Spanish. Then she handed me a rock. I didn't understand but smiled. She had one, too.

The *caballeros* rode by single-file then lined up outside the arena. I recognized the man at the gate. He was a Los Islotes groundskeeper. Pedro noticed Lief and me and waved. Then he opened the gate and the first of our team trotted inside. Our guy backed his horse into the stall, Pedro opened the door to the chute, and a white calf flew out. Our cowboy was off. He circled his lariat above his head three times then spun it toward the spirited yearling. His rope caught the animal around the shoulders, just as intended. Dalys' grandmother banged her rock against the metal fence in front of us. She looked over at me and nodded her head encouragingly. Dalys' sister picked up a rock and banged alongside her grandmother. Everyone was cheering. The racket was deafening. I laughed and started banging, too.

The next rider entered the arena. "That's my dad," Dalys said. I didn't recognize Dalys' father. He looked twenty years younger in his rodeo gear. "Your father still competes?" I said.

"Oh, yes. This is a very important day for him. He has never missed a rodeo since the year he met my mom here." Dalys' father was out of the stall in a flash and had his rope around his calf's shoulders in a second-and-a-half. It was the fastest time of the day.

Too soon, our two-week family reunion was over. Lief and I

AT HOME AT LOS ISLOTES
Finding Our Way On This Veraguas Coast

stood at the top of the driveway to see the kids off. Jackson backed out first. "Thank you for everything," he and his friends called from their open windows. Harry pulled out next. I blew kisses and waved as he and Kaitlin drove down the hill. We watched until both cars were out of sight. Lief went inside. I stood in the spot a moment longer to take in the moment. It would be another bright and sunny summer day. I started back toward the house, mood high, but our spirit tree stopped me. It continued to struggle. I searched carefully but, as had been the case for too long, found no sign of life. *It'll come back*, I told myself. *It always has before.*

Dora and Smokey sprinted toward me. I hadn't seen them since I'd let them out the front door before breakfast. Now they were soaked and muddy. "You two have been in the estuary again, haven't you?" I said. They darted around in circles at my feet, barking and playing. "Come on. Let's go around back. I'll give you quick baths. The kids are gone. It's just us again. Let's think about what adventures we can get up to today."

Alone again with Los Islotes, Lief and I settled into a routine. We were up before dawn. The way our bedroom is configured we have windows on all four sides. The sunrise colors the sky rosy and the interior of our bedroom, too. We basked in it as we showered and dressed each morning. We were in the office by 7:00 a.m. Live And Invest Overseas now had teams not only in Panama City but also in Paris with Harry and Kaitlin and in Waterford

ARIADNE
Chapter XII

where we'd reconnected with contacts from our *International Living* days. We spent mornings on video conference calls. One of our Los Islotes crew would bring us lunch from Dalys' mom's restaurant. Quebro's answer to take-out. Afternoons were for Los Islotes. The stables were almost finished. Next on the list was a clubhouse. Luis was finalizing construction drawings.

We were advancing on all fronts. After years of trying, our kitchen garden delivered a bumper harvest. I'd been tongue-in-cheek blaming the soil for previous failed attempts, but it wasn't lost on me that everyone else around was able to grow corn and tomatoes no problem. Finally, we were, too. We'd also planted blackjack, pennywort, marshmallow, and cilantro, our starter healing garden. Dalys had shown me how to prepare teas from the leaves of these plants to treat everything from fever, infections, and wounds to digestive disorders and joint pain. Our mare Señora Cortez delivered another healthy colt. We called him Santiago. "We're going at a good pace, don't you think, Señora Kathleen?" Dalys remarked in passing one day. "Yes, Dalys," I said. "We are indeed." Days turned into satisfying weeks and months.

Then more good news. Kaitlin called to say that she and Harry were expecting their first child. Lief and I rejoiced. We were happy for all the reasons anyone is pleased to hear they're about to become a grandparent for the first time, but the announcement carried additional weight. It meant our efforts at Los Islotes had a future not only beyond us but also beyond our children. The

AT HOME AT LOS ISLOTES
Finding Our Way On This Veraguas Coast

instant I heard of her existence, our decades of legacy-building efforts were worth it. Ariadne was the point.

That's what Kaitlin and Harry had already decided they'd call their daughter. I appreciated the literal translation. "Ariadne" is Greek for "most holy." Kaitlin and Harry chose the name for the legend. Cretan princess Ariadne helped Theseus escape the Minotaur but then died tragically. Dionysus traveled to the Underworld to bring her back to life so he could marry her. Dionysus gave Ariadne a crown to wear for the wedding. After the ceremony, Ariadne threw the crown to the heavens where the jewels turned to stars and formed Corona Borealis, the brightest constellation in the sky. What better metaphor for our first grandchild.

Lief and I remained at Los Islotes through September. We spent a few weeks in the office in Panama City then met Kaitlin and Harry in Baltimore for a family baby shower late October. We returned to Paris altogether. We enjoyed a quiet Christmas then settled in for the countdown. Ariadne was due to join the family the third week of January.

That date came and went, then, 2:00 o'clock in the morning a week later, I got Harry's text. It was time. Lief had had to travel to Belize to host our annual conference in Belize City. Jackson and I called him from the taxi on the way to the hospital. "Give everyone my love," he said. "I'll be on the first possible flight back." Jackson and I sat up the rest of the night in the waiting room. Harry came out just before dawn to tell us that Ariadne had made

ARIADNE
Chapter XII

her debut. Mother and baby were doing beautifully. Life was almost too good to be true.

Lief and I stayed two months more in Paris, long enough to help Kaitlin get back on her feet and to get to know our granddaughter. Then, just as we were about to reposition to Panama, we, like the entire rest of the world, had to recalibrate. In response to the global pandemic, borders closed. We were locked down in Paris. Back in Panama, strict quarantine mandates took effect. Offices were shuttered, and construction halted countrywide.

We kept in touch with Dalys by WhatsApp and video calls. "We'll be back to work as soon as possible," we assured her. She passed the message along to Martin and the guys. As soon as possible was more than a year later. One week after Tocumen International reopened, we returned to Panama City, but travel within the country remained restricted. It was another two months before we could make the trip to Los Islotes. After a year-and-a-half away, our reunion with Dalys and Martin was joyous. We were all eager to rebuild momentum. The first order of business was reclaiming gardens and parks. Left on its own, the jungle had taken back some of its territory. Everywhere were more flowers, more trees, and more wildlife. Noticeably augmented populations of monkeys, deer, iguanas, and gato solos roamed the hillsides, and we noticed birds we'd never seen before. Our first day back in the house, I met a katydid resting on my potting bench and a praying mantis on our bedroom balcony. Our welcoming committee.

AT HOME AT LOS ISLOTES
Finding Our Way On This Veraguas Coast

Our extended absence had the opposite effect on the situation with our neighbor. The woman I'd almost called a friend years earlier was now like a stranger. Roberta wouldn't return my waves when I drove past her house. Lief and I had energy to burn post-pandemic lockdown. We wanted to make up for lost time. Top of the list was our new grander entrance. This meant finally starting on the fence and wall in front of Roberta's compound. My Spanish was too limited to have a conversation with her directly. Plus, I thought Roberta might take the news better from Dalys. Roberta had known Dalys her whole life. Dalys made a heroic effort to assure Roberta of our good intentions, but Roberta shut her down.

"She won't speak to me, Señora Kathleen," Dalys reported after two weeks of stopping by Roberta's place every morning on her way to work. "She tells me that she will not allow a wall or a fence. That is all she will say. She says 'no' then she tells me to go away."

Roberta had become our enemy. I didn't understand. Probably I never would. The cultural gap between us is canyon deep. I'd been aware of the divide all along but had hoped—maybe naively—that we could build a bridge. Lief had never been interested in coddling Roberta. Now, after having sat in the cab of Dalys' pick-up watching the woman brandish a machete at our crew, neither was I.

XIII

Spirit Tree

LOS ISLOTES
2022

No one spoke as Dalys drove us back through our front gate and around the bend to the work yard. She dropped off the men and their tools then started up the hill to our house. Lief's hands were shaking. My husband has a temper. I've learned to give him time to cool down before engaging. Dalys followed my lead. When we reached our driveway, Lief was out of the truck before Dalys had brought it to a full stop. "Come back by, Dalys," I said as I climbed out, "after you've filed your reports with the Justice of the Peace and the police in Quebro. So we can regroup and make a plan for next steps."

"Copy that," Dalys replied. She waved out her open window and pulled away smiling. What would I do without unflappable Dalys? I pray for resilience like she has.

Lief was inside the house. He'd slammed the front door behind him. I was in no hurry to catch up. I was worn out trying to help

AT HOME AT LOS ISLOTES
Finding Our Way On This Veraguas Coast

him keep perspective. I was as frustrated as he was and as tired. Right now I had nothing for him. I needed to process the events of the morning for myself. Fourteen years into Los Islotes, I was again close to crying uncle. What a roller-coaster ride it'd been. Now we'd hit another bottom. I couldn't remember the last night I'd slept more than a few hours. Or the last twenty-four hours that'd passed without Lief and me arguing. On days like today it was hard to say why we'd started down this road. And too many days were like today. The machete scene was extraordinary, but the struggles it sprang from had become our normal.

Our feud with Roberta had been the talk of Veraguas for two years. Recently, Dalys told me a woman she has known her whole life approached her on the street in Mariato. The woman, a friend of Dalys' mother, wanted to shame her. "You shouldn't build a wall without making sure it is okay with your neighbor, Dalys," the woman said. "You know that is not our way. That is not how good neighbors behave."

"What did you say in response, Dalys?" I asked.

"I didn't say anything," Dalys said. "What can I say, Señora Kathleen? She is a nice woman, but she does not understand. The mayor, he stopped me, too," Dalys added. "And, you know, that made me mad. For many months I have asked him to come to Los Islotes. I want him to meet our crew. I tell him that we have thirty-five people working here now. That means thirty-five happy families all around because of Los Islotes. Thirty-five fam-

SPIRIT TREE
Chapter XIII

ilies with six, seven, eight people in each one, now they all have money they've never had before in their lives. These people are living better. They say it to me all the time. The mayor should want to see for himself. These are the people of his town. But he always has some reason, and he never comes.

"Then, last week, he came to me outside the bank in Mariato. He said he heard we are building a wall. 'But you do not have a permit,' he said. I told him that our staff has been in touch with his office three times. Three times we have come for a meeting to arrange for the permit. Each time, the mayor's people, they say they are too busy to meet. They send us away. This man, this mayor, is harassing me on the street because we are building a wall without a permit, but we have been trying to pay for the permit for months. I didn't say that last part. I only said yes, of course, we want to pay for the permit. 'Okay,' he said. 'Let's go to my office now.' I told him great. I smile and say, 'Thank you, Mr. Mayor. Thank you so much for your time, blah, blah, blah.' So now we have the permit. But still the mayor doesn't come to Los Islotes. He only has time for me when he thinks he can get a fee from us. I want him to come to see what we are doing. He doesn't understand either. No one understands. I cannot educate all Mariato." The speech came out in a rush, like a flood of feeling Dalys had been keeping to herself a long while.

Dalys was right. We couldn't change the mind of an entire population, and maybe we didn't have any business trying.

AT HOME AT LOS ISLOTES
Finding Our Way On This Veraguas Coast

While I waited for Lief to cool off, I looked over at our spirit tree and remembered how we'd come to call it that.

In preparation for construction of our house, our crew cleared the lot. They chopped down all the trees, including this one. A few days later, this tree resprouted. They hacked away the new growth with a machete, but the tree resurrected again and again. One day, when the guys were pouring concrete for our foundation and cursing this tree that wouldn't die because it was in their way, they decided they'd dig out the stump. "Please, no," I'd said. "Please let it be." The tree was a survivor. It deserved support. Begrudgingly, the guys agreed.

A month later, I arrived to find the tortured trunk covered with cement. "Would you please have someone scrape the concrete off that tree stump out front?" I asked Dalys.

"Yes, of course, Señora Kathleen," she said. "I know the tree you mean. The spirit tree."

"Spirit tree?"

"Yes, Señora Kathleen. That is more than a tree. That is an energy. Don't worry," she'd told me. "That tree will only grow." I replay that confident refrain over in my head often. Times like now, I lean on it. Our spirit tree has become a metaphor for our attempts to keep going with Los Islotes. What if Dalys was wrong? What if it finally dies? The old me would have shrugged off such worries. It's a tree. Sometimes trees die. That reality has nothing to do with the challenges Lief and I face at Los Islotes. But I'm not the

SPIRIT TREE
Chapter XIII

same woman I was before Los Islotes entered our lives. The new me believes that this near-dead ceiba in my front garden's future could portend our demise.

Standing by the tree, my mind flashed back to images from just minutes before of Roberta in our dirt lane. I couldn't reconcile that woman with the woman I'd known for years. I thought of the first day Lief and I stopped for lunch in her restaurant and how later that afternoon she'd met us in the road bearing gifts from her granddaughter. Roberta closed her restaurant after a few years. She told Gary she was tired of being tied to her stove all day. We lost touch after that. All I'd known of Roberta in recent years were the rumors. People on this coast have a lot of time on their hands. They like to gossip. After they got to know him well enough, they began telling Gary stories about Roberta and her practice of the black arts. They referred to her as *bruja*. Lief and I would chuckle when Gary and then others over the years since relayed the tales. It was entertaining local color. Ha, ha, our neighbor is a witch.

Now I didn't know what to think. The scene I'd just witnessed had me in shock. I'd done what I do. I'd projected onto Roberta. I'd let myself believe she was what I wanted her to be. The weakness has led me to bad partners and unfortunate staffing choices and now it'd had me believing that, in Roberta, I'd found a kindred female soul in this frontier world. Clearly that wasn't the case. Roberta wasn't a witch. That notion was silly. But she wasn't

AT HOME AT LOS ISLOTES
Finding Our Way On This Veraguas Coast

an ally either. She was a threat. It was time for me to own up to that truth.

It was also time to go inside and face Lief. The current situation was largely of my making. Roberta had been bullying us for two years. Lief had wanted to stand up to her from the start. I'd defended the woman but no more. It was time to fight back.

XIV

Showdown

LOS ISLOTES
2022

After our heart rates had returned to normal the morning after Roberta held our crew hostage in our dirt road with her machete, Lief, Dalys, and I called our attorney in Santiago. Fernando helped Dalys file complaints with the court in Santiago, which mandated a pause in construction of the fence. We obliged. Six weeks later, after reviewing the case, a judge found in our favor. He ordered the Quebro justice of the peace to step aside and instructed the local police to uphold our property rights. *At last*, we thought with a sigh of relief. A resolution. We could move on from the drama and return to our work.

The next day, Dalys sent our men back out with post-hole diggers. Roberta, her husband, and their children reappeared. The bunch of them held their machetes at their sides while they taunted and threatened our guys. When Dalys realized what was happening, she sent our men to join the crew working on the

AT HOME AT LOS ISLOTES
Finding Our Way On This Veraguas Coast

stables again. She had to do some sweet-talking, but she got them to agree to return to the road in front of Roberta's house the next morning and again the morning after that, but each day Roberta and her family harassed them, making their work impossible.

Each day, Dalys filed a new complaint with the Quebro police. And, each day, again, she reported back that the police had barely indulged the conversation. On the fourth day, Lief and I joined her at the station. I sat on a plastic folding chair in the unpainted concrete block reception room while Lief stood before the handmade wooden counter. He relayed the most recent experience, explaining how Roberta and her family were continuing to interfere with our work on our land and reminding the police chief that the Santiago judge had found in our favor and ordered both his police department and the justice of the peace, who was standing in the doorway of her office next-door eavesdropping, to protect our land and our men. The police chief leaned back on his heels and looked down at his big belly. Then he waved his arm dismissively in Lief's direction and shook his head. "There's nothing I can do," he said smugly. "It's out of my hands. You must wait for the process."

"We have waited for the process," Lief replied. Now he was shouting. I didn't blame him. It was all I could do to stay put in my chair. I have a long fuse, but I wanted to scream at the arrogant man, too. If the Santiago judge's ruling meant nothing to these people, what were we to do? I felt desperate.

SHOWDOWN
Chapter XIV

"We have the judge's ruling," Lief was still shouting. "You must defend it. It is your job." Lief held out the stamped paper showing the judge's directive in our favor. The police chief refused to look at the paper. He just kept staring down at his belly. When he waved his arm in Lief's direction again, this time to indicate that the conversation, as far as he was concerned, was over, I wanted to punch him in the nose.

Fernando filed more complaints. The judge in Santiago called for an official inspection to settle the matter once and for all. Our surveyor, Cristian, had checked the boundaries three times, but Señor Sanchez and Roberta rejected our topography. A date was set for an independent review, but the court surveyor never appeared. Dalys called him to ask why.

"He said he had car trouble," Dalys explained when she came to my office to report back on the phone call. Lief was sitting in the armchair across from my desk. We'd been reviewing plans for the clubhouse at the beach that we hoped to break ground on at the start of next dry season. It'd be positioned between Panama Jack's and the small amphitheater I wanted to build back from the sand. I had a new pie-in-the-sky objective. I was going to reach out to Jimmy Buffet. I'm a lifetime fan. I grew up on his music then raised my kids on it. Los Islotes is his kind of place. Maybe he could be persuaded to perform a concert on our beach as a fundraiser for my Los Islotes school. Lief laughed off the notion, but I held on to it. I continued to tell myself the Los Islotes plan

AT HOME AT LOS ISLOTES
Finding Our Way On This Veraguas Coast

was on track and moving ahead even though our current day-to-day reality made a strong case to the contrary.

"Were you able to reschedule?" I asked. No point commenting on the lame excuse. All that mattered was that the guy hadn't shown up. We needed to try again to get him on site. Eye on the prize.

"No, Señora Kathleen," Dalys said shaking her head slightly. "He said he didn't know when he'd be able to come."

A light came on that brought me up short. Our road dispute with Roberta was a clear-cut case. Yet, after months of appeals for help from the authorities, it remained open.

"Lief," I said, "could there be something going on behind the scenes? I mean, do you think somebody could be, you know, paying somebody off?"

"Yes, I do," Lief said simply.

"Señora Kathleen, that is what I think also," Dalys offered. "I am sorry to say it, but I believe people are not being honest with you about this."

Lief and I have been doing business in developing-world markets for decades. I've worked hard to continue to believe that it's possible in places like Panama to operate transparently and to count on others to do the same. Over the decades we've been spending time and money in this country, many have had their hands out. Lief has been pulled over by traffic cops asking for a *mordita*, or a little bite, dozens of times. "It sure is a hot day," they

SHOWDOWN
Chapter XIV

say. "I could use a cold beer." The implication is that you should buy them a drink. Pass over a US$5 bill with your driver's license and the imagined infraction is forgotten. Lief ignores the game. He pretends he doesn't speak Spanish. He makes the conversation so difficult and lengthy that the cop loses interest. The officer realizes he's wasting time that could be spent pulling over a more obliging gringo. I've witnessed the scene many times but have fended off cynicism to hold on to my naturally romantic perspective. As Dalys would say, I've stayed a sucker.

We arranged a meeting in our office with Fernando. "This country is run by the rich and connected Panamanians," Fernando told us when he joined us at our conference table. "Panamanians without money or connections don't stand a chance. Foreigners, even foreigners with money and connections, don't stand a chance either. Rich and connected Panamanians only work with each other. They look out for each other. They do favors for each other. If one is in trouble, another who is a cousin or a friend of the judge makes a call and the ruling is changed." The Sanchezes weren't rich, but they were connected. The family has led this coast for generations.

"Yes, Señora Kathleen, Señor Lief, that is the way of things," Dalys confirmed. "It is not the right way, but it is the way. The law does not always win. It makes me angry and ashamed for my country.

"Do you remember," Dalys continued, "last year when MiAm-

AT HOME AT LOS ISLOTES
Finding Our Way On This Veraguas Coast

biente came to Los Islotes one day? I wrote an email to tell you and Señor Lief about it."

I remembered. We'd faced many delays over the years at Los Islotes, but MiAmbiente's constant calls for more reports, more inspections, and more proof that we weren't harming the ecosystem we were developing had been the costliest. It's not that Lief and I object to the oversight. From day one, we've welcomed help protecting the gifts Mother Nature offers at Los Islotes. But we have no tolerance for developing-world bureaucracy and MiAmbiente was a quagmire of red tape.

"MiAmbiente came that day with no warning," Dalys continued, "because someone had told them that Los Islotes was pouring oil into the estuary." Dalys made air quotes when she said the words "pouring oil."

"Who would have done that?" I wondered.

"I don't know," Dalys said shrugging her shoulders slightly and looking nervous. "We'll never know, but, some around, like we've talked about in the past, Señora Kathleen, they don't understand what we're trying to do here at Los Islotes. They feel threatened by our plans. We can't worry about them." I knew she was right, but not worrying doesn't come easily for me.

"When MiAmbiente showed up at the office that day," Dalys continued, "and told me I must take them to the estuary. I said, okay, no problem. Come, see the estuary. It's beautiful. We are not putting oil in the estuary. That is crazy. We are not putting

SHOWDOWN
Chapter XIV

anything in the estuary. I showed them the estuary. Like I'd told them, there was nothing to see so they left.

"I was so mad that day, because what about the rice farmers. That's what I wanted to know. The farmers in our area clean their machines and pour their chemicals into the rivers. They kill thousands of iguanas and frogs and fish every year. I know this. Everyone knows this. We see the farmers dump oil and things into the river and then we see the dead things. People complain to MiAmbiente. But no inspector comes to the offices of the rice farmers insisting on proof that they are not hurting the environment. Nobody does anything. That is because the rice farmers are friends with the other rich Panamanians in Santiago."

Bribery, skimming, profiteering, and old boys' networks are facts of doing business in the developing world, but Lief and I hadn't faced this level of corruption before. Panama is a civil law country. In common law countries like the United States, case law and judicial opinions inform decisions. Interpretation and precedent count. In civil law systems, codified statutes rule. As long as a document has been signed, sealed, stamped, and filed away, that's the black and white. As much as I resented hearing it from the police chief, I knew he was right. The process was all that mattered. I'd come to hate the word. Panamanian attorneys, bureaucrats, and politicians pull it out to pass the buck. "It's not my fault. It's the process," they insist. The process continues as long as someone is willing to pay the associated costs. I'd blamed

AT HOME AT LOS ISLOTES
Finding Our Way On This Veraguas Coast

Napoleon until I remembered he based his code on Justinian's. The Romans set us up for this fight.

Lief and I agreed we'd stay the course. What was our option? To throw down in the mud with the rest and begin paying off government officials like everybody else? The thought lit a fire in me. I wouldn't be brought that low. I wasn't going to play the game. We asked Fernando to keep following the rules of the process.

"It is your land," Fernando assured us every time we called for an update. "The judge has confirmed this. Legally, there is no question. You can do what you want on your land. The police should keep the neighbors away." Maybe so, but who was going to make them? It's not like we could call 911. Veraguas has no such system. And we couldn't call Fernando in real time during a moment of crisis because there's no cell service in the road by Roberta's house. I could identify no path forward. The local police would do what they wanted no matter what the judge in Santiago said. Roberta and her family counted on it.

Finally, Fernando's efforts resulted in a new order stating that if the justice of the peace did not recuse herself she would be removed from her post and a new justice of the peace will be named and instructed to support our legal rights. "Now you can proceed," Fernando told us confidently. "That woman would be a fool to interfere anymore. She will lose her job."

We planned for blitzkrieg. We would build the wall and the fence in a single campaign. Dalys found a Nicaraguan in Torio

SHOWDOWN
Chapter XIV

who was eager for work. "It is better this way, Señora Kathleen," she said. "Nica doesn't know anybody in these parts. He doesn't care about Señor Sanchez and he isn't afraid of Roberta." I wondered if he minded being called "Nica." "He doesn't answer if I call him anything else," Dalys said. "And why would he mind? He is Nicaraguan, after all." Nicknames are common on our coast, and political correctness isn't a thing. It's refreshing.

Nica hired eight men, all from Torio and north. No locals. Dalys ordered cement and rebar. When it arrived, she had the guys stack it with the fence posts and rails they'd cut. Nica and his team would use our Bobcat to carve a ditch from the start of our property to our front gate. Then they'd lay rebar and pour concrete. "We can have our wall in two weeks, Señora Kathleen," Dalys told me. "And the fence one week later." Sounded great to me. If Dalys thought we could do it, I was all in.

D-Day arrived. Nica and his team were to arrive by 7:00 a.m. Dalys was standing outside the door waiting for me as I pulled up to the office. "Good news, Señora Kathleen," she said as I climbed down from my Jeep. "Roberta is in Santiago today. One of her sons was arrested yesterday. He beat his wife badly."

"That doesn't sound like good news, Dalys," I said.

"Well, no, not for the poor woman who took the beating, but it creates a window for us. Roberta has to figure out that mess. She will be gone some time. Señor Sanchez is in Santiago, too. He has a medical appointment. So Nica has a chance to do his

AT HOME AT LOS ISLOTES
Finding Our Way On This Veraguas Coast

work. He is out front now with the Bobcat. I'm going to check his progress."

Dalys returned twenty minutes later to say all was well. Then, 3:00 o'clock that afternoon, our gate guard called the office. "Dalys, Dalys, come quick!" he cried frantically over his radio. Lief, Dalys, and I drove to the front. One of Señor Sanchez's sons was standing in our dirt road shouting at Nica. Dalys pulled out her phone to take photos, as Fernando had instructed her to do. Nica appeared calm in the face of the drama but he was nervous. "I don't want any trouble," he said in Spanish as Lief and Dalys approached. "Don't worry," Dalys assured him. "We aren't doing anything wrong." The workday was nearly over and Nica's crew had finished their ditch so Dalys told them to go home. "*Hasta mañana*," she called out as they pulled away in their beat-up red pick-up. Nica nodded and smiled back. He hadn't been scared off. He'd be back.

The next morning Dalys was again standing by the door when Lief and I arrived at the office. "Señor Lief, Señora Kathleen," she said, "I am sorry to have to tell you that today we have trouble. Señor Sanchez and all three of his sons are in the road. They have filled in Nica's ditch. All Nica's work from yesterday is lost. I tried to speak with the Sanchezes, but they are angry. Mateo came at me with his machete. He called me very bad names. Why do they have to be so mean?"

"I'm very sorry, Dalys," I said. What was it with these people and machetes? "Are you okay?"

SHOWDOWN
Chapter XIV

"Oh, yes, I am okay. They hurt my feelings calling me names, that is all. They do not make me afraid. They make me want to fight. They are wrong to be doing what they are doing. It is enough."

"Yes," I said. "It is time for this to end."

Dalys got into the Prado with Lief. I followed them out our front gate in my Jeep feeling like we were headed for the O.K. Corral. When we arrived, Nica and his crew were in a huddle across the road from Señor Sanchez and his sons. Nica smiled in Dalys' direction. It wasn't his battle. He barely knew us. But he and his men were standing with us in the face of danger because they believed it was the right thing to do. Moments like this show of solidarity by Nica are the reason why I haven't lost hope for us humans.

Lief jerked the steering wheel putting the Prado on the wrong side of the road then he stopped short. Dirt and dust went flying. Lief jumped out of the car. "You're trespassing," said like a rancher in a John Wayne movie. "This is private land. You need to get off it now." Roberta's "husband" of the moment, Mateo, stopped shoveling. He, his brothers, and their father stood in a row atop the mound of dirt they'd made filling in Nica's ditch. Señor Sanchez stepped forward. "This is my land," he said. "I will not let you build a wall on my land." His wagging finger reached dangerously close to Lief's nose. Señor Sanchez's three sons surrounded the old man for support, but Lief on his own was more intimidating. He was done messing around.

AT HOME AT LOS ISLOTES
Finding Our Way On This Veraguas Coast

I'd parked my Jeep behind Lief's Prado so I could video the scene with my phone. I imagined the headline, "American developer arrested in land dispute with Panamanian neighbors. Wife's video tells whole story."

I watched from my Jeep as Señor Sanchez continued ranting and shaking his finger in Lief's face. His son Yuhenio snarled in Lief's ear. I continued filming. I expected shouting, but when Lief finally spoke, his voice was calm. He was on the other side of his anger. I almost felt sorry for the Sanchez clan. They didn't recognize the dragon they'd unleashed by pushing Lief as far as they had. They'd refused our pleas for reconciliation for months. They'd wanted a fight. They had one.

"Señor Sanchez, stop," Lief said, looking the man in the eyes. "Stop now," Lief said again with steel in his voice, and the old man did. Señor Sanchez's arm fell to his side. He took a half-step back. Yuhenio quieted down, too. Silence. Could the resolution be as simple as a firm instruction? I felt a flash of faith.

When Lief negotiated the purchase of the Los Islotes finca, he insisted it include a stretch of land wide enough for private access from the public road. It was one of the smartest moves he's ever made. He wouldn't accept a guarantee of an easement. The property required for this entrance was owned by the senior Señor Sanchez.

"Señor Sanchez," Lief said even more calmly, "you know that you sold this land. I know you know that this is my land now. And I want to build a wall on it."

SHOWDOWN
Chapter XIV

"I did not sell this land!" Señor Sanchez shouted. He was agitated all over again. "I would never sell this land." He was so certain in his tone and in his posture that he almost had me wondering. Could Lief and I somehow be mistaken in our understanding of the situation?

"Okay, where is your title?" Lief asked quietly. "If you own this land, show me your title."

"It is in the house," Señor Sanchez said to Lief. Then, to his son, "Go. Get the papers."

Mateo returned with a document. I leaned far out my window. I could hardly hold myself back. What was this document? "May I see that, please?" Lief asked in Spanish. Mateo handed over the papers, and Lief began to read. When he reached the final page, Lief leaned his head back and looked up at the sky with his eyes closed. He was composing himself but why? What did the paper say? Lief looked back at me. He was half-laughing, half-crying. His eyes were desperate. I kept filming.

"Señor Sanchez," Lief said, as though in pain, looking the old man in the eye again, "this says that this land is owned by Los Islotes. This is a copy of *my* Los Islotes title. Look, right here. Here is your signature," Lief said holding out the paper for Señor Sanchez to see. "And here is the name of the registered owner of the land. It says 'Los Islotes.' This shows that Los Islotes is the buyer. That is my company. I am the owner." Señor Sanchez looked at the paper blankly. Lief looked at the ground, waiting,

AT HOME AT LOS ISLOTES
Finding Our Way On This Veraguas Coast

but Señor Sanchez didn't respond. He kept staring straight ahead. *Could it be*, I wondered. Lief had the same thought at the same time. "Señor Sanchez," Lief whispered, "can you read this?"

"No," Señor Sanchez replied so softly the word was barely audible.

Lief was still a moment then looked at Mateo. "Can you read this?" he asked. Illidro shook his head. Then, to Yuhenio, "Can you read this?" Finally Lief turned to Señor Sanchez's third son, Pablo, and held out the document. Yuhenio and Pablo both looked down. They couldn't read either. They'd presented this document with confidence as proof of their position but they had no idea what it said. The fight left me. I looked at Lief who was looking at me. *What now*, I mouthed. How could we persuade this man to accept reality when he couldn't read the proof? He wasn't going to suddenly take our word for it. Why would he? We're the big bad outsiders. The man is hard-wired not to trust us. I felt a rush of sympathy.

Lief turned back to Señor Sanchez. "That is your signature, isn't it, Señor Sanchez. Even if you can't read these papers, you recognize your signature, right?" Señor Sanchez nodded. "*Sí*, that is my signature," he said, still whispering. "Well, okay, then," Lief said, relaxing a little. "That settles things."

"No," Señor Sanchez responded fiercely. "That is my signature. But I did not sell this land! This is public land. It has always been public land. This is a public road." What was this man saying now? He couldn't have it both ways. The road couldn't be both

SHOWDOWN
Chapter XIV

his land that he'd never sell and a public thoroughfare. Had the man lost his mind? Did he understand what he was saying? Then, as though in response to my unspoken questions, Señor Sanchez went one step further. "If you want to build a fence here," he said to Lief, "you will need to buy this land. If that is what you want, you should have said so. You should have come to me. We could have talked like men. If you want to have this land for a fence, I can sell it to you. I can give you a price." I was no longer sorry for Señor Sanchez and I was no longer laughing. This man had been playing us all along. He knew he didn't own this land. And he knew that we did. His antics so far hadn't worked so now he was trying a new scheme.

The air went out of Lief. He was spent. The courts were rigged, the justice of the peace operated by her own rules, and the police sided with the locals, who, in this case, were common swindlers. Lief handed the title documents back to Mateo. He looked at Señor Sanchez as though to say something but thought better of it. He glanced at me and nodded slightly. I closed my window and put the Jeep in drive. Lief opened the door to the Prado and climbed inside. Dalys got in the passenger side. Lief turned the truck around and headed back to our gate. I followed. In the rear-view mirror I saw Señor Sanchez and his three sons standing again in a row atop their mound of dirt. They appeared victorious, holding their shovels like planted flags. They'd gotten what they'd wanted. We wouldn't be building a fence today.

XV

La Bruja

LOS ISLOTES
2022

The day after the scene in the road with Señor Sanchez and his sons, I invited Dalys to lunch, just the two of us. I wanted her honest impressions of things. We met at her mom's *fonda*. Hundred-foot Panama trees grow all around the open-air structure keeping temperatures cool even at midday. "*Hola, hola, buenos días,*" Dalys said to the room as we entered. "*Hola, hola,*" I offered behind her, smiling. We made our way to the only empty table. I recognized a couple of surveyors. Dalys knew everyone. They greeted her in turn as we passed.

"What do you recommend?" I asked as we pulled over chairs from the edge of the room. In the months since it'd opened, Lief and I had been visiting Dalys' mom's *fonda* for lunch two or three times a week. Some of the dozen tables were plastic, but ours was made from a thick round slice of hand-hewn wood set atop a tree trunk base. "Ah, you know the answer to that, Señora Kathleen,"

LA BRUJA
Chapter XV

Dalys said. "I always recommend the chicken. My mother is famous for her chicken. It's so good because it's fresh. Mom kills the chickens every morning. She lines them up just behind there," Dalys said, pointing over her shoulder, "early in the morning while it is still dark. Then she cuts their throats. She does it quickly. She doesn't want them to suffer. My sister and cousin, they don't like that part. But I don't mind. I help my mom when she has to kill a lot of chickens, like on Saturdays." On cue, four chickens darted between my legs. They were taking a shortcut from one side of the yard to the other. I heard their brethren clucking out back.

"My mom is very proud of how her business is growing. We all are. My mother is gaining a reputation. Workers from other villages come to her *fonda* for lunch. They have other choices that are nearer to them, but they come here. Every day is like today, full."

The coastal road from Santiago had been paved for the first time the year Lief came to Los Islotes. In the decade-and-a-half since, the climate, the annual rains, and the overweight rice trucks had taken a toll. The asphalt had become spectacularly broken and potholed. The trip down the coast that was originally a comfortable ninety minutes was now two-and-a-half rib-rattling hours. For years, we heard rumors of a new road. Finally, in 2018, loads of rock and sand were dumped at staging areas. Cranes, loaders, mixers, rollers, graders, excavators, and forklifts arrived next, then hundreds of workers. The project would take more than two years.

AT HOME AT LOS ISLOTES
Finding Our Way On This Veraguas Coast

Dalys' mom saw the opportunity. She opened Mama Regina's a month later.

"My mom named this place for my father's grandmother," Dalys said. "When she and my dad decided to move to live with me here in Quebro, this is the spot they chose. Mama Regina lived up the hill, just there, on the piece of land where I am making my own house now. My mother became almost a daughter for Mom Regina. Since she was always around, she was an important part of my childhood and my values, too. Mama Regina's represents the strength of business and of women. It is a symbol of our matriarchy in Quebro and it is my mom's legacy. She has built something that can continue making money for my sister, my cousins, and me even long after she is gone." Most women in Quebro live at the mercy of men who take them for granted and abuse them. But some rise.

When the work first commenced, Lief and I rejoiced. We'd longed for the renewal of our coastal road for years. Now that it was materializing, I was ambivalent. Like everything to do with Los Islotes, it was a double-edged sword. Better access would make it easier for the outside world to make its way here.

"These people believe you will get tired and give up," Dalys said after she'd told her mother that we'd both have the fried chicken. "What do you mean?" Typical Dalys. Straight to the point.

"Well, Roberta and Mateo have done this before, many times, and not only with foreigners. They are like a, what do you say in

LA BRUJA
Chapter XV

English? Like a syndicate I think you call it." Roberta and Mateo were the local mafia dons? This was a twist I hadn't expected.

"Do you remember the first time we went to Santiago together? When we passed by Roberta's house that morning you asked me if I knew her. I wanted to tell you more about her then. I should have. There are things about Roberta and the Sanchezes that you and Señor Lief should know. I should have said these things before now, but they are hard things."

"Go ahead, Dalys," I said. "Don't worry."

"Well, it is like I'm saying. Roberta and Mateo, they take other people's land. Sometimes the other Sanchezes are in on it with them, sometimes another man, too," Dalys continued. "Right now, they say they own land over there," Dalys said pointing to the right, "and over there," pointing to the left. "These are *fincas* owned by local Panamanians. People with families. Roberta and Mateo don't care. They say the land is theirs. They have always done like this, as long as I can remember. In the past, the people get tired of fighting and move away. That is what they count on." I was glad I'd suggested this private conversation. Dalys was giving me insider access I'd never gotten before from her or anyone.

"Years ago Roberta told a man from Norway that his land on the beach was her land. That fight became violent. I was a child when this happened, but my mother saw the man from Norway in the office of the *juez de paz* one day. He was bleeding from his head. He was trying to make a complaint about Roberta, but the

AT HOME AT LOS ISLOTES
Finding Our Way On This Veraguas Coast

juez de paz wouldn't listen. That man left these parts and never came back. Then Roberta and Mateo had his land. They built a house on it. That is what they think again now. They are sure that if they keep pushing, you will give up like the others and leave these parts."

"The guy was bleeding," I asked. "What do you think happened to him?"

"I can't say I know what happened because no one would talk about it. But I know what happened and so does everyone else. Roberta attacked the man with her machete."

Watching Roberta wield her machete at our men in the road that day three months before, I'd been concerned but not scared. The woman was posturing, I'd figured. Making a dramatic show to scare us off. I didn't imagine she'd actually cut anyone. I couldn't reassure myself with that thought any longer. Now I knew Roberta was capable of real physical harm. This was a different ballgame. Lief and I hadn't shared the Roberta drama with Kaitlin or Jackson. For them, Los Islotes is an idyllic escape. I wanted it to stay that way for them, untainted. But if the situation remained unresolved by their next visit, I'd have to tell them so they'd know to give Roberta and her kin wide berth.

Since the day Lief told me he'd decided to close on the purchase of Los Islotes without Dan the investor's money, I've gotten few good nights' sleep. By nature, I'm a powerhouse of positive energy. My glass is always nearly full. I hop out of bed by

LA BRUJA
Chapter XV

sunrise to embrace whatever adventures the day holds. I thrive on work and challenge. I'm good at juggling and navigating. I persist and persevere. I'm resourceful and resilient and constantly ready to regroup and try again. After a slip, I rally quickly and look around to see who I can pull back up onto their feet to continue onward with me. But fourteen years of lying awake in the dark worrying about cash flow and construction and questioning my and Lief's sanity while building a business and raising a son had worn on me.

At first, I'd ignored Roberta's bullying. I was more resolved back then. When Roberta pushed back on the news that we intended to build a wall, Dalys and I agreed that the best strategy was calm reassurance. Eventually the woman would realize that we meant her no harm. If we didn't fight back, she'd lose interest. That's how bullies work. I thought I was waiting her out, but she and her mini-mafia were only biding their time, pursuing a proven strategy. Dalys' description of Roberta's history of evil-doing reminded me of something else I'd long ignored, something Gary had told us about Roberta years before.

"Dalys, do you think Roberta is a witch?" I asked without preamble to see Dalys' reaction. When she shrugged her shoulders and twisted her face up, I had my answer. It wasn't the first time she'd considered the idea. "Well," Dalys said, "she has been known as '*bruja*' since Roy McKana."

"Roy McKana?"

AT HOME AT LOS ISLOTES
Finding Our Way On This Veraguas Coast

"You haven't heard about Roy McKana? Ah, this is a story you must know if you want to understand Veraguas."

"Roy McKana came to Panama in 1980 or so," Dalys continued, "something like that. He had a wife in Canada, but I don't think he ever intended to return to her. He came to Santiago to work for a Canadian company that was exporting oil from coconuts. Roy was an adventurer. He was happy in Veraguas. When the Canadian company went out of business, Roy decided he would stay. This was before I was born, but everyone knows about Roy McKana." Dalys' cousin came to the table with our plates. "*Buen provecho*," I said as I cut into my chicken breast. Our days at Los Islotes begin before dawn. By noon, I'm starved.

"Roy McKana came south, to Mariato, looking for opportunity," Dalys said, returning to her story. "Mariato was like Quebro is now. Just a *pueblo*. Roy liked it even better than Santiago." Mariato today is the only town on our coast with a bank and, until the bramador, its three chinos were the only shopping options outside Santiago. Chinos are grocery, hardware, and sundry shops. You find them everywhere in Panama. They're called "chinos" because their owners are Chinese. The first Chinese came to Panama to help build the Canal. Their descendants sell cheap kitchenware, gardening tools, and flip-flops imported by containers full from the other side of the globe.

"People in Mariato have always grown rice," Dalys continued. "They grow what they need, poking holes in the earth with sticks

LA BRUJA
Chapter XV

to put the seeds. Roy McKana thought he would grow rice, too, but in bigger amounts. You know, to sell. He bought equipment from the Canadian men he had been working for and he put it on a boat like *La Fortuna* to be carried down the coast."

"Then Roy McKana started buying land, a lot of land. The rice he grew in Mariato and eventually in fields as far south as here in Quebro was transported on horseback to Puerto Nance and from there by boat to Montijo. Roy McKana built a whole industry that is still today the biggest part of our economy in Quebro.

"After a while, you wouldn't have known that Roy McKana was Canadian," Dalys said. "He became like all the men of Veraguas. He took one girlfriend and then another. Eventually, he met Roberta. Right away he called her 'Bruja.' It was a joke maybe, I guess, but I think he saw it in her. Roberta is strong-willed and peculiar. She has never frightened me. I am strong, too. But around these parts people have always been afraid of her.

"One piece of land Roy bought was in the center of Quebro. He built a house there where he and Roberta lived together for years. It was a long affair. Roberta had three children by Roy McKana. Then Roy moved on to his next woman, and Roberta had another son with another man. When that man moved on, that's when Roberta and Mateo Sanchez got together."

"How long ago was that, Dalys?"

"At least fifteen years ago, Señora Kathleen. Before you and Señor Lief came to Los Islotes."

AT HOME AT LOS ISLOTES
Finding Our Way On This Veraguas Coast

"Roberta and Mateo decided to move to the Darien," Dalys continued. "I couldn't say why. I mean, who moves to the Darien? There is nothing there. Not even a road." The Darien is the easternmost province of Panama at the border with Colombia. It's home to Emberá Indian tribes, drug smugglers, and FARC terrorists. The Darien Gap, a roadless expanse of jungle, is the missing link of the Pan-American Highway.

"Roberta sold the house in Quebro that Roy had built for her to get money for the move," Dalys said, "but Roberta and Mateo weren't gone long."

Roberta, Mateo, their daughter, and Roberta's four other children returned to Quebro less than a year later, Dalys explained. Roy, to his credit, caring enough to want to make sure his children had a roof over their heads, bought back the house he'd built for Roberta. She and Mateo moved in with all the kids, but they had no income.

"That's when they all went to Mateo's father's house," Dalys said. "That's Señor Sanchez," Dalys added to make sure I was keeping up. "But that was a lot of people to live in Señor Sanchez's house, Señora Kathleen." The senior Sanchez lives in a two-room shack with a dirt floor and a thatched roof across the road from Roberta. He's just a few minutes' walk away from our gate but hidden by the jungle. He built the house decades ago for his wife. The couple has been together since they were teenagers. They're married in the Quebro way.

LA BRUJA
Chapter XV

"Señor and Señora Sanchez, they are truly in love, Señora Kathleen," Dalys said. "I feel sorry for Señora Sanchez. She is a sweet woman whose children grew up bad." *They must take after their father*, I thought.

"After a while, Señor and Señora Sanchez couldn't stand all those people in their little house. Señor Sanchez moved Roberta and Mateo and all the kids to another house he owned on another piece of land in the center of Quebro. Today another daughter of Roberta's from another man lives in that house," Dalys said. "Some years after that, not too long after you and Señor Lief came to Los Islotes," Dalys said, "Roberta decided she would move to where she is today, on your road."

"Gary used to tell us stories about Roberta, Dalys," I said, "and other women around Quebro, too. He talked about a woman named Minton, at Playa Plaza. He said people say she is like Roberta. That she is also a witch."

"Yes, that's what people say," Dalys said. "Minton lives in a hut with a high wall in front. She built the wall so no one can see the things she does. She says she is a healer. That she can cure anything, even cancer and very serious things like that. She holds ceremonies behind her wall. She kills chickens there, on the beach. Then she smears their blood on rocks. With those rocks, she builds an altar. She says that when she prays at these altars she becomes possessed by a very old woman. The old woman is the spirit who heals people. For a fee, of course," Dalys added. "I

AT HOME AT LOS ISLOTES
Finding Our Way On This Veraguas Coast

know it is a scam, but people believe it. Roberta does the same kinds of things. At least that's what people say.

"Stories of witches have always circulated in these parts," Dalys continued. "There are places in Quebro where we wouldn't go when we were young. We were afraid. They were the places where witches gathered. Mostly on the beach. Sometimes they killed animals and used the blood for their ceremonies, like Minton. I saw it once myself."

The conversation had moved beyond my comfort zone. When Gary'd told me the witch rumors, I'd laughed. Ha, ha, funny stories, I'd thought then put them out of my mind. But I was having more trouble dismissing Dalys. Could witches really exist? Roberta certainly had a hold on the local population, but Dalys' revelation of Roberta as a syndicate boss made more sense to me as an explanation for why.

"What do you think people mean when they call these women witches?" I asked.

"Well, people say that these women have agreed to be the devil's girlfriends," Dalys said. "In exchange, the devil gives them powers. They use those powers to do bad things. They put curses on people who they don't like or who are getting in the way of something they want. People come from as far away as Colón, all the way over on the Caribbean side, to meet with the *brujas* of Quebro. The witches in these parts are said to be very strong. I've heard of some people paying witches in these parts one thousand

LA BRUJA
Chapter XV

dollars to do bad things for them. This is an enormous amount of money for the people who give it. My grandfather Bocho has powers, too," Dalys added before I could interject.

"Your grandfather is one of the devil's girlfriends, Dalys?" I couldn't help teasing her. We'd crossed into the realm of fairytale.

"No, Señora Kathleen," Dalys said, laughing. "Not everyone with powers is a bad witch. Some are good, like my grandfather. He knows prayers for healing. He can cure his cows and his horses when they get sick. He knows a walking prayer, for example, that you can say before setting off on a long trip. When you say the prayer, you get where you are going in an instant, even if it is very far away." If most anyone else had told me these stories, I would have dismissed them as nonsense. But hearing these things from Dalys, I had to wonder. Dalys is one of the smartest women I've known. If she believes in good witches and walking prayers, maybe there's something to them. My time on the Veraguas coast was causing me to question everything I thought I knew.

"The evil side of witchcraft is *perros negros*," Dalys continued. "Black dogs. My grandfather talks about 'people who know.' He means people who know about *perros negros*. He would point them out to me at dances and rodeos when I was little. He wanted me to know to avoid those people. 'Never speak to them, Dalys,' he would tell me. 'And never speak about them.' The stories of *brujería* and *perros negros* are the stories of my childhood," Dalys

AT HOME AT LOS ISLOTES
Finding Our Way On This Veraguas Coast

continued. "They are the stories of Veraguas. They come from the practices of our ancestors. I don't believe them. Well, not all of them. But I respect them."

"What do you believe?"

"I am very spiritual," Dalys said. "I believe in God but not in the way my grandmothers believe. God for them is the Catholic church. I am not interested in the Church. I don't see the point. God for me is Nature. That is how I feel connected, through the natural world. And my ancestors. I speak with them every day. I count on them. They guide me. They help me to channel positive energy." The Spanish imported Catholicism. Dalys' sense of the divine harkens back to the beliefs of this world before the invaders found it.

Dalys is of Veraguas. She is rational and intelligent, but she follows the ways of her ancestors. She keeps a clear glass bowl of water under her bed at night. She'd told me once, "In the morning you can see all the bad stuff in it. The water attracts all the negative things from around and traps them in tiny bubbles." Each morning, Dalys takes the bowl outside, climbs the hill behind her house, and throws the water into the jungle. Then she rinses the bowl and puts it back under her bed. "That's how I keep my house happy," she'd said.

Like Dalys, I was raised Catholic. My mother was baptized Protestant and attended Protestant services with her family every Sunday growing up. When she was in her twenties, she converted

LA BRUJA
Chapter XV

to Catholicism. My father's sister, Margaret, was a big influence in my mother's life. Aunt Margaret was Catholic. I've never asked my mother why she turned away from the religion of her parents, knowing it would upset them and create family drama, which it did. I think she wanted Aunt Margaret's approval. I attended Catholic schools from first grade and graduated from a Catholic university. For years, I went to Mass more than once a week. I know all the prayers and carry two rosaries in my purse. I've wanted Catholicism to be the guiding light I've sought my whole life, but it isn't. It doesn't ring true for me.

Dalys and I finished our chicken, thanked her mother for another delicious meal, and started back to Los Islotes. As we approached our entrance, I saw Roberta standing outside her house watching the road, like she was waiting for us. It's not possible to drive fast on the dirt lane so Roberta and I had time to consider each other. As we neared, she stepped in front of our vehicle. Dalys had to turn the wheel to avoid her. When we stopped for the guard to open the gate, I looked back. Roberta was still standing in the road, her arms at her sides. As I watched, she lifted them both above her head then lowered them in front of her and held them there, outstretched in my direction. I felt a jolt and turned away. I looked in the side mirror. As Dalys drove through the gate, Roberta was still there with her arms stretched out in front of her. A chill went through me. What was this woman up to now?

AT HOME AT LOS ISLOTES
Finding Our Way On This Veraguas Coast

A couple of hours later, my stomach bothered me. I had painful cramps and diarrhea. I never take off early, but I had to go up to the house to lay down. Maybe it was the chicken from Dalys' mom's *fonda*, I thought, though I'd eaten there many times and had never had a problem before. I had no appetite for dinner and went to bed early. That night, I tossed and turned more than usual. The next day was worse. I managed to work until 5:00 o'clock, but I couldn't concentrate. My legs ached, and my intestinal symptoms persisted. Maybe I'd caught the flu. A week later, I was no better. I couldn't keep anything down.

Lief and I returned to Panama City for staff meetings. Our first day back, I went to the clinic around the corner from our office. As we remind our Live And Invest Overseas readers, health care is another thing Panama does better than anywhere else in the region. The standard of care is as good or better than you get in major U.S. cities but a fraction the cost and more personal. Clínica Einstein, named for the life-sized bust of Albert in the park across the street, requires no appointments and charges US$35 for a visit. We've sought medical care here for a decade-and-a-half. The primary physician, Dr. Sucre, has become a friend. "I think you might have a parasite," he told me when I described my symptoms. Ah, that would explain things. Lief and I had both had parasites before. They're not uncommon in this part of the world. The onsite lab tests came back positive. I started the treatment that day, but my symptoms grew more severe. The diarrhea was debilitating.

LA BRUJA
Chapter XV

Two weeks later, I returned to the Einstein Clinic. "The medication I gave you was strong," Dr. Sucre said, puzzled. "You should be improving by now." But another round of lab tests confirmed that the parasites persisted. I started a new treatment. Two weeks later, I was even sicker. When I'd had parasites years before, in Nicaragua and Belize, I'd recovered quickly. After the third medication he prescribed didn't work either, Dr. Sucre grew concerned. I was unable to eat or drink and was losing weight.

By the next Sunday morning I was miserable. Constant diarrhea had kept me awake all night. I was lightheaded and weak, and every part of my body ached. It was all I could do to make it to and from the toilet. Lief sleeps like a log under any circumstances. When he finally woke up and looked over at me in bed, he registered my distress levels. "Come on," he said. "We're going to the Emergency Room." He pulled a pair of my jeans and a T-shirt from the closet and helped me dress. He had to prop me up for the walk to the car and then into the ER when we arrived. I couldn't sit upright for the intake questions. A nurse got me into a bed and on an IV. Eight hours of intravenous fluids and antibiotics later, I was released. I was revived enough to walk to the car under my own steam, but what was going on.

A couple of weeks later, we were scheduled to travel to France for the holidays. I didn't want to miss the chance to see the kids so, sick as I still was, Lief and I flew to Paris. The day after we arrived, I went to see another doctor. He, too, diagnosed parasites

AT HOME AT LOS ISLOTES
Finding Our Way On This Veraguas Coast

and prescribed a stronger drug that came with side effects. I suffered through Christmas and spent most days in bed.

Lief and I returned to Panama a month later. I'd finished the new course of medication, but my symptoms continued. I was beginning to fear I was doomed to spend the rest of my life in this condition. I was exhausted and desperate. Seated on the plane, I reached into the seatback pocket for the in-flight magazine. The cover got my attention. The focus of the issue was Latin American healers. Flipping to the article I saw the smiling face of Iya Janina Walters of Panama. "I work to help a person find their Destiny and the best way to fulfill it," read the caption beneath her photo. "I focus on Nature Spirits and our surrounding environment. And I look for a person's Ancestral Spirits and how to connect with them. These things help us to follow our talents and gifts to find our true purpose, our place in the universe, and peace."

As recently as a few months earlier, I would have laughed at the magazine article about Iya Janina, too. Now, for reasons I couldn't explain, I felt drawn to the woman.

Much as I was shocked to admit it, a bizarre possible source of my illness had flashed through my mind. I wanted to dismiss it as foolishness but couldn't. What if Roberta had cursed me? I shook my head. That couldn't be. I didn't believe in witches, and I didn't believe in curses. But how else to explain that I was still sick even after doctors in two countries had done their best to cure me? Crazy as it was, I couldn't dismiss the idea. I was ready to

LA BRUJA
Chapter XV

admit that I needed help. I'd get in touch with this spiritual healer Iya Janina. If anyone would entertain a discussion about a witch's curse, it could be her. The article included an email address. I'd send one when we landed in Panama City.

XVI

Iya Janina

LOS ISLOTES
2022

The day after our return flight from Paris to Panama City, I sent an email to Iya Janina. "I am reaching out to you," I wrote, "though I'm not sure why. I have a story to tell that I think you will understand. I don't mean to be cryptic, but I don't know how to begin. I believe you are in Panama? I am in town for several weeks. I would like to meet in person if possible. Hope to hear from you."

"Yes, I am in Panama," Iya Janina replied. "I live in El Dorado and would be pleased to meet. Were you referred by someone?"

"I read about you in the online magazine of my Copa flight," I explained. "Would you be able to meet tomorrow for coffee at Petit Paris? Do you know it?"

"Yes, sure. I know Petit Paris. Marbella. See you there at 3:00 p.m."

I recognized Iya Janina from a half-block away. Her smile was

IYA JANINA
Chapter XVI

as warm and friendly in person as it had appeared in the article photo. I'd decided during the walk from our Panama City apartment around the corner that I'd be direct. I thought I might be suffering under a witch's curse. No way to make that sound less kooky so I'd come right out with it. I'd chosen Petit Paris as the meeting spot because it's nearby and lively. Plus, since Jackson and Valerian had graduated high school and gone off to college, I hardly saw Muriel and Loic. This would be a chance to say hello. I'd introduce Janina as a new friend. They didn't need to know she was my spiritual advisor called in to cure an imagined plague.

Petit Paris is like a sidewalk café in its namesake city but with palm trees. I made my way through the maze of tables to where Janina waited. "Hello," I said. "I'm Kathleen Peddicord." Iya Janina's smile was even brighter up close. I'd never met a spiritual healer in person before. I wasn't sure what to expect. Janina's bright eyes and easy manner made me feel at once at ease. "Please have a seat," she invited. Muriel saw me and waved. We ordered coffee, tea, and a plate of pastries.

"You wrote that you have a story to tell me," Iya Janina said after the waitress had walked away. No way to delay the conversation further. Time to admit out loud that I'd lost my mind.

"Yes," I said. "I'll start at the beginning."

I told Iya Janina about our purchase of Los Islotes, about Lief's plan for selling lots and building houses, and about my dream of creating a city to rival the greatest cities the Spanish built in

AT HOME AT LOS ISLOTES
Finding Our Way On This Veraguas Coast

the region centuries ago, a new city of light. I told her about the museum we'd inaugurated and the library and school I intended. Then I told Iya Janina that I'd been sick for months. Doctors in Panama and Paris had diagnosed parasites. I'd tried five rounds of treatment, but the symptoms persisted. The doctors were stymied. I was frantic. I had a theory for the cause of the illness that I hadn't shared with the medical professionals, I said. Finally, I told Iya Janina of Roberta and the feud over our access road. "People in Quebro call her *bruja*," I said. For the first time I could remember, I exhaled fully. Finally, I'd said it all out loud.

"Yes, she is a witch," Iya Janina said simply. "And, yes, she is the source of your problems, both physical and mental. You are very stressed," she said. "And tired. You don't sleep well, do you?"

"I haven't had a good night's sleep in more than a decade," I admitted. I hadn't spoken of my sleeping troubles to anyone, but I wanted to open up to this woman. I'd known from the moment I'd sat down across from her that she would help me.

"This woman Roberta has powers because people believe she has powers," Iya Janina said. "You have let yourself believe she has powers, too. And you are having a bad time as a result. The way to deal with a witch is to fight back. Show her you are not afraid of her. Show everyone that you are not afraid of her. Roberta is a bully. Turn her sorcery against her. Throw her evil back." So simple and so huge.

Months earlier, I'd invited Madrigal to spend a weekend with

IYA JANINA
Chapter XVI

Lief and me at Los Islotes. I craved a friend. Madrigal and I walked to the islands at low tide and climbed to the top of the cliff between our two beaches. Lief grilled hamburgers for us at Panama Jack's, and we invited Dalys for dinner Saturday night. The four of us played poker and drank too much wine. Sunday morning, Madrigal and I nursed our hangovers in the pool. I have many favorite spots in the house that Ricardo designed for us. The back terrace is one of them. The edge of the infinity pool is lined with hibiscus and red ginger. Beyond are the black walnut trees that the monkeys like. Then it's jungle down the cliff to the sea. Seated on the edge of the pool, Madrigal and I had views of the estuary and the ocean pounding the rock face far below us. In each place I've called home, I've been blessed with a true friend. In Baltimore, it's Beth. In Ireland, Morette. In Paris, Emanuela. In Panama, it's Madrigal. Madrigal knows every detail of our troubles with Roberta. I trust her so I posed my question plain.

"Do you believe in witches, Madrigal?" I asked.

"I know people in Veraguas do," she said nonplussed. "They are part of the culture. I hear the stories. People talk about ceremonies on the beach with animal blood. Here in Quebro the tradition is even stronger than in Santiago," Madrigal said. "Dalys told me the other day that Juni on your crew thinks Roberta has made a voodoo doll in the shape of your excavator. He was joking, but there would be truth in it. And fear. People in these parts believe witches can harm them."

AT HOME AT LOS ISLOTES
Finding Our Way On This Veraguas Coast

I thought of a story Dalys had told about her friend Maria getting lost on her way home one day. The girl was following the same route to her house that she'd traveled her entire life but missed a turn. It was late afternoon and would be dark soon. "Maria needed to get home to help her mother with dinner for her boys," Dalys had said. "But, before she realized it, Maria had driven past the bridge she'd crossed every day for twenty-three years." But this time she didn't recognize it.

Maria made the next left turn and in a few minutes was back at the river. When she got to the edge, she stopped, climbed off her motorbike, and walked into the water. For some reason, she started crossing the river on foot. "She knew what she was doing was crazy, but she couldn't stop herself." That was how Dalys had put it. The water was deep, but Maria continued across then climbed out the other side. She was wet and cold and started walking down one path then another, until there was no path, only jungle. "Maria pulled at the branches and vines in her way," Dalys had told me. The girl was wearing flip-flops. After a while, her hands and feet were bloody. There was no moon. She went around and around in circles in the dark until she had no idea where she was. "Then she tripped and fell, Señora Kathleen," Dalys said. "On her knees, she started to cry. Then she started to pray. Maria is like me," Dalys said. "She never prays. But this night Maria prayed the Our Father over and over. Finally, the sun came up and she could see her way again." With the sunrise, Maria recognized the

IYA JANINA
Chapter XVI

hills and found her home. "Maria is certain it was a witch," Dalys had told me.

"That's silly, Dalys," I'd replied at the time. "There's no such thing as witches."

But my time in Veraguas has helped me to become more open to new ideas about how spirit manifests. When our new office was built, I started keeping a clear glass bowl of water on my desk as Dalys does in her home. At the end of each work day, I dump the water into the toilet and rinse and refill the bowl then return it to its position at the corner of my desk. I don't know if I believe that the water purifies my environment, but I like routine. This one has no downside, and every time I notice the bowl on the other side of my laptop, I think of Dalys and that brings me comfort.

"Dalys tells me about the witches of Quebro," I said to Madrigal. "She says she doesn't believe the stories but that she doesn't not believe them either. Do you believe these women are witches, Madrigal?"

"I believe in God," Madrigal said. "With God, I don't have to worry about anything. I don't think these women are witches, and I don't think they're not witches. I don't think about them. I have God, and, well, God is God. That's all I need." Madrigal is an old-school Catholic. She's confident in her faith the way I'd always wished I could be. My time in Veraguas had adjusted that position, too. I'd come to think that maybe the point isn't what you believe but that you believe at all in something.

AT HOME AT LOS ISLOTES
Finding Our Way On This Veraguas Coast

Iya Janina gave me a prescription. "Problems are resolved when you change your beliefs and your behaviors," she told me. "You need to see Roberta differently and you need to take action against her. You need to take control of your situation. Here is what I advise."

Iya Janina told me to think of three key spots around Los Islotes. "Three points of defense," she said. "In each of these three spots, plant a tree with white flowers. And place, at the base of each tree, three white candles."

Iya Janina also recommended exercise. "What do you like to do?" she asked. "I like to walk," I said, "and I like to swim." "Excellent," she told me. "Take a walk or a swim every day. Plant your trees and move your body. You will sleep better."

I paid the check and thanked Iya Janina. Her recommendations were simple but encouraging. I didn't know if following them would make a difference, but I was despairing enough to try anything. Iya Janina gave me a hug then went to the corner to catch a taxi home. Walking back to our apartment, I felt calmer than I had in a long time.

Lief and I returned to Los Islotes the following Saturday. I asked him to stop at the *vivero* outside Santiago. I chose three white lilies. In the grocery store I bought nine white candles. The next day, I planted one of the lilies outside our front gate and buried three candles in the ground beside it so they weren't visible. I planted the second at the end of our driveway and put three

IYA JANINA
Chapter XVI

candles beneath it. The third I placed partway up the hill between our two beaches. Here I didn't bury the candles. No one climbs this cliff except me. No need to be covert. Over the weeks that followed, I checked my lilies often. Each took well to its spot. All three grew and flowered.

A couple of months later, Lief, Dalys, Martin, and I met at the point between the two beaches to discuss ideas for improving our beach access. We'd always referred to the beach to the right as our "swim beach." I'd suggested we give it a proper name. "It's the best spot on the property for watching the sunset," I'd said. "Let's call it Playa Sol." We planned steps down the hill to a deck where people could enjoy sundowner cocktails. Martin would cover the concrete stairs with slate. In the center of each wide step he'd create a mosaic with pebbles and shells in the shape of a sun with six points inside a circle. At the base of the deck he'd install the same mosaic bigger along with "Playa Sol" in white coral. The contrast against the black slate would be striking. As Dalys reviewed the details of the plan, I looked over to see two of our guys running down the hill from midway up the point. One carried a big flower. The other held something in his hands I couldn't make out. They were calling out to Dalys. They seemed panicked. As they got closer, I realized what they had. They'd found my offerings.

"What are they saying, Dalys?" I asked.

"They are freaking out, Señora Kathleen," she said. "I sent

AT HOME AT LOS ISLOTES
Finding Our Way On This Veraguas Coast

them up there today with machetes to clear the path. I know you like to hike up there. While they were working, they found that white flower planted in a special spot with the candles around it. They think they have found a witch's hiding place. They say one is using our point to make spells. She is lighting candles and doing bad things up there."

"Dalys, I put those candles up there," I said. "And I planted those flowers." The man with the lily had raised it over his head. He was about to throw it into the ravine. "Please ask him to stop, Dalys," I said. "Pease tell him not to damage the flowers. Explain that the lily and the candles are mine. Ask them to put it all back where they found it, please. And give the plant some water. Its roots look dry."

"You planted those flowers up there, Señora Kathleen?" Dalys said. "And you put those candles?" She was laughing so hard she doubled over. I hadn't told her about Iya Janina or my worry that Roberta had cursed me.

"Yes," I said. "I want those things up there." I was too embarrassed to explain further.

After she regained her composure, Dalys relayed my message to the guys. They stood motionless for a minute, stupefied. They stared at Dalys but wouldn't look at me. Finally they turned around and climbed back up the hill.

"That was a good idea, Señora Kathleen," Dalys said. "Now those guys think you are a witch. They will tell this story to ev-

IYA JANINA
Chapter XVI

eryone. By tonight all Quebro will think you are a witch. Roberta will hear this story. Now she will know that you have powers, too." Dalys wasn't teasing me. She was serious. She knew that this story would have a big impact on the people of this coast.

I'm not sure about witches, but I know bullies exist. Standing up to mine had the healing effect Iya Janina had predicted. Okay, planting flowers on my own property wasn't particularly brave or dramatic, but it'd had a big psychological effect. By taking even that small action I'd taken back control. Roberta's antics no longer dominated my daily thoughts meaning I was able to direct more attention to more deserving subjects. A few days later, as if by magic, the symptoms that had plagued me for months were gone. I felt well enough to begin swimming every day before dinner. And my body finally remembered how to sleep.

The resolutions to my physical and mental maladies could be chalked up to mind over matter.

What happened next couldn't be explained so easily. Two weeks after the scene at the point by Playa Sol when our guys discovered my secret gifts we got an email from our attorney Fernando. I was in my office, Lief in his, and Dalys in hers, but we all read Fernando's note at the same time.

"For the past three months," he wrote, "we have pressed for a response from the government. Finally we have achieved that goal. All three expert reviews have come out in our favor, and the court has issued an ultimate ruling based on this. This is from the

AT HOME AT LOS ISLOTES
Finding Our Way On This Veraguas Coast

highest court. It cannot be dismissed or ignored. This is the news we have been waiting for."

I stood up to walk to Lief's office. He'd had the same idea. We met in the middle just as Dalys came through the front door. We were all afraid to believe the news. Could this really be the end of the battle? We'd been told of favorable rulings in the past. They hadn't kept Roberta and her family from continuing to terrorize us.

"Does this mean we can return to our work on the fence and the wall?" Dalys wrote to Fernando. "And, if we do, how can we be certain Roberta won't attack our men again?"

"Yes, this means you can do whatever you would like to do on your land," came Fernando's response. "And this time the court will send a representative from Santiago to oversee the work." For the two years we'd been at war, we'd been holding our breath. At last, we exhaled, all of us.

Recovered from my physical challenges, I was reborn. Liberated from the legal battles, we were all renewed. Time to get back to work. I still couldn't say where the road we'd been traveling would lead and I had no doubt that the Los Islotes roller coaster would continue its wild swings, but I was finally certain we were on the right path.

XVII

Old Ways

LOS ISLOTES
2022

Fernando assured us that the latest ruling from the Santiago judge was irrefutable. We could restart construction of our new entrance, including the wall in front of Roberta's place. We should have been thrilled, and briefly we were. Hugs all around. But it wasn't long until joy was overtaken by uncertainty. If we sent Nica's guys out to the road again and the Sanchez clan again made their work impossible, then what? We didn't want to find out that this so-called final decree was no different from the useless orders that'd preceded it because then we might have to admit that we'd run out of recourse. After the initial moment of jubilation, Lief and I actively avoided the subject.

Two weeks later, Dalys acknowledged the elephant in the room. "Should I contact Nica to ask when he could come back to build our front wall?" she wondered at our regular Monday morning meeting.

AT HOME AT LOS ISLOTES
Finding Our Way On This Veraguas Coast

I didn't want to take responsibility for a course of action I feared. After a long pause, Lief did. "Yes," he said. He'd been looking down at his desk. He raised his head slowly to look Dalys and then me straight in the eye. "It's time to finish what we started."

"Should I say anything to Roberta?" Dalys wanted to know.

"No," Lief said. "Don't say anything to anyone except Nica."

Intellectually, I knew Lief was right. We should keep our plan to ourselves. There was nothing to be gained by warning Roberta what was coming. On the other hand, I had the urge to reach out to her. My experience with her had been complicated. I'd welcomed her as a fellow female entrepreneur. She'd reciprocated with gifts and hospitality. Then she'd grown so apprehensive about our plans for change that she threatened our men with a machete, and, if I allowed myself to believe my crazy suspicion, put a curse on me.

Her behavior was outrageous but maybe understandable. Madrigal's father had told me the history of this place, and Dalys had shown me its ways. The people of this Veraguas coast suffered greatly at the hands of their earliest attackers. Isolation became their armor. Geography supported the choice. The region was difficult to access. Until the world's front-running property scouts, like my husband, realized its beachfront was the only unexploited stretch of Panama's Pacific, no one was motivated to make the trip all the way down to the bottom of the western half of this

OLD WAYS
Chapter XVII

peninsula. The world left Veraguas alone, and the people of Veraguas were happy in their separateness.

Roberta was wrong to raise her machete against us, but I couldn't say she was misguided to revolt against the modern-day invasion we represent. I respected Roberta's dread. I shared it. I didn't want the outside world to encroach farther down this coast either. I wondered if I could speak with her directly, woman to woman, about this shared goal. My Spanish was too basic for that level of conversation, but Dalys could translate. The cultural gap was enormous, but I could try to bridge it. The real impediment to one-to-one peace talks was Lief. He'd flip out at even the suggestion of the idea. In his cowboy world, Roberta's the one in the black hat. You don't broker peace with the enemy. You protect against them. It's a simpler approach to life. Sometimes I envy it.

Dalys' stories of Roberta the *bruja* haunted me, but not everything of this place was mine to understand. My way of life is night and day from Roberta's, but she and I aren't light and dark. Lief and I showed up uninvited with an agenda founded in greed. I've never believed Los Islotes was our path to riches. Fifteen years in, I don't care if we make a penny out here. This place doesn't owe us anything. Rather, I feel an obligation to it. We had gifts to share with each other, this Veraguas coast and me. Lief would still prefer to make money than not, but profits are no longer his driving objective. He wants to create something we can be proud of that will live beyond us. Ariadne has clarified

AT HOME AT LOS ISLOTES
Finding Our Way On This Veraguas Coast

that purpose for both of us. We want to leave a place for her that's worthy of her. Could we forget and forgive and reboot with Roberta as friendly neighbors? I was sure enough of Lief's response to that question not to pose it. For Lief, Roberta would always be the woman who'd stood in the way of his wall. But I still wanted to allow for the possibility of eventual détente. Lief and I weren't going anywhere, and neither, I figured, was Roberta. Who knew how our two paths proceeded from here. I'd keep an open mind.

Dalys came to Lief and me the day after the Monday meeting when she'd returned us to the conversation about the wall to say that she had confirmation. Nica and his crew were ready to recommence work any time.

"Great," I said. "Lief, I guess we ask Fernando to arrange for the witness from Santiago?"

"Yes," Lief said. "As soon as the representative from the court can be on site, that's the day we restart our wall." Dalys said she'd coordinate the timing.

The next day, after my morning conference calls, I walked over to Dalys' office. I wanted to check on the design for the brick paths around the stables. It was hours past starting time. Dalys hadn't been in the yard, and she wasn't at her desk. That never happened.

"Dalys' family had a death last night," Fernanda said in Spanish from across the room when she saw me looking around. "She said she would be in touch with you later."

"Who died, Fernanda?" I asked.

OLD WAYS
Chapter XVII

"Her grandfather, Bocho."

Dalys is Veraguas royalty. She traces her ancestry to the earliest Indians on this coast. She is distantly or directly related to most every soul in Quebro and beyond. Her grandfather Silverio worked for the same company as Roy McKana. They were friends. After the Canadian export operation went bust, Roy moved to Mariato and Silverio returned to Quebro. He decided that, like Roy, he'd go into the rice business. Roy rented Silverio some of the equipment he'd ferried down the coast from Santiago so Silverio could plant his fields.

"My grandfather Silverio was very successful," Dalys told me once. "He had two Cessnas and flew around the country with Torrijos and those guys. He used the money he made to buy more land. His business grew and grew. But he was kind, too," she said. "He donated the land for Quebro's first school. His downfall was women. He liked them a lot. He had many girlfriends. When he died, Silverio left land to all his children, legitimate and not. He wanted to be fair, but it was a mistake. His holdings got all split up. Now, only two generations later, all the land that Silverio worked so hard to buy has been chopped into little pieces."

Dalys' other grandfather, her mother's father, Bocho, was also an entrepreneur who also invested in land. Between them, when Silverio was still alive, the two men owned all the land from Mariato south to Flores. When I first confided to her that I was

AT HOME AT LOS ISLOTES
Finding Our Way On This Veraguas Coast

feeling protective of the Veraguas coast that Lief and I had adopted, Dalys understood right away. "Just like my grandfathers," she'd said.

"Silverio and Bocho were businessmen," she'd continued. "They put their money into land because they believed it was the most valuable thing. They were looking to make money, of course. But they also wanted to take care of this place. They realized how special it is. Just like you and Señor Lief."

Silverio had died not long after Dalys came to work for us, but as long as they lived, Dalys had visited both her grandfathers every week. "I would sit with them all day and listen to their stories. I've always liked talking to old people," she'd told me on our first day out together in Santiago. "My mother," she'd continued, "tells one story about me that she loves. She says that, when I was two years old, and she was outside behind the house working around, I invited an old man inside. Mom doesn't know how, but I made this man coffee. When she came back inside, I was sitting drinking coffee with an old man she'd never seen before."

"I'm so sorry to hear about your grandfather," I told Dalys when she called that afternoon.

"It is okay, Señora Kathleen," she said. "Bocho was eighty-seven years old. He lived a good life. He was a leader of the community, respected and loved. He died happy."

"When will the funeral take place?" I asked.

"Tomorrow will be the mass," Dalys said. "Then we will have

OLD WAYS
Chapter XVII

the wake. That lasts nine days. It will be at my grandfather's house. We will clean him and dress him nicely and lay him on his table."

"You'll put him on a table in his home?" I asked.

"Yes, sure," Dalys said. "What else?" She had a point. The nearest undertaker was in Santiago and would cost money families in Quebro didn't have.

"Will you be there for the wake the whole time, Dalys?"

"Yes, of course, Señora Kathleen. The whole family will join. The closest family members will sleep in the house together, all around my grandfather. We will leave the doors and windows open all day and all night so everyone's prayers can leave and so my grandfather's spirit can come and go."

Dalys explained that the first night after a death the family builds an altar of white cloth. On it they place white flowers, a rosary, a cross, and a photo of the deceased. Neighbors and relatives come to pray with the family. Everyone stays awake for the next nine nights saying the rosary. It is believed that, during this vigil, the deceased walks around his house, inside and outside, preparing for his transition.

"I don't pray, Señora Kathleen," Dalys said, "but I will pray for Bocho."

"You will stay awake for nine nights, Dalys?" I asked.

"Well, we will sleep a little now and then. But, yes, we stay awake. It is a show of support for my grandfather. To help him with his journey."

AT HOME AT LOS ISLOTES
Finding Our Way On This Veraguas Coast

On the last day, everyone meets in the home of the deceased for a feast.

"We are expecting more than three-hundred people," Dalys said. "Many from Quebro village plus people from all around Veraguas. Even some from Santiago and Panama City will come to say good-bye to my grandfather. He had a big life. It is a nice thing that so many people will come but we will have to feed them all the whole time. We will slaughter a cow to have enough food for everyone."

When night falls on the ninth day, the family prays the rosary a final time and dismantles the altar little by little. Then everyone sits in silence. They believe that, in this moment, the spirit of the deceased walks our earth one last time then is gone.

"The next day the body will be transported to the family tomb," Dalys told me. "Sometimes this is on horseback but Bocho will go by truck. We will all follow behind on foot."

Lief and I joined the procession through the village. When we got to the gravesite, men pushed aside the rock at the entrance to the tomb. Dalys had told me that many families cannot afford coffins. They bury their deceased without them. Bocho had a casket. Eight men lifted it from the back of the pick-up, carried it across the grassy clearing, and placed it inside the chamber. Bocho was laid to rest just as his father and his father's father had been, his body atop their remains. Lief and I had never discussed after-death plans. Watching Bocho's burial I knew what I

OLD WAYS
Chapter XVII

wanted. I'd ask Lief to return me to the earth, here in Veraguas, like Bocho, without pomp or circumstance. With that thought, I realized just how connected I'd become to this land Lief and I had adopted. I was choosing Veraguas as my eternal home. I added a cemetery to my Los Islotes city plan.

XVIII

New Ways

LOS ISLOTES
2023

The court in Santiago told Fernando that the soonest a representative could be onsite at Los Islotes to oversee the return to work on our wall would be in four weeks. It was early February. We should have known better than to try to schedule an appointment at this time of year. Los Carnavales were around the corner. Nothing would happen before, during, or for days after. The country shuts down.

As I'd had to do many times, I pushed the Roberta situation from my mind. I'd agonized long enough. Worrying didn't ameliorate anything and kept me up nights. Fernando assured us we could finally build our wall. I'd believe that until I couldn't.

I was still swimming each evening before dinner. Sometimes Lief would join me at the pool. He'd sit in a lounge chair and read the news on his iPad. One evening, he stood at the edge when I emerged. "Let's plan a Los Islotes summit," he said when I came

NEW WAYS
Chapter XVIII

up for air. "Two full days of meetings with everyone. We finally have a real team. Let's sit down with them around a table altogether. I want to review all aspects of what we're doing here—infrastructure, amenities, home designs, etc. We can prioritize projects, set budgets, and make a five-year plan."

"I want to dig into everything," Lief said, showing enthusiasm he isn't known for. "We need a road map for where we're headed." He was taking the reins in both hands. I felt lighter. No more jockeying for position. We could move forward side-by-side.

"Oo, oo, oo!" Lief called out suddenly.

"What?" I asked as I climbed out of the water. Was my husband having a stroke?

"Ah, ah, ah!" Lief replied in the direction of the black walnut trees. I looked behind me. Six howler monkeys were jumping from limb to limb.

"Ah, ah, ah," they cried back at Lief.

Lief and I walked to the other side of the patio for a better look. There we saw another troop. These were capuchin monkeys, in the next tree over. I'd never seen howlers and capuchin mix.

"Oo, oo, oo!" It was Lief again. My husband wasn't in need of medical attention. He was having fun. Los Islotes had worked its magic on him, too. The monkeys came closer. "Oo, oo, oo!" they responded.

"I'm going inside to start dinner," I said. "You stay and play with your friends."

AT HOME AT LOS ISLOTES
Finding Our Way On This Veraguas Coast

"Ha, ha," Lief said. "I'll be right in." But he wasn't. Forty-five minutes later I walked out onto the living room balcony to tell him it was time to eat. It was dark but clear. Starlight lit the scene below. Lief was asleep in his lounge chair. The monkeys were in the trees above him still and silent.

Two weeks later, after the Carnival holiday, Dalys, Martin, Fernanda, Luis, Joaquin, and Madrigal joined Lief and me at our conference table. "Could I see your *cronograma*?" Madrigal had asked when Gary brought her to Los Islotes to meet with Lief and me for the first time. We hadn't been able to show Madrigal our construction timeline that day because we didn't have one. We hadn't focused on master planning at first because Lief intended to get in and get out. By the time we realized we weren't going anywhere anytime soon, we were too consumed by real-time challenges to think through a long-term plan. It was all we could do to get through each day. At last we were past that stage. Lief was stepping up to true our path.

"Welcome to our First Annual Los Islotes Summit," he said to the group our first morning together. "We've never held a meeting like this before because we haven't had a team like you before," he continued. "You guys are the future of Los Islotes. Let's talk about what that means, exactly."

Seated around the table with our Los Islotes team for Lief's Summit I believed for the first time without doubt that my vision, ambitious as it was, was more than a daydream. It'd come to be.

NEW WAYS
Chapter XVIII

We just needed to stay the course. That conviction would carry me across all the hurdles still to come.

XIX

The Way Forward

LOS ISLOTES
2023

Of course, the court witness was delayed. Two weeks post-Carnival, he was still a no-show. No matter. We'd gotten good at taking disappointment in stride. Dalys would update us when she had news. Lief and I carried on with our work. We'd been alone together at Los Islotes for weeks. I appreciated these extended stays. They allowed me time to focus on long-term writing projects, and they were a chance for Lief and me to reconnect as husband and wife. Lief would read to me from newsfeeds on his iPad as we ate breakfast. We'd mark the end of each day with a walk on the beach, hand in hand, then a glass of wine by the pool before dinner. Of the two of us, Lief is the better cook. I'd prep. Our garden off the kitchen was delivering cilantro, basil, thyme, oregano, spicy peppers, and mint. The mint was for Lief's mojitos. I'd choose other herbs for the evening's salmon or pasta then keep Lief company as he did his thing at the stove.

THE WAY FORWARD
Chapter XIX

We had found our power balance. We were comfortable in ourselves and in each other and partners in every sense. But, after three or four weeks in our Los Islotes bubble, I missed the other parts of our world. Our far-flung Live And Invest Overseas team is good company. And it includes our family. Lief and I don't have enough opportunity to enjoy the community we've worked decades to create. We decided we'd host a retreat for Live And Invest Overseas employees. The long weekend would return Kaitlin and Harry to Los Islotes, and they'd bring Ariadne. This would be her first trip to Panama. A grand occasion.

We wanted to put our best foot forward. Dalys and Martin took the lead. They worked around the clock to prepare the property. They directed crews to repaint the front gate, repair fences in the horse corrals, repave sections of road that had washed out during the rainy season, and collect driftwood for a bonfire on the beach. Sunday a week before the event, Dalys sent an update from Panama Jack's. The time stamp showed it was nearly midnight. "Solar power working!" she texted beneath a photo of Martin in front of the bar. He was in his Sunday uniform—white swim trunks covered with pink flamingos. We'd built a bridge across the creek that flows between Panama Jack's and the beach and positioned lampposts at each end. In the photo Martin had his arms spread wide, pointing to the lights of the bar overhead with one and the lights of the bridge outside with the other. I could almost hear his, "Ta, da!"

AT HOME AT LOS ISLOTES
Finding Our Way On This Veraguas Coast

We'd bought more paddle boards and kayaks, and the guys had rebuilt the pier at the estuary. That's the best launch point. They erected a volleyball net on the beach and hung hammocks in the shade. Shrubs were pruned, gardens manicured. It was showtime.

The day before the retreat, our eldest mare Guadeloupe gave birth to a baby girl. Guadeloupe's newborn was the first filly born on the property. Horsemen along our coast have been impressed by our lineages. No one could remember a finca with seven male births in a row. Now we had another matriarch. Reyito, who manages the horses, suggested a name for the foal. Lluvia. She'd been born in a thunderstorm.

Fernanda made reservations for our Live And Invest Overseas staff at the bramador hotel. We installed a porta-crib in Kaitlin and Harry's room. At the last minute, Jackson's professors gave him the okay to participate in classes virtually the three days he'd miss, so he would be joining us, too.

Los Islotes had three-dozen property owners, including three couples who'd built houses. Lief and I now shared the property with six full-time residents. We'd invited them to join the Saturday afternoon cookout at Panama Jack's. We all surfed and kayaked, competed at volleyball, and tossed a football on the sand.

Saturday night, Lief grilled steaks and ribs. After dinner we roasted our managers, both Live And Invest Overseas and Los Islotes. Dalys' certificate named her "La Jefa." Martin won the "MacGyver Award." The two groups mixed effortlessly and truly

THE WAY FORWARD
Chapter XIX

enjoyed getting to know each other. I stood off to the side, alongside the bridge at Panama Jack's, to take it all in. The positive energy was palpable. A sign of things to come.

The Live And Invest Overseas staff returned to Panama City Sunday afternoon. Kaitlin, Harry, Jackson, and Ariadne stayed another night. We spent Monday at the sea. The long surf beach at Panama Jack's gets visitors' attention, but I prefer Playa Sol, in the shadow of the cliff point. I held Ariadne's hands at the ocean's edge. She screeched with joy each time a wave covered her little feet. She wasn't afraid. She wanted to dive in. She was at home.

Tuesday morning after breakfast, Lief and I walked to the end of our front walk for good-byes. The sky over the distant mountains was clear. That's where our weather comes from. Dalys taught me that the day we moved into our house. We'd shipped furniture and boxes from Panama City and stored everything in our garage until Alonso completed construction. Dalys came to help me unpack. Unwrapping the sofas and chairs and opening the cartons that'd sat untouched in the dark, steamy space for months, we found mold, mice, cockroaches, crabs, and a few scorpions but thankfully no snakes. We washed each thing then set it in the driveway to dry in the sun. About two that afternoon, Dalys looked over at me. "Señora Kathleen, I think we should bring everything inside."

"Why, Dalys?" I asked. "We still have a few hours of daylight."

"Do you see those clouds over the mountains?" she said. "That

AT HOME AT LOS ISLOTES
Finding Our Way On This Veraguas Coast

rain will be here in twenty minutes." The clouds Dalys pointed toward were far in the distance and motionless. Her prediction was specific. How could she be so sure? I was skeptical. "If the clouds come closer, Dalys," I said, "we'll bring things back into the garage. But I think we can continue for a while longer."

Dalys smiled and nodded and returned to work alongside me but kept glancing at the mountain horizon. Twenty minutes later the dark clouds were directly overhead. All at once, they released a deluge. Dalys and I rushed to drag everything under cover. Dalys didn't say anything, but I'd learned my lesson. That was the last time I didn't pay attention to advice from Dalys.

We'd have no rain today. Three hawks circled overhead. Butterflies played in the hibiscus. All around, birdsong. Costa Rica is known for the diversity of its wildlife, but Panama actually has more varieties of many animals, including birds. Dalys had given me a guide. *I'll pull it out after everyone is gone*, I thought, *and try to identify the tiny pointy-beaked bluebirds making a home in our Guanacaste tree.*

Jackson was the first out of the driveway. "Thanks for making the trip, bud," I said as he paused and turned down his window. "Safe travels. Send a text when you arrive back in New York!" I shouted as he started down the hill. "Love you," he called back.

Harry and Kaitlin were next. Through her open window in the back, Ariadne waved her little hand. "Bye, bye, Gigi! Bye, bye, Guandi!" she smiled. The year before Ariadne was born, Lief and I

THE WAY FORWARD
Chapter XIX

traveled the Silk Road in western China. At the end of the Great Wall is a temple to a third-century Chinese general named Guandi. He was both a warrior and a poet and revered by his troops. Lief liked the story and took Guandi as his granddad name.

The retreat was a recharge, as I'd hoped it would be. The next day, Lief and I returned to our routines refreshed. "Any news from our court witness?" I asked as I joined Dalys at our meeting table.

"No, Señora Kathleen," she said. "But I do have good news related to the wall."

"We can always use some of that," I said.

"Well, you know how I've told you that everyone is always talking about us and Roberta? In Mariato, in Quebro, all around. It's the favorite gossip. Well, the story is changing. I helped my mom at her *fonda* yesterday." Dalys said. "I guess people didn't realize I was there. I stayed in the back, behind the wall in the kitchen. But I could hear the talk. It was all about our wall."

"Why is everybody so obsessed with our wall?" Lief asked. "They should mind their own business."

"Quebro is a small place, Señor Lief," Dalys said. "People here don't have a lot of other things to talk about. In the past, people took Roberta's side. They would say that you and Señor Lief don't belong here. That you don't understand our ways. That you should move on to different parts." Dalys had never been so direct about this before. She'd always focused on the positive feedback from her mom and her sister and our workers' families. It stung now to

AT HOME AT LOS ISLOTES
Finding Our Way On This Veraguas Coast

hear that many folks around didn't want us at Los Islotes.

"But yesterday," Dalys continued, "people were taking your side. They were saying that Roberta is wrong to be making trouble with you over your wall. And they were saying that Señor Sanchez isn't very smart to be with Roberta the way he is. Roberta doesn't have anything to lose, but he does."

"People understand that Roberta doesn't own the land where she has built her house?" I asked.

"Yes, they understand. They know she shouldn't be there. Everyone knows that you can't build a house so close to the mangroves. Everyone knows that land is owned by the government. People around aren't stupid, Señora Kathleen. They know that if you wanted, you could sue Roberta and the Sanchez family. They are interfering with your business. But if you decided to sue them, what would Roberta care? She doesn't have anything to lose. But Señor Sanchez could lose his home and all his land. People know this. They say Señor Sanchez is being like a fool. That was the talk at my mom's *fonda* yesterday." Dalys had spared us the hurt she knew we'd feel hearing that we weren't completely welcome in Quebro, and I was glad. We'd been working all along to show our neighbors that we came in peace. Hearing now that they not only no longer wished we'd moved away but also sympathized with our position in the conflict with Roberta felt like the greatest reward I could imagine for having persevered to this point.

"What do you think has caused the change in people's think-

THE WAY FORWARD
Chapter XIX

ing, Dalys?" I asked.

"Like I said, Quebro is a small place. So many people from town work at Los Islotes now. It is making a difference. People like working here. They are happy with Martin and with me, too. I tell them all the time how lucky they are, and they agree. I tell them that we should all be paying you and Señor Lief for the training that you give us."

"Hey, there's an idea," Lief said.

"Don't pay any attention to him, Dalys," I said. "Thank you for the support and the feedback. We really appreciate hearing that people are happy with Los Islotes. It is especially nice to hear that they are no longer wishing we'd go away."

"That's right, Señora Kathleen, People don't want you to leave. People see what it means having you here. People working for us are building bigger homes for their families. They are living better. Everyone around sees it. People ask me every day if we are hiring. I add their names to a list I keep and I tell them that I will be in touch when we need more help. People around want to work, Señora Kathleen, and they want to be part of Los Islotes. Well, most people. Some are jealous and nasty, but some people are always that way."

"I have other news, Señora Kathleen," Dalys said changing her tone of voice in a way that got my attention. "I went to Mariato yesterday. Martin sent me for some supplies. While I was in the chino, an old man came over to me. I had never seen this man

AT HOME AT LOS ISLOTES
Finding Our Way On This Veraguas Coast

before, Señora Kathleen. You will never believe what he came to say."

"Not bad news, I hope."

"No, no, but funny. This man told me that he is planning to run for mayor in the next election. I told him congratulations. I thought he wanted me to say I would vote for him."

"That wasn't it?" I said.

"No," Dalys said, laughing. "He wanted to know if I would run with him. He wants me to be his deputy mayor. Can you believe that?"

"Yes, in fact, I can," I said. I knew Dalys was gaining a reputation. I was proud of her, but now I was also a little worried. I sure didn't want to lose her. "I'm not surprised at all," I said sincerely.

"Well, I sure was," Dalys said. "So I asked him, 'Why me?'"

"What did he say, Dalys?"

"He said he is old. He wants a deputy mayor who is young. And he said that he has been hearing about me. He said people all up and down the coast are telling stories about me. No one can believe that I run Los Islotes. After all, I am just a woman. And only thirty years old. But this man, he said that he has heard that I am a woman who is not afraid to speak up to men. He said someone told him a story about being at a meeting in the mayor's office last year where I stood up and spoke to the mayor and everyone in the room. I remember that day. I was the only woman there. I guess I should have been afraid, but I wasn't. These men,

THE WAY FORWARD
Chapter XIX

they were all in suits and feeling so good about themselves. They had their chests puffed out, you know, how men do. They were talking and talking, blah, blah, blah, but not saying anything, you know. Just kissing up to the mayor, playing that game. So I stood up. 'You know, we have real things to talk about,' I said. 'We have things in these parts that need to be fixed,' I told them."

"How did they respond?"

"Oh, you know men. They didn't want to listen. But I kept talking anyway. 'We need more things for our schools,' I told them. 'That is the most important thing,' I said. I told them about our plans for a school at Los Islotes. That is the story that the old man heard. About me talking about our school."

"What did you tell the man, Dalys? About running as his deputy mayor?"

"I told him I have a job. At Los Islotes." Dalys spoke nonchalantly, as though to state a thing she took for granted. I wondered if maybe she was more intrigued by the offer than she was letting on. She'd never want to disappoint me, but she must be at least a little interested in seeing where a conversation like this could lead.

"Yes, of course, Dalys," I said. "You have your job with us. But, you know, Lief and I would never want to be the reason you missed out on another opportunity. Would the position be full time? What does the deputy mayor do exactly?" Maybe this wasn't an either-or situation.

"No, it is not full time, Señora Kathleen. The man told me I

AT HOME AT LOS ISLOTES
Finding Our Way On This Veraguas Coast

would only need to go to some meetings and show up at some speeches. Things like that. He said he understood about Los Islotes. He said I could still keep my job here."

"Do you want to run for deputy mayor, Dalys?" I asked.

"I don't know, Señora Kathleen. It is an honor to be asked. I am very flattered. And there are lots of things I would like to do. I would like to make this place better. It is my home, after all, and I have many ideas, Señora Kathleen, just like you."

"Dalys," I said, "it sounds to me as though this is something you'd like to consider. And I think you should. Lief and I would support you. It wouldn't affect your job here. Never worry about that."

"Okay, Señora Kathleen," Dalys said. "Then I will think about it." She sounded relieved. She didn't need my permission, though I appreciated her seeming to feel like she did. I was thrilled for her to have this chance to try to make a difference for the better in her "beloved Quebro."

"Oh, and one more thing," Dalys said as she stood up to leave. "Martin has news, too. He has bought a piece of land. He is building a house for him and Sophia. They want to have a family. Martin is very excited."

"That's wonderful news," I said. "Thank you for letting me know. I'll congratulate him next time I see him."

"Yes, it's a big deal," Dalys said. "They are not getting married in the way you think, but for us this is like getting married. I am

THE WAY FORWARD
Chapter XIX

happy for them. And for us, too. This means Martin is here at Los Islotes to stay."

"That *is* excellent news for us."

It was quitting time. Lief and I packed up our laptops and drove up the hill to our house. *Deputy Mayor Dalys*, I thought as I let the dogs out of the back of the car. I was thrilled for her to be acknowledged in this way. She sure deserved the recognition. Plus, wouldn't it be nice to have Dalys on the other end of conversations with the mayor's office? Maybe when the old man was ready to retire, Dalys could run for mayor. Politics is an ugly business in this country. Dalys wouldn't change that, but it would put her in a position to support our projects, starting with the school.

I stood at the end of our front walk. I couldn't bring myself to continue past the spirit tree. It was time to admit that it was dead. Every branch had been bare for months. I picked up a stick and poked at the trunk. It was rotting. Mushrooms had sprouted around the base.

Lief came up alongside me. "What do you think?" he said. "Finally time to chop it down?"

Lief would have cut the tree down long ago, when it started the long downward spiral that'd led to the current state. He was worn out with this tree's cycle of rebirth. The reality was that much of the time we had a dying tree in our front yard. But Lief knew this tree had become important for me. I'd been hoping for another miracle recovery, but now the thing was decomposing. It'd never

AT HOME AT LOS ISLOTES
Finding Our Way On This Veraguas Coast

been lifeless for this long.

"Yes," I said. "I guess it's time to let it go."

"It's just a tree, you know," Lief said.

"Well, it is and it isn't. It's also a symbol. Cutting it down is giving up. It means we're admitting defeat."

"What are you talking about?" Lief said. "It's a dead tree, and it's in the way. When we remove it, new life will fill the space. The garden will be nicer than ever. You'll see. I'm going to ask Danillo to take it out in the morning. The sooner the better if you ask me. I'm tired of looking at it."

Lief went inside, but I stayed put staring at our dead spirit tree. It'd been a source of hope. This tree never said die, and neither did we. But Lief had a point. Clearing it away would make room for the future. Dalys had said this tree had an energy. I'd drawn strength from it for years. Now it was a mass of toxins. Doing away with it would be saying good-bye to all the struggles it'd supported me through. The death of our spirit tree didn't signify our end. It marked the beginning of our next stage.

"I'm going down to the beach," I said to Lief as I walked through the front door. "It should be low tide. Want to join me?"

"Sounds good," Lief said. "Let me change my clothes."

I've searched all my life for something to believe in. From that first day when I hiked in in the rain then surrendered to the surf, I've suspected. Now I know. Los Islotes is the meaning I've sought. It is my purpose. It has blessed me with the opportuni-

THE WAY FORWARD
Chapter XIX

ty to create something lasting, a place for my children and their children to connect with a nearly forgotten world with secrets worth preserving.

Los Islotes has also brought me face to face with my greatest fear. I've always been afraid of running out of time. Now I wonder if I've found the real reason I've been pushing myself so hard my whole life too late. Do I have years enough remaining to build the Los Islotes I imagine? Even a year ago, that question would have been one more thing to keep me awake at night. The trials and tribulations of the past decade-and-a-half on this Veraguas coast have pushed me, finally, through apprehension and out the other side. Now I don't worry. I just keep moving forward.

As soon as the court provides a witness, we'll send Nica and his guys back out to our dirt road. They'll try again to build our wall. If that attempt is thwarted, we'll make another plan. We'll reconcile with Señor Sanchez or we won't. Roberta will stay put or move along. I can't predict the next complication, but it doesn't matter. As I've taken to reassuring Dalys, more for my benefit than hers, it'll all be alright. We'll make it alright. I have faith.

"Meet you at the car," I called to Lief. "Let's go toast the sunset at Playa Sol."

Lief drove around the bend from our house then down the long hill to the coast. He stopped at the foot of the point between the two beaches.

"I'd been thinking we could sit for a while on the deck at the

AT HOME AT LOS ISLOTES
Finding Our Way On This Veraguas Coast

beach," I said as I reached into the back seat for the basket I'd packed with wine and glasses, "but what if we hiked to the top of the cliff instead?" Lief and I hadn't made the climb together in a long while.

"I didn't realize this outing was going to require exercise," Lief said smiling, "but okay. I'll get my machete."

Lief carried the basket and led the way. We were glad for his machete. The journey is steep, and the trail hadn't been cleared in weeks. I placed my boots carefully, putting each foot where I'd seen Lief place his and reaching for his arm every time I slipped. When we got to the top, Lief hacked away limbs and bushes to create a small clearing on the ground. I hadn't thought to bring a blanket. We sat on the earth with two big rocks for support and looked out our keyhole view. Framed before us were the sea, the sky, and our three islands. The sun had begun its descent. One more day down. No problem. We'd done what we could. Tomorrow would be another chance. Lief opened the wine and filled the two glasses. We didn't speak. The only sound was the surf crashing against the rock face below. The sky was turning orange and pink at the horizon. *We shouldn't stay too long,* I thought. It'd be slow-going back down the hill in the dark. But I didn't want to rush the moment. I slid my arm through Lief's, took a long, slow sip from my glass, and watched the setting sun paint the sky. I was at peace. I was at home. And I was ready for whatever came next.

Would You Like To Stay In Touch With Kathleen?

Follow Her Global Adventures Here...

The world's savviest, most experienced, and most trusted source for information on living, retiring, and investing overseas

Kathleen Peddicord's Live And Invest Overseas has helped countless readers take advantage of the world's best opportunities for living better, retiring well, and chasing adventure. She shares her ongoing experiences around the world both through the www.liveandinvestoverseas.com website... and also through email. Kathleen's ***Overseas Opportunity Letter*** is a daily dispatch from her, with contributions from her far-flung network of editors, experts, friends, and advisors. Each day you'll find out about the best opportunities for international living, retiring overseas, and investing in real estate around the world.

Overseas Opportunity Letter is a completely free service. You can find out more at www.liveandinvestoverseas.com.

Have You Read The First Book In Kathleen's "At Home" Series?

AT HOME IN IRELAND

Kathleen Peddicord was pulling herself up the corporate ladder when given the opportunity to chase a dream she'd had since girlhood. She'd been editor and publisher of a magazine focused on options for Americans interest in living and investing overseas and finally had the chance to take her own advice. Kathleen charged headlong into her move from Baltimore to Ireland only to run headfirst into the Irish way of life. Ireland forced her to dismantle and doubt every belief she'd held as she struggled to start a business and open herself up to new romance while restoring an Irish Georgian country ruin.

Praise For At Home In Ireland

"Kathleen does a phenomenal job at transporting the reader to Ireland during a pivotal time in her life. Her characters come to life with great detail and she tells a wonderful story about not only her life, but life in general on the Emerald Isle. Highly recommend picking up a copy for a quick, thoughtful, and inspiring read." —*Amazon Customer*

"This book set the stage for Kathy's amazing journey. It only covers Ireland and I know she has many more places where she has explored. I only hope this means the next memoir is called 'At Home in Paris!' Excellent writing. It was a quick read on the beach." —*Carolyn B. Wescott*

"Overall, a highly readable and enjoyable memoir. Perfect for anybody who's ever had an interest in Ireland or becoming an expat." —*Ryan M. Healy*

Order At Home In Ireland Here:

Made in the USA
Monee, IL
20 May 2024

58706521R00177